ECONOMIC GEOGRAPHY

To,

Suresh M. Sethna

About the Author

V.A. JANAKI was educated in Madras and later at Oxford and Cambridge and headed the Department of Geography of the Maharaja Sayajirao University of Baroda since its inception in 1952. She has taught economic, political and historical geography to graduate and post-graduate students for about thirty years and also guided students for their post-graduate dissertations and doctorate theses. She has several publications to her credit including monographs on the *Geography of Padra Town; Some Aspects of the Political Geography of India; Kandla Post, Surat: A Study in Historical Geography; Vanadha Chalamli: A Study in Rural Dynamics; Gujarat as the Arabs Knew it; The Trade of Cambay from Early Times to the Nineteenth Century,* etc. She has contributed several articles to the *Encyclopaedia Britannica,* the *Gujarat Gazetteers* and to journals.

INTRODUCTION

THE field of geography is very vast. It is concerned with the cultural or man-made phenomena and the natural or physical phenomena of the entire earth. It embraces all sciences : social, physical and biological. Geography is a method of study rather than a subject. The geographer's efforts are directed towards discovering the combined impact of interrelated phenomena (both physical and human) on an area, and explaining the causes for areal differentiation on the surface of the earth. But there are legions of phenomena in different degrees of relationship and combination which give character to an area. The geographer, therefore, has to sacrifice the less important phenomena and highlight the more important ones to throw light on the problem he is investigating. In the choice of criteria to explain areal uniqueness, the physical phenomena of the earth are in no way more important to geographers than the cultural or the human phenomena in all places at all times. Time was when geographers explained human activities and behaviour as controlled by a relentless nature. That was in the nineteenth century. Very few geographers today subscribe to such a deterministic point of view. Geography is not a science of relationship between man and his physical environment. When geographers speak of the 'environment' they mean the total environment, the physical, the economic, the cultural, the social, the historical, the political and even the aesthetic and invisible environment. Every areal feature is the result of a combination of phenomena, both human and physical, in interrelationship. The geographic method is best grasped when areal studies are problem-oriented. The geographer's fields of investigation are so wide that he must of necessity specialize in certain aspects and certain areas of the earth in order to understand the purpose and method of geography.

Economic geography is one of the branches of geography. It deals with the economic and commercial aspects of man on earth and the influence on these of the environment in its broadest sense. The adjective 'economic' confines the geographer to the economic problems and systems of man and as such he must know something of the principles of economics. Economists, till recently, have been preoccupied by theories of value, price and income, while economic geographers have emphasized the physical realities in area and their relationship to economic life. But both are now pushing their investigations into borderland areas in their search for reality. While the economists are realising the futility of mere theories without reference to the physical and other environmental factors in area, geographers are also pushing upward from the physical basis to the region of the social and cultural sciences to discover the causes of areal differentiations in economic patterns. Somewhere the two disciplines must meet. But theories and definitions as such are of no value to the geographer unless they help to explain areal differe-ces. Certain basic forces produce a particular pattern on the ground in terms of economic, social, cultural, political, physical or otherwise. Where these forces function, the theory helps to explain or understand the pattern. But where they are not in operation the theory is of no use for geographical interpretation. To the geographer, therefore, the correct identification of the basic forces or factors influencing a ground pattern, is more important than theories and definitions. The areal pattern, which is the fundamental concern of the geographer is dependent as much if not more on human reactions to the total environment than on the physical environment. The response of man to his physical, social, cultural and political environment changes from people to people, place to place and from time to time and it cannot be limited by theories. Each area, each structure and pattern on the ground has to be studied in the context of the influencing factors (basic forces) which produced it. Since these patterns are likely to change, the criteria used at a given time in a particular place are not applicable to the same place at all times nor to any other place. Hence the futility of sweeping theories in geography or any branch of it. Each problem and each areal uniqueness calls for a full investigation of the basic forces that created it.

The geographer is not content with just a mere description of the differences in the economy of the different parts of the earth, but, like specialists in other branches of geography, he seeks out the causes for the areal differentiation in economic development and patterns on the earth. The why, when and how of things in particular areas are more critical to a geographer's investigation than a mere 'where' of things. The adjective 'economic' in no way deters the geographer from the geographic method.

The economic development of the different countries and regions cannot be explained by the availability of the physical resources alone. In reality such resources are inert and only of cartographic value until man develops them and they are put into active relationship with the consuming centres by man's genius, skill and organization. It is only then that a natural resource becomes an economic resource. Further, nature produces regardless of cost and the return value, but man always asks the question "how much will it cost, what will be the profit?" The uneven economic development which causes areal differentiation is thus the result of a host of factors such as advances made in technical skills, accessibility of markets, availability of labour, capital and transport facilities, attitude of the people to a particular type of development and their goals, government policies, trade agreements, cut-throat competitions, international controls, etc. The gifts of nature alone do not explain areal differentiation in economic structure and development. If this were true, how did Japan become one of the leading economic powers in the world? How did Germany recoup herself and re-establish her industries after World Wars I and II? How did the USSR succeed in growing potatoes and cereals in the cold deserts ? How can the USA produce rice more cheaply than the monsoon lands of Asia ? Why is India's iron and steel industry lagging behind those of the USA and UK? Why is England facing a crisis in unemployment ? Why is she restructuring her industries and seeking greater self-sufficiency in food? It is the search for an answer to such questions that leads to the geographic method in economic geography.

The location and structure of economic activity keep changing according to the basic forces or factors of influence which operate at a given time. In the under-developed world where man's skills are rudimentary, his activities may be largely controlled by the physical environment. In other areas the burden of traditions and a long history may be powerful factors in the determination of the structure and location of economic activity. In yet other areas the demands of a growing market and easy accessibility to it may stimulate production. Governments may decide to protect or encourage certain activities by bounties, subsidies, import tariffs etc. Cultural and political factors may demand the economic development of particular areas. Trade may be channelised through particular routes and ports because of government concessions or cut-throat competition. Lack of a common currency or unfavourable rates of exchange may impede trade. It is left to the economic geographer to choose the influencing factors intelligently in order to explain the economic pattern in the area under investigation.

Economic geography can be studied in many ways, the most common approach being regional economic geography. It is rather a specialized picture of the economic patterns in particular areas. The stability of these areas as distinct economic regions is dependent on the factors of influence that produced them. When these factors cease to operate, the region will also change its form, structure and function. These economic regions are as ephemeral as any other geographic region, even more so than some of them, because the factors that built up an economic region are mainly human. The human element in geography is very unpredictable and liable to more rapid changes than the physical element. The technique of the average regional economic geographer is to halt a motion picture as it were, to describe the economic patterns at a given time. But by the time he completes his study, it is likely that all parameters would have changed. Unless such 'regional studies' focus on the changing nature of the causative factors that gave uniqueness and character to the region at a given time, they are of little worth. They tend to be descriptive and static and fail to recognize the fundamental purpose of geographical investigations: the why, when and how of things. Such a study is only of transitory interest. It does not train the student to intelligently choose the relevant factors of influence for a given economic pattern in an area nor does it lead him to the geographic method in economic regionalisation.

There are others who emphasize a 'systematic approach' to economic geography. They aim at a systematic study of production, industry, agriculture, trade, population and transport of the world, or a particular country. The focus is on the phenomenon rather than the region. All these phenomena are no doubt part of economic geography. The nature and characteristics of economic phenomena and their general distribution are essential to the understanding of economic geography. But they do not equip the student to understand the causes of regional variations in economic systems and patterns. Unless such systematic studies are applied to particular regions, it makes economic geography a dry-as-dust subject. It is the continuous need for discovering the forces that produced the uniqueness of an economic region that makes the subject dynamic and worthy of study.

A reasonable and intelligent approach to economic geography is, therefore, to acquaint the student with the various possible factors which influence the economic activity and the economic structure in any area at any given time and leave him to choose the best criteria (influencing factors) which explain the regional economic patterns or problems in the area of his choice. In such an approach the student is trained in independent thinking, while seeking the causes for concentrations of economic activity in particular areas or the lack of it in other areas. He has to discover the combinations of these phenomena, their relationship in the region of his choice at the time of investigation. Such knowledge of the possible influencing factors and the way they operate in economic geography are of lasting value. They would be applicable to any region at any time, the only consideration being the degree of their importance in a given region at a given time. The foundations of geographic research are based on the capacity of the student to choose the most important combination of phenomena to explain the patterns in particular regions. It is the capacity to identify the correct basic forces which create a particular economic pattern on the ground that equips the geographer to understand the regional method.

Once the student grasps the importance of certain combinations and interactions of phenomena in an area for the development of an economic region, he is equipped not only to explain the reasons for economic concentrations but also to plan an economic region. Planning is the right arrangement of phenomena in an area to achieve maximum returns from a particular type of development. A geographer who is trained to recognize the causes which produced a thriving economic region is also equipped to suggest the right arrangement of phenomena in area for an ideal planning region. A geographer's 'synthetic' approach to regions makes him invaluable as a planner.

This book emphasizes the factors of influence or the basic

forces that operate in economic geography and the nature of the impact of these phenomena on economic development. It leaves the student to choose for himself the best criteria and the most important combinations to explain the economic concentrations in the region of his choice.

CONTENTS

1

ECONOMIC GEOGRAPHY AND PHYSICAL PHENOMENA

WITH the technical developments of the last few centuries, it is more or less accepted that nature does not dictate the economic progress of man, that man himself is, to a large measure, the agent whereby civilization advances. But while his importance in changing the environment is recognized, the physical environment and the works of man through the ages in a given area, condition and influence, his present activities. Where technical advancement and skills are minimal such influences are greater than where technology is advanced. Every technical advance in a given area calls for a reappraisal of its geographical values. The economic patterns and types in a region are not static but are ever changing phenomena which have to be continuously studied and reassessed to understand the relationship between nature and man.

In the economic development of an area, physical factors, such as the position of the area, its accessibility to other regions as well as to raw materials and markets, its topography, climate, vegetation and soils, its geological and the biological factors, all may have a direct bearing on the type and the pattern of economy it develops.

POSITION

The position of a region or country is not always a static feature from the point of view of the economic geographer. The mathematical location (latitude and longitude) of a region which is a fixed phenomena affects its climate, vegetation and soils which in turn have a bearing on the use of land. But attitudes towards these phenomena are different in different regions. The relative location of a region or country to other economically developed or undeveloped areas is again dependent on the changing economic patterns in these areas. Such changes in the neighbouring or distant areas may have an impact on the availability of raw meterial and on the markets of the region under study, thereby necessitating a shift in its economy.

Likewise the position of a country or region in relation to the major sea and land routes of the world is changeable with the development in transport and the shifting emphasis down the ages on particular sea routes in world commerce. In the ancient and medieval periods the Mediterranean and the Indian Ocean were the important commercial seas and access to these were considered an asset for trade. Today the North Atlantic and its tributary seas are of prime commercial importance. A favourable location in relation to these seas is an advantage for developing a commercial economy to meet the requirements of a world market. But with the rise of the USA and the USSR as giant economic units, together with the fact that some of the overpopulated and economically backward areas of South East Asia flank the Pacific Ocean, it is likely that this ocean might become commercially important in the future. A sea frontage to the Pacific Ocean may then be considered of greater commercial significance than one to the Atlantic and its tributaries.

Further, technical developments in transport may change the significance of the location of a region or the use of it as a nodal area. The advent of the steam ship in the nineteenth century and the shift of world commerce from overland routes to overseas routes on a large scale made the coastal fringe-lands of the world more important commercially than during the days of trade by land. Goods came to be carried in bulk across the wide expanse of the seas at lower costs than by land. The nodal centres on the major land routes of the world such as Tashkent, Bukhara and Samarkhand on the silk route, Kiev and Novogorod in the Russian plains and many other trade centres in Europe and Asia lost the significance of their natural location in mountain passes, gaps, foothills and plains.

The large steamships of the nineteenth century also needed well equipped ports and harbours with facilities for loading and unloading of goods in bulk, docking, storing and linkages with wide hinterlands so that the initial cost of setting up a port and maintaining it economically required a huge capital outlay and a well managed organization. It became uneconomic to provide such facilities at all the anchoring places of the world where a sailing ship could easily dock without much man-made facilities. Rather a concentration of these facilities at particular ports became necessary for economic reasons. The world's commerce was channelized through these ports and trade was concentrated there. The small ports on rivers and creeks became obsolete and lost the significance of their location. Much of the 'drive to the sea' of some continental countries is due to the importance of the sea as highways of commerce and the advantages of access to the sea routes. Russia's drive to the Baltic and the Black Sea right through her history, her demand for the Polish coast, her anxiety to effectively occupy the Pacific coastal lands and the efforts she is making to conquer her inhospitable Arctic Sea Coasts are all partly due to the shift of world, commerce from land to sea. Likewise Germany's thrust to the Baltic, her interest in the Rhine-Rhone Corridor, (its outlet to the North Sea), her ambitions in the Polish sea frontage, Britain's desire to confine Germany to land after the First World War by creating the political units of Belgium and Holland at the Rhine mouth, are all reflective of the need for control of a sea frontage to cope with the commercial rivalries amongst the highly developed nations with surpluses to export to an overseas market. In the future, carriage of goods by air might create other nodal centres of commerce and economic activity. But at present carriage of goods by air is costly and its weight limited. Water transport continues to be the cheapest mode of transport known and hence it is the most economically suitable. A position accessible to the sea routes of the world is therefore considered of some economic significance for the development of a region.

ACCESSIBILITY

The real economic significance of land is its accessibility. Accessibility is the keyword in economic geography. Isolation from centres of population and economic activity leads to retardation and stagnation. Accessibility however is a changeable phenomenon. Distances on the ground can be shortened by adequate facilities in transport, increasing the speed of transport and by bringing down its cost. Accessibility in terms of economic geography is not related to the actual distance on the ground but also to other factors such as the time taken to transport goods and government policies in subsidising the cost of transport. With the technical developments achieved in transport in the nineteenth and twentieth centuries, many areas which were inaccessible before now became available for use. But while minor landforms have been conquered by man's skill, major landforms have remained a challenge to him and a hindrance to easy economic movement of goods. The conquest of nature by man always involves cost, which in turn increases the cost of production. Areas of isolation therefore remain retarded because the major concern in production is the cost factor.

Man has also increased his speed considerably in the last two centuries, creating new space relationships. In ancient Greece and Rome it took nearly one day to travel from one end of the city to the other. Today travel from one end of America to the other is possible in less than ten hours, thereby changing the concept of accessibility in Economic Geography. Man increased his speed from a mere jog trot to about 96 km an hour (the average speed of trucks and trains) after centuries of experimentation but in the last few decades he has increased his speed to that of the jet plane, (about 480-960 kms per hour). Further, telecommunications enable him to conduct and organize huge business concerns across land and sea. This achievement of speed in contacts has made it possible to set up large economic units and regions not known before. The small Greek City State as an economic unit and the traditional self-sufficiency of the Indian village developed in the context of a transport system whose speed was limited to four to five kilometres an hour. But today economic regions spread over miles of land, particularly in the developed world.

Africa is said to have remained a 'dark continent' to the European explorers for a very long time because of its inaccessibility from the sea. Africa has a very long coast but the coastline is unbroken in most parts and devoid of suitable harbours. The greater part of Africa is a plateau extending from the Guinea Coast to Somaliland and from the northern margins of the Sahara to the central districts of the Cape Province. The straight shoreline, with no great indentations was hostile to the sea-faring adventures of medieval Europe. Added to this was the fact that most of the rivers fall abruptly over the edge of the Plateau to the low coast, making their lower courses tortuous and unserviceable as communication lines to the interior. Sandbars along the coast were also obstructions to the sailing ships of the period. Further, the continental shelf of Africa has an abrupt descent to great oceanic depths, making sea navigation risky except in the more hospitable Mediterranean coast, the Horn of Africa and off Cape Province. Such difficult access between sea and land made the interior of Africa an unknown land. If Africa figured as an important supplier of gold, ivory and other valuable products in the ancient trade of the Indian Ocean, it was mostly because of the enterprise of the Arabs and Indians who exchanged goods at suitable ports. Some of the Negro communities brought the valuable commodities of the interior by land and by river, across tortuous paths and mountains, to the coast, but they were not a sea-faring people like the Arabs and the Indians. Trade of this kind, however, did exist long before the advent of the Europeans. But the penetration of the Europeans to the interior was delayed because of its inaccessibility.

The same is true of Brazil. Brazil is endowed with a large share of the world's mineral wealth. It has 20 per cent of the world's iron resources and a large quantity of manganese. Over 80 per cent of its land is highly productive. Yet it has remained backward in industry and agriculture partly because of its inaccessibility. Most of Brazil, like the Congo, is in the Tropics covered with thick jungles. Moreover, as in Africa, the Plateau is inaccessible from the coast. 'From Salvador to Porto Alegre in Rio Grande du Sul' the coast is backed by a steep rocky wall known as the Great Escarpment which rises to elevations of 792 meters, and in certain parts is surmounted by ranges reaching elevations of 2,133 to 2,438 meters. 'Between latitude 18° and 30° south, the Great Escarpment is crossed only by two deeply-cut river valleys, those of Rio Doce and Rio Paraibo. In only two places, between Santo and Sao Paulo and between Parnagua and Curitiba, is this Escarpment concentrated in one sea-facing slope. Along most of its course it is broken into a series of steps forming parallel escarpments with deep valleys in between". The rivers of the Plateau, therefore, turn inwards and drain the Plateau or descend over its steep edge in rapids and falls so that there is no natural communication between coast and plateau. With the development of Rio de Janeiro and Sao Paulo as ports of export (wheat and coffee respectively) to Europe, in the nineteenth century, man-made communication lines do focus on these ports. But, the connections of both Rio de Janeiro and Sao Paulo with the interior are still inadequate.

In the Andes also the economy of the mountains and the valley are independent of each other because of lack of contact between the two. Such areas of isolation are found throughout the world and they are bound to have retarded growth because of the lack of accessibility needed for development.

The degree of accessibility of a region or area can, however, be increased with adequate transport and by reducing the cost of the carriage of goods. Developments in the Mackenzie River and Peace River valleys in Canada were stemmed because of their remoteness from the existing population centres and areas of development. But today the need for Petroleum has created the incentive to break the barrier of distance with adequate transport.

In certain parts of the world Nature itself provides easy accesibility so that these areas obtain priority in economic development. In such areas, community with even a primitive economy can achieve a degree of self-sufficiency or even surplus production. The ancient agricultural civilizations were possible in the river valleys in Egypt, Mesopotamia, India and China partly because of their accessibility.

In addition to the accessibility of an area, the occurrence of raw materials within easy reach is also important in economic geography. The successful development of economic activity requires it to be located at nodal points which are central to access of the required raw materials. For example, the modern machine age, iron and steel form the basis of an industrial economy. No country can claim to be economically advanced unless it has a well developed iron and steel industry. Iron without coal is inarticulate. Hence the accessibility of iron to coal is an incentive to set up a steel industry. The north-eastern coalfields of England held the lead in the British coal industry because of accessibility to iron ores. Even when iron was exhausted necessitating its import from the continent, the coastal location of the north-eastern coalfield proved an advantage. Again the Donbas coal of Russia, situated near the Krivoyrog iron field, had an early industrial start in Czarist Russia. In north-eastern India coal has the advantage of being situated near to the source of iron.

On the other hand, the rich coalfields of Siberia were only of cartographic value still Communist Russia decided to develop the region and lay the foundations of a sound economic structure for the hitherto neglected land of Asiatic Russia. The Siberian coalfields are now gradually being brought nearer to the Mangnitogorsk iron fields through the construction of railways and roads. The distance being still too great to make the full exploitation of the Siberian coal economic, attempts are being made to discover new sources of iron in the regions near the coal deposits. In the same way the remoteness of the Shansi, Shensi and Schezwan coalfields of western China from the iron fields of the lower Yangtze valley was the greatest hindrance to Communist China's industrial ambitions. The problem was one of locating the iron and steel industry in the inaccessible coal regions of west China or developing it in the populated and agriculturally advanced iron regions of the east. It engaged the attention of the planners in China necessitating changes in the patterns of the location of the iron and steel industry after the Communist take-over. Hankow in the lower Yangtze valley is now connected by rail, road and water to the Schezwan coal and also to the industrial north. The industry is gradually shifting to the iron and the market region. The Manchurian coal on the other hand witnessed an early development through Japanese enterprise partly because of the availability of iron in the nearby areas.

Accessibility to the market is another incentive to economic development. Some economic activities are better situated in the Market area while others derive advantage from a location near the raw material area. Usually consumer goods industries seek a location near the market while heavy industries like iron and steel seek the raw material areas. Nearness to the market therefore is advantageous to certain industries. 'Nearness' in economic geography, however, is related to the cost of transport and not to the distance on the ground.

TOPOGRAPHY (RELIEF)

The topography of a region is significant to its economic development because it decides whether the land should be made available for cultivation or for industrial development. Both industry and agriculture consider flat land as the most suitable for development while others are treated as marginal or second priority lands. The first revolution that transformed human economy from a hunting stage to that of crop cultivation (the Neolithic revolution) took place in the fertile valleys of rivers subject to floods. The pre-and proto-historic civilizations of West Asia, India and China were built on surplus cereals which, in the context of the techniques available at the time, could be cultivated only in the plains with a natural flow of surface water. An agricultural economy is perhaps more dependent on topography than an industrial economy. But industries also require flat land for buildings, plants and more important, for the construction of transport lines to link the manufacturing centres with the market and raw material areas.

The configuration of land also affects transport. Rails are limited to fairly gentle slopes. A locomotive on a grade that rises one foot for every 100 feet (one per cent grade) can cope with only one-fifth of the load pulled on level ground. Even the Andean railway has only a four per cent grade. Railways, therefore, avoid mountains and follow valleys and streams. When mountains cannot be avoided tunnels are built. Such structures add to the initial cost so that only a voluminous traffic can justify their construction. Its running cost is also high as the load carried, given the same pulling power of the engine, decreases with steepness.

Other topographic barriers of railroads are swamps and water (rivers). Narrow and shallow water-bodies can be bridged but large ones have to use ferries or be avoided. Break of bulk at the ferries, building of bridges and so on add to the cost of transport.

In mountainous countries roads are more economic than rails. Automobiles can climb steeper gradients than locomotives. Roads can penetrate into mountainous areas inaccessible to the railways. Roads are also cheaper to build than railways and trucks can ply on these roads.

Water transport also require level terrain. Inland waterways can be developed only where nearly horizontal streams are available. Canals usually maintain a horizontal level. Even a low range of hills may completely bar waterways. A series of locks and steps can be made available for climbing slopes on a waterway but they slow down the speed of boats and also make water transport expensive. Even ocean transport uses sea level plane of water. At the terminals (ports) the terrain factor becomes crucial for waterways.

Aeroplanes are more independent of terrain conditions. Neither steepness of slope, depth of sand nor bogginess affect aeroplanes. But the critical terrain factor for aeroplanes is the terminal area. A long flat piece of land is essential for taking-off and landing.

Where none of the above types of transport can be used, because of the limitations placed by topographical factors, only human beings and animals can penetrate. The mountain lands are still the stronghold of pack animals such as the donkey, mule, horse, llama, and yak. Movement of goods in such areas is, therefore, necessarily slow.

The successful laying out of pipelines underground, usually used to carry petroleum and water, also require flat terrain.

The construction of ports is carefully planned after studying topographical features. Many of the world's well-known commercial ports are situated at a distance from the sea. They are river ports and suitable to accommodate the sailing ship and later, steamships. Their channels to the sea, once sufficient for the merchant ships of a century ago, had to be kept at a depth sufficient for the modern leviathans, by the constant dredging to prevent the ancient seat of a thriving sea commerce from becoming a mere inland village. Many well-known ports of the world developed before the steamship age such as London, Manchester, Bordeaux, Antwerp, Amsterdam, Hamburg, Nantes, New Orleans, Houston, Calcutta, Bombay and many others. Hamburg, to avoid becoming an inland city, increased her dredging operations creating depths to keep pace with the increase in vessel crafts. The channels to the port of Calcutta have to be kept clear by dredging. However, dredging to keep the channels clear of silt for ocean-going vessels is a costly affair. The best ports are those near the sea coast, where the harbour is accessible without change in the ship's course and where the channels are wide and deep. Ports which have room for manoeuvre and good holding ground, are convenient for modern shipping. Port Charleston, for example, is closer to the open sea than any other port on the US coastline. Vessels here have to change course only twice between sea and berth. It has a wide deep channel and ample room with a good holding ground. At Hampton Roads an entire navy can be anchored. Where man has to cope with a hostile Nature, the cost of production is pushed up reducing the region's capacity to complete with other regions better endowed.

Topography also determines problems such as erosion, draining of the marshy areas, reclamation of land, making bad lands productive and so on. To overcome topographical defects for economic development, requires technical skill and financial investment. Steep gradients accelerate erosion by water leaving land uncultivable. Marshy lands are also difficult to develop. The Pripet Marsh of Russia is the largest marshy area in the world. With all the technical skill available to the Russians today the marshes are still not fully conquered. The problem of bad lands in South Dakota and the adjacent parts of Wyoming and Nebraska has been a challenge to even the technically skilled Americans. There are several thousand acres of bad lands in these states. The land is mostly of heavy clay and is so steep that it washes badly. The earth absorbs so little water that it is devoid of vegetation. The bad lands are the result of running water on impervious clay. The lands become so gullied and bare that they are useless for either pasture or agriculture. The formation of soil itself in this manner is related to topography.

Topography further has a direct bearing on the distribution of human settlements. Population tends to concentrate in the plain regions of the world except where climatic conditions drive them to higher altitudes or bad drainage makes low-lying regions unhealthy. With man's occupation of the plains, economic activity is also oriented towards the plains.

CLIMATE

Climate is a composite phenomenon which includes temperature, precipitation, evaporation, wind and humidity.

Temperature

Temperature has a direct bearing on crop cultivation. There are certain limits of temperature at which crops can be grown. An annual average temperature of 10°C is necessary for intensive crop cultivation. More important to crop cultivation, is the number of frost free days in the year. Most grains need about

110 frost free days to attain full growth. In Russia where the summers are very short, the growing period is limited to a short period. In certain areas, Russia has only 100 frost-free days on an average and artificial germination of the seed has to be utilized. Vernalisation is practiced in such areas. The seeds are subjected to a slight increase in temperature and moisture through artificial means, before they are sown, so that they may sprout earlier and get the required number of days with adequate temperature for its growth. But this practice is now giving way to new techniques.

The limits in temperature during the growing period of the plant are concerned with more than the direct heat of the sun. Soil temperatures and the cooling of the air in spring depend on the snow cover in winter in Russia. The spring in Russia progresses from west to east and the transition from winter to summer may last for weeks depending on the thickness of the snow cover. Air temperature does not rise rapidly until after the whole snow cover has melted and the wet ground has dried a little. The spring may be a long period of killing frost. The last day of the frost is the beginning of summer and the growing season. If this last day of frost is abnormally late, crops are likely to suffer. As a rule, if the depth of the snow to be melted is great, then spring in Russia can be raw and cold and summer, slow in coming. Where there is little snow cover, spring is pleasant and warm and soon gives place to fine summer-like weather. If the growing season is less than 90 days artificial means like vernalisation or electrical heating of the soil have to be resorted to, to cultivate crops. In Siberia, a great area is covered by the Tundra, Taiga or even the Steppes where at no great depth, a layer of frozen subsoil is found. In Kozhevnikov Bay in Northern Yakutia, the ground is frozen to a depth of 518 metres and more at times. The farmers' spade rings as it strikes the ground and ploughing is very difficult. These low temperatures make lands beyond 60° latitude difficult to cultivate unless relieved by other features such as a hot current or periodic hot winds. They are what are known as frontier lands, expensive and difficult to be cultivated except with a highly developed technology and heavy capital investment. The 'moving frontier' owes much to technology and the capacity for capital investment.

Temperature conditions also cause seasonal barriers in transport. Transport has always been a major problem in Russia partly due to the freezing up of the rivers and ports, and partly because of the frozen soil which make construction of roads and rails difficult. In the Tundra the ground is sometimes domed up by pressure of the underground circulating water which is unable to escape as a normal spring because it is imprisoned beneath a layer of thick frozen soil. Sometimes this dome explodes and large blocks of earth are hurled in all directions. Roads and railways are often damaged and buildings are known to have collapsed in the lake Baikal region.

Most of the Arctic ports of Russia remain closed during winter due to the low temperature and consequent snow cover. The progression of the summer being from west to east, the Arctic ports of Siberia are affected more by the low winter temperature than those of western Russia. Russia's search for an 'all-the-year-round' port has driven her to the Baltic and the Black Sea in the west and to her southern Pacific coast in the east.

Temperatures have also a bearing on demand (that is, the Market). This is very evident in regions with distinct summers and winters than in regions where temperatures tend to be uniform throughout the year. Demand for certain goods in such areas change with the seasons. There is a peak demand for power in winter in the northern latitudes. Industrial lighting requires more power in winter. Domestic heating also creates a seasonal demand for power in the winter. Switzerland, which depends mainly on hydroelectric power for its industries and transport, runs short of running water in winter when the glaciers in the mountains become frozen. In summer when they melt, the water is abundant but the surplus has to be stored to meet the rising demand for electricity in winter. Such conversion of water for use in winter makes hydro-electricity expensive. Even the cost of water in the towns goes up.

Seasonal markets are also created for woolen clothes in winter, fruits and milk in summer and for many other products. To meet the market requirements, organisation, planning and conservation of surplus resources necessitate over the seasons. Economic patterns in such regions have to be viewed in the context of these problems.

Precipitation

Precipitation comes into all economic activities. Both industry and farming are affected by precipitation. But in assessing the effect of precipitation on economy it is necessary to understand (i) its type, (ii) its distribution over the year, (iii) its reliability and (iv) whether the total precipitation received is used for more than one purpose.

(i) Precipitation in a region may be in the form of snow and ice, rainfall or dew. The type of precipitation is of importance to economic activity. Crop cultivation requires rainfall or water from the melting of the snows. Industry is also dependent on the availability of water. In the form of snow and ice, precipitation is of little importance to industry and agriculture, till it melts.

Precipitation in the form of snow seasonally prevent navigation by water. Rivers like the Yukon, the Mackenzie and the Yenisei can be navigated only after the spring when the snow melts and the frozen surface softens. The New York Barge Canal usually closes in December and opens in April. The north and south portions of the ocean are seriously affected by ice. The steamship route across the Atlantic has to be shifted sometimes because of the polar ice. The North West Passage (N. America) is blocked by ice and the North East Passage (along N. Asia) is useful only for a short period in summer.

The roadways are also temporarily blocked by ice. In certain areas of the cold latitudes where precipitation is in the form of ice, it is difficult to keep the highways open. In thinly populated regions like Canada people change their forms of transport. In countries of freezing winters the roads are subject to thawing and freezing, necessitating yearly expenditures of large sums for their upkeep.

Railways are the most dependable under variable weather conditions. The most troublesome weather element for rail traffic is precipitation in the form of snow. Snow ploughs have to be used and snow sheds have to be built. Precipitation in the form of water also damages rails when it is violent and seasonal. Floods and erosion are common in the tropical rainy climates.

Weather conditions at the terminals especially at the time of landing are very important to air transport. Visibility is the most essential single weather element for aeroplanes. Radio telecommunications make it possible for a plane in flight to be directed to an open airport. Eventually blind landing or fog dissipation may become possible. Weather is responsible for at least one-fifth of the air accidents. Such accidents, damages and seasonal suspension of traffic reduce the dependability of all forms of transport. Delays in transport of goods cause economic regression. Continuity in transport has to be bought at a price which increases the overhead costs.

(ii) Secondly, a region might get all its total rainfall of the year in a short period of two or three months or it may be spread throughout the year. Rhodesia, for example, may get a rainfall of 101.6 mm in an hour which results in swollen rivers, floods, great erosion and waste of land. The seasonal rainfall of India can also cause floods and great damage to crops. Erosion and run-off effects are great in regions with seasonal rainfall. The transporting and eroding power of running water increases with its velocity. A rapid stream carries more material and particles of larger size than a slow stream. Seasonal precipitation and the sudden increase in the velocity of rivers can cause great erosion in countries like India, China and so on. Large areas are left behind as unculti-vable land.

Further, in an area of seasonal rainfall the growing season is confined to the season of rainfall. The dry season presents problems, as crops can be cultivated during this season only if irrigation is available. The generation of hydro-electricity also becomes difficult when the rivers shrink in the non-rainy season. The problem for both industry and agriculture is one of conserving the water for use in the non-rainy season.

Heavy seasonal rainfall sometimes makes the tides violent, damaging ships and harbours. In certain coastal areas of western India. particularly those within the limits of the tidal waters, the tides bring in sea water and cover the soil with a thin layer of salt. This feature is present even during normal tides. In the dry season the salt dries up and the ground shrivels into thin flakes of salt which are blown about by the hot winds of summer blighting the crops, damaging the soils and making life generally uncomfortable.

Seasonal rainfall has also a direct impact on soils. During the wet season the downward movement of water causes leaching of the top soils while in the dry season the upward movement of water (capillary action) due to the heat of the sun, brings the minerals of the subsoil, particularly salt, to the top. If the salt content is very high it is detrimental to crops. Laterisation is also a common feature in regions of seasonal rainfall having siliceous rocks.

In regions where the rainfall is spread throughout the year the growing season is long. It may be possible to cultivate the land all the year round without the aid of irrigation. A total annual rainfall of 1,524 to 2,540 mm. spread over the year is more economically beneficial than a concentration of it in one season. It reduces run off and erosion and prevents dryness in the soil.

Precipitation also affects communication lines. Transport has to be dependable. Climate and weather affect the dependability and in some cases even the possibility of certain forms of transportation.

Waterways depend on an adequate amount of water for navigation. Dry climates and seasonal rainfall are not ideal for waterways fed by inland water. The Suez Canal runs through a desert but its water comes from the Mediterranean at sea level. The Panama Canal gets it water from a tropical river. When a river flow is seasonally low like the Indus, the Nile or the Sacramento, navigation must stop or diminish during the dry season unless artificial means are adopted.

(iii) Another factor in precipitation which is important to the economic geographer is its reliability, not only seasonal reliability but also in the day-to-day rainfall during the rainy season. Reliability of rainfall or water supply is very essential to both industry and agriculture. Cultivation is impossible in the face of unpredictable rain. A certain element of luck and a consequent blind dependence on the forces of Nature creeps into the minds of settlers, which retards progress. In India, the regions with 889 to 1016 mm of rainfall in the year are subject to failure in rainfall and are considered as regions prone to constant famines. These are regions where the rainfall is adequate for cultivation in a year of normal rainfall and as such irrigation has been neglected. But it is also a region of unreliable rainfall. The day-to-day rainfall during the Monsoon also has an impact on crop cultivation.

(iv) Finally, the economic geographer has to consider whether the water received in a region is used for more than one purpose. Water is used for generating hydro-electricity, for crop cultivation, for industrial and domestic purposes, for recreation and for other purposes. Some of these uses do not compete with another.

However, the use of one resource for more than one purpose calls for a fair distribution over the many users. Such problems become crucial when the region has only a limited supply of water as in the semi-arid regions of the world. In areas which are very highly developed and heavily populated or where demand exceeds supply of water, organizations are set up for a fair distribution of the water over the users to ensure the welfare of the whole. The 'sharing of waters' over border areas can also create political friction.

Evaporation

The fact that a certain amount of water on the surface of the earth is evaporated by the heat of the sun is of economic significance. The total rainfall (gross rain) received by a region is of less importance to economic activity than the amount that is left after evaporation (net rain). Where the temperatures are high, evaporation is greater leaving less moisture in the soil for crop cultivation and less surface water for man's various uses. If the region is also semi-arid, evaporation might have grave consequences on the economy of the region. In America, for example, wheat can be grown in regions with 381 mm of rainfall because the temperatures are low and evaporation less. The 'water balance' in the soil is adequate enough to cultivate the crop. In India on the other hand the limit of wheat cultivation is roughly the 762-889 mm rainfall line because the heat of the sun causes greater evaporation than in the temperate climates, and the soil is left dry. Certain regions in the prairies of America, however, have so little rain and evaporation is heightened by strong winds and high temperatures. The water balance in the soil is extremely important to crop cultivation.

Wind

Wind, like all other climatic elements, is an economic factor. It enhances evaporation and affects temperatures. Sometimes they are beneficial. The Chinook wind experienced along the eastern side of the Rocky Mountains in Canada and USA is a mountain and valley wind like the Fohn wind of Switzerland. Such winds are found in other parts of of the world as well, under different names. The characteristic features of these winds are their dryness and high temperatures. The Chinook normally blows on the southern side of a depression which is moving generally across the continent, eastwards. Its direction is conditioned by the local landforms but normally it is south westerly. The descent from the Rockies dries up and raises the temperature of the wind so that it can raise the temperature of the atmosphere sometimes more than 4° C. in 15 minutes which is a contrast to the prevailing anticyclonic cold. The hot winds melt and dry the winter snow making grazing possible throughout the winter. In the regions stretching from southern Colorado in USA to the Mackenzie river in Canada, the Chinook is of great economic importance. Frequent and strong Chinook winds provide a mild winter and the pastures are rich throughout the winter. An absence of the Chinook is followed by a severe winter which causes great loss to livestock.

The direction of the wind partly determines the course of rainfall as well as the currents in the oceans. Peru in Latin America has many climatic peculiarities which are caused by the wind and the consequent direction of the currents along the coast. It affects the economy of the land considerably. There is an exceptional richness of microscopic marine organisms or diatoms along the coast of Peru. It is the result of the chemical composition of the water and the protection of the coast from sunlight by clouds. These organisms provide food for a large number of fish. The fish in turn is preyed upon by a bird population. Pelicans, cormorants and gannets fly close to the water, hover over the schools of fish and dive for their food. The excrement of these birds guano contains nitrogen and used as a fertilizer. It is deposited in the islands and is preserved in the arid climate. It forms one of the notable resources of Peru. A million birds can provide 10,000 tons or guano enabling the Peruvians to raise crops year after year without any aid of other fertilizers. But the situation changes when winds from across the equator bring southward a back eddy of warm water which spreads over the surface of the cold water. The back eddy appears regularly round Christmas or during January, February and March and is therefore called the Christ Child (El Nino). In normal years it forms only a thin layer of warm water over the cold and soon gets dissipated. But at irregular intervals the north wind is stronger and the warm water covers the cold water upto northern Chile, sometimes raising the temperature of the water to 26·6°C. The humidity of the air is increased with the warm water resulting in giant cumulus clouds which bring a deluge of rain. The fish depart from the coast and follow the cold water. The birds starve to death and Peru is left without its valuable fertilizer. Floods destroy the irrigation system. Buildings, built for a dry climate crumble and roads and bridges are washed away. Insects plague the air bringing distress and misery to the inhabitants. Since such disasters are rare, protective measures are not undertaken.

Winds are reported to have caused great harm to crop cultivation in the prairies of the US. In 1933 the newspapers gave a new name, "the Dust-Bowl" to the great plains when series of dust-storms had occurred. The topsoil of the Great Plains from Denver to Dodge city and from the Dakotas to middle Texas was literally blown away to the sea. The wind had been blowing since January and became worse in spring. Buildings, fences and highways were buried in the soil drift. Traffic was stopped, and it was so dark that lights burned during the day. In Kansas the wheat fields were turned into mounds of soil four feet deep. Then came a severe drought in 1930, 1934 and 1936 and the soils were blown by the wind.

The Scottish highlands do not grow forests because of its exposure to wind. The Norwegian highlands, which are colder than the highlands of Scotland have better wealth of timber because they are sheltered from destructive winds. The timber position of Britain is, therefore, precarious compared to that of Norway.

The regions of loess soils are generally the creations of wind. The loess is a deposit of fine soil or loam, believed to be transported by wind. It covers wide areas round the margins of the arid interior of Asia. In northern China, where it has enormous extent and thickness, the loess is a fine loam, rich in lime, and yellowish in colour. Its great advantage is its extreme porosity. Rain sinks quickly into it but its surface is normally dry. However, when irrigated and humus added, it is highly fertile. There are also extensive loess deposits in Europe and Central United States. Mixed with a high proportion of humus it also forms the fertile Black Earth of USSR. Rivers cut very deeply into these loess soils.

In most of the desert regions winds are very strong and cause discomfort, blowing the dust and sand which are low in moisture and high in temperature. Severe sandstorms cause undue inconvenience to travellers. Bare rock and pebble pavements are usual sights in the deserts. In such regions human occupation is temporary or absent.

Humidity

Humidity affects the distribution of plants and gives rise to fungoid diseases in plants. It also influences the distribution of animal population and man.

In West Africa, Europeans were not able to settle down because of the high humidity and adverse climate, whereas, the white man has made himself quite at home in East Africa. The economy of the two regions thus presented a contrast. In the west was a one-crop exploitation economy based on native labour hired by the Europeans who were temporarily settled there. In the east, on the other hand, the Europeans were permanent settlers and introduced a diversified and advanced farming. Political independence of some of the African countries is changing their economy but often independence is given in return for good will and continuance of the old economic pattern.

The effect of climate on man needs no elaboration. Diseases which sap the energy of the people are many in the tropical countries. Small pox, lung diseases, measles, malaria, sleeping sickness, all are found in the tropical climates. The Tsetse fly in South Rhodesia which affects the animals necessitates the sheltering of cattle in dark stables even during the day. The family sleeps in the middle of a round hut and the cattle are tied all round. In Nigeria such a hut is known as Tum Tum. Stock rearing is, therefore, not a success in the hot-wet regions. The value attached to cattle as bride price and the social states of a man being assessed on the heads of cattle he possesses is partly due to the cost of rearing them in humid climates. The economy in such regions tends to be wholly agricultural and often exploitational.

There are diseases in the temperate regions also. But on the whole temperate climates are the best suited for man's health.

Vegetation

Vegetation is an indication of climatic factors. Most plants require a certain environment. Natural vegetation is indicative of the best use of land but it does not indicate the best use of land in terms of world demand. At certain stages it is best to maintain natural vegetation. Man cannot overtax land. The tropical forests, for example, live in a state of equilibrium. When the forests are destroyed the soil is deprived of the humus. Lack of cover raises the temperature of the soil and there is further destruction. Heavy rain percolates into the soil and there is leaching of the soil. The soils are also washed away. Laterisation is a very common feature in the tropical areas where vegetation has been removed and the rain is seasonal.

Vegetation holds the soil and cheeks soil erosion. But if soil has to be held by natural vegetation it means that the area available for cultivation will be less.

Vegetation can also be a barrier to development. The forests of Congo and the Amazon are impenetrable. It is difficult to construct adequate transport lines in thick jungles. Thick forests still harbour only very technically backward people.

The clearance of forests gives rise to many problems such as the leaching of the soil, laterisation and erosion. To maintain the the balance between natural vegetation and human demands needs careful planning. The carrying capacity of land, in part, depends on the fertility of the soil which in turn is partly dependent on vegetation because it provides the humus, so necessary for crop cultivation.

Soils

Soil is an important economic factor particularly to an agricultural country. Soil is the loose material, consisting of very fine to coarse rock particles, deposited on the rock mantle, through a continuous weathering process. The mineral content of the soil depends on the chemical composition of the parent rock from which it is derived. Over 90 per cent of the dry substance of the average soil is mineral matter. But once deposited, climatic conditions, vegetation cover and so on change the characteristics of the soil. Soil contains humus which is generally derived from decaying vegetation and animal matter. It also contains liquid and gaseous matter all of which are necessary for the growth of plants.

To the agriculturist only the top soils are of importance. The shallow roots of plants derive their food and moisture from this top layer of soils. But the depth of these soils varies from place to place, from a fraction of an inch to several feet, depending on the rate of deposition and erosion.

Soil is the link between the inorganic and the organic world. It maintains this link through a series of cycles, of which, the hydrologic and the nitrogen cycles are important. The great reservoir for the hydrologic cycle is the sea. Water goes from the sea to the air through evaporation, by condensation to clouds, to the earth in the form of precipitation, and back to the sea in rivers, in groundwater and so on. But during its temporary stay on the earth some of the water sinks into the soil, combines with other simple substances and is turned into organic compounds (living things) whose bodies are half water. The water in the organic compounds enter the bodies of living things only through the soil and the plants that grow on it.

Just as the great reservoir for the hydrologic cycle is the sea, the nitrogen in the atmosphere is the reservoir for the nitrogen cycle. Nitrogen exists in abundance in the air and acts as a diluent to oxygen. It is an inert gas. Certain bacteria living in the soils can convert the atmospheric nitrogen into nitrites which is worked upon by other bacteria and converted into nitrates. Nitrates are the only compounds of nitrogen that can be used by most plants. They suck them up from the soil water where it is found in dilute solutions. In the nodules of some plants live certain bacteria which can convert the nitrogen in the air to nitrates. These are the leguminous plants like clover, lupins, peas, beans which cultivators rotate with plants that exhaust the soil of nitrogen, as they are 'nitrogen-fixers'. Nitrogen is very important to plant growth. All these bacteria which convert nitrogen into nitrites and nitrates and make it usable for plants are called 'nitrifying' bacteria.

The plant builds the nitrates into amino acids and proteins. The animals feeding on the plant, absorb the amino-acids and proteins in the plant and build new proteins. The urine and dung of animals are nitrogenous wastes and they are returned to the soil. When dead, their bodies are worked upon by other bacteria in the soils and the proteins are broken into simpler substances of which ammonia is one. It escapes into the air, and being easily soluble in water, is returned to the earth with rain. Once again the cycle repeats itself.

The cycles in Nature are broken when man decides to clear forests, cultivate the land for his own crops or build industries and houses. But he is also capable of maintaining Nature's balance in the soil by man-made fertilizers and manures, irrigation and by scientific rotation of crops.

Soil is also closely linked with the parent rocks, vegetation and climate. These three together determine the nature, type and characteristics of the soil. The Coniferous Belt of Siberia has long cold winters and a short moist summer. The vegetation here is coniferous forests. The parent rock is ancient igneous and metamorphic to fairly thick sediments which does not weather easily. The hard pine needles of the coniferous trees contribute little to the organic matter of the top soil. On the contrary they are acidic. The melting snows of the spring and the summer rains wash the acids down. There is very little capillary action in the soil as the temperatures are never very high in these latitudes. The prevalent movement of water is downwards. The acidic rain water dissolves and removes most of the minerals from the upper layers of the soil leaving beind the resistant quartz grains. The resultant grey soil has very little humus or organic matter. It is, however, very loose and friable containing a large percentage of quartz. Although infertile it can be worked easily. The lower layer of the same soil, where the salts have been precipitated, undergoes chemical changes and is quite rich in potential plant foods. The deeper rooted coniferous trees thus find a favourable environment. In such a climate coniferous trees can always grow provided the trees are not felled and the balance is not upset. For purposes of cultivation such a soil will need manures on the top soil to make up the loss of minerals and humus by the downward movement of water. These are the podsolic (ash grey) soils of Russia, hungry, and unproductive but quite yielding and easy to plough.

In some of the heaths of England podsolic soils are found. The local rocks are poor sands and the vegetation is coniferous. But the climate is not so extreme as in Siberia. The percolating ground water dissolves the iron oxide of the parent rock. The decaying plants contribute enough humus to make a film of top layer somewhat black, but beneath, is a layer of leached light grey sand.

In such areas where the prevailing movement of water is downward, because of the cool moist climates, the soils are leached. They are poor in lime as carbonate of lime, which is easily soluble even in slightly acid solutions and so is the first mineral to be carried away with the percolating water. Such soils are grouped together as Pedalfers *al*, aluminium and *fer*, iron). They are non-lime-accumulating soils.

On the other hand, in warm, dry climates the upward movement of water in the soil is more prominent (capillary action). The soil loses more water than it gets because of the heat of the sun and the consequent evaporation, during most part of the year. This is the situation in the prairies of USA and the steppes of Russia. The natural vegetation in such areas can only be grass. The upward movement of water brings the salt to the top layer of soils. The grass does not provide enough humus on decaying and the soil is, therefore, poor in organic matter. Since lime is the most important of the salts that accumulate at the top, these soils are grouped together as Pedocals (*cal*, Calcium). They are lime-accumulating soils. These soils are very rich for a time. But if continuously ploughed or if they are left uncovered during the long dry season, they tend to become loose and friable, lacking in humus, and are blown away by the wind. But some of the soils of the prairies and the steppes are amongst the richest in the world. However, they can be easily destroyed by bad management.

Tropical soils also live in a state of equilibrium. Percolation of water leaches the soil. Soluble matter such as lime, potash, nitrogen, phosphoric acid and humus are very little or absent in the top soils. Felling of the trees reduces the humus content of the soil. Lack of cover increases the soil temperature and there is further destruction. Erosion is accelerated. Laterisation is also common in tropical soils. Laterites are quite infertile as they contain hydroxide of aluminium and hydroxide of iron which cannot be assimilated by plants. Laterites are also impermeable and they harden on exposure. Irrigation has no effect on it and chemical manures are harmful to laterites as they produce toxic soluble salts of alumina. Most tropical regions where vegetation has been removed are subject to laterisation, sometimes called pedological leprosy. It occurs particularly in hot-wet climates with alternate dry and wet seasons. In the dry season the capillary action brings to the surface hydroxide of alumina and iron and forms the laterite on the top layer. Heat and rain are required for leaching of the soils. An equatorial climate without a dry season will not produce laterisation. A monsoon climate as that of India is particularly suited for the formation of laterites. Laterite is formed at the expense of silicate rocks. Limestone areas in tropical regions are not subject to laterisation like the siliceous rocks. But limestone is hostile to agriculture because of the lack of surface water.

Soils, therefore, are the result of the combined interaction of the parent rock, vegetation and climate. The relationship between them change when trees are felled and the effect of climate on soil undergoes change through time. Erosion, transportation and deposition by water, wind and ice also affect the characteristics, properties, distribution and type of soils.

The geological factor

The availability of minerals, their accessibility to man, the quality of the ore, their location and economic exploitability are all dependent on the geological factor to a great extent. Geology also plays an important part in the mineral content of soils as already noted.

Taking coal for example, which serves modern industry in many ways and influences the location of heavy industries, it has its origin in the vast tropical like swamps with luxuriant plant growth which during the course of millions of years underwent chemical changes and was converted into coal. Rocks which were on the earth before the advent of vegetation (that is before the carboniferous period of the Palaeozoic era) such as the rocks of the older Palaeozoic (Cambrian, Ordovician, Silurian and Devonian) and those of the pre-Cambrian era, therefore, cannot contain coal. In India, these correspond to the Archaean (Dharwar-Aravalli systems), the Purana group (Vindhyan and Cuddapah series) and the upper Vindhyan series of the Dravidian group including those of Madhya Pradesh, Kashmir and the Central Himalaya. The lower carboniferous period corresponds to the upper Dravidian period in India. Most of the coals of India are found in the Aryan group of rocks corresponding to the upper carboniferous to the Jurassic. The lower, middle and upper Gondwana Coals belong to the Aryan group. Coals formed during the Eocene Period of the Tertiary and later are not of good quality as they are of recent (geologically) origin.

Likewise if the heating underground takes place too quickly (as during a volcanic eruption and lava flow) the vegetation is burnt out and cannot form coal. Instead igneous and metamorphic rocks are formed. Igneous rocks therefore do not contain coal.

The accessibility of coal to man does not only depend on the area of its occurrence but also on the depth at which it is found. The carboniferous period of the earth's history, when vegetation first made its appearance, was some 280 million years ago. These sediments have been superimposed by the deposits of the Permian period of the Upper Palaeozoic, the Triassic, Jurassic and the Cretaceous periods of the Mesozoic, the Eocene, Oligocene, Miocene and Pliocene of the Tertiary and the Pleistocene of the Quaternary, stretching over a period of some 300 millions years. When first deposited, the stratified rocks were usually laid down in almost horizontal beds or strata. If later earth movements had not tilted the earth's crust the coal would have remained at very great depths, inaccessible to mankind. But during the course of its long history, the earths' crest and mantle have undergone many changes. Vertical and horizontal movements have folded and tilted these stratified rocks. Folds and faults have created huge anticlines and synclines, rift valleys and other structural changes which have brought these coals sometimes nearer to the surface of the earth for Man's use. Man can now reach these coal bearing rocks through mining. Of these the coals on anticlinal formations are the easiest and most economic to mine as the coal bearing strata is more continuous than in a faulted structure. In overfold and overthrust formations also the continuity of the coal bearing strata is lost. The miner will have to rediscover the coal bearing rocks and the existing mine may have to be closed down. The coals of the Pennines of England occur on an anticline whose crests have been eroded leaving behind the coal on its flanks. But the region has been further disturbed by faulting, making mining more costly and difficult.

Coals are also of different variety ranging from anthracite, semi-anthracite, bituminous, semi-bituminous, sub-bituminous, lignite and peat. The quality of the coal, its heating capacity in fuels and so on, accidents in mines due to roof collapse, seepage of water are all due to the geological factor. This is true of all the ores and minerals. (see Chapter 7)

Geology also affects the quality of the soil. The mineral content or the chemical composition of the soil as mentioned is dependent on the parent rock from which it is weathered. It may be further mixed with other soils or transported to other regions where the parent rocks are different. Certain of these minerals are not only useful but necessary for plant growth, while in excess some of them may be detrimental. Three of the minerals which can be easily identified in soil are quartz, clay and calcite. Quartz cristals are found in the form of sand. They are hard and do not weather easily. The grains are too large to be carried away by wind. Such sandy soils are found in deserts. Although it is a dry soil lacking in humus, it is friable and easily worked. It lends itself to irrigation.

Feldspar is the source of clay and mineral salts in soil. Hornblende also decomposes into clay and soluble salts. Clay soils are very difficult to plough. They crack into cakes with the heat of the sun. They are sticky, impermiable and illdrained. But it is very rich in plant foods and can retain water. A good crop can be grown in these soils and often irrigation is not necessary. The cracks formed in the soil during the dry season help the water of the rainy season to sink in.

Calcite is the chief constituent or chalk of limestone. Lack of lime in soils can make it infertile although too much of it can be detrimental. Such soils however, cannot retain water.

Every soil contains one or more minerals. Some are easily identifiable while others need more elaborate analysis. The fertility of the soil depends partly on the presence of the various minerals necessary for plant growth, in the right measure.

Geological factors further have a direct impact on the laying out of transport lines. Roads and rails require a hard bed rock. In Russia the absence of a hard bed rock in certain parts, makes building of roads a problem. Important railways follow the line of moraines which mark the stage in the retreat of the Scandinavian ice sheet. The routes avoid low lying marshy areas. The railway line from Daugavpils to Leningrad and the famous high way to Moscow (used by Napoleon and later by Hitler) through Minsk, Orsha, Smolensk and Bondino, both run along the crests of end moraines. Transport also seeks the gaps in the mountain regions which are often the result of geological formations.

Geological factors are also responsible for the presence of underground water, artesian wells and the level of the water table, all of which have a direct bearing on agriculture and industry. Water is trapped underground when pervious rocks are underlain by an impervious stratum which checks the downward percolation of water. A crack in the top rock can release the underground water in the form of a spring or wells can be dug to tap this water.

The biological factor

The biological environment is of significance to economic geographer. Animals require protein, carbohydrates and fats just as man does. The extent of the livestock industry has an impact on the allocations of land for cultivating crops and for grazing. This forms a relationship between the species that eat and those that are eaten.

As populations grew, the relationship between man and other living things changed. A large number of them have become extinct due to widespread encroachment on forest land. Ever since the neolithic period methods to increase food supply have been sought. But while man has exterminated many pests, there are others which prey upon the increased food supply. Certain species have also increased in number since the disappearance of their natural enemies. Many of them are pests and a source of disease in plants, animals and men. Black fly on broad beans; white butterfly on cabbages; boll weevil in cotton; pests that infest grain fields, warehouses and storehouses such as rats, mice and cockroaches; moths on clothes; meal worms; house flies; sparrows and so on, are a few among the host of pests. There are also plant pests such as the microscopic plants (fungi) which cause blights, mildews, moulds, bunts, smuts, rust and diseases of cultivated plants. Most of the advanced countries now have strict legislation to control the influx of carriers of disease.

The cotton boll weevil came to the US from Mexico. It strongly influenced the distribution of cotton and the type of cotton grown. The weevil generally runs through several generations in one growing season so that it becomes a serious pest if cotton is allowed to stand long on the ground. But the best cottons with the longest and finest staples are those that take a long time to mature. These are the ones which are usually affected by the boll weevil. Planters in the USA were forced to grow short-growing varieties with coarser fibre after the boll weevil pest. It also forced the farmers of the South to diversify agriculture and grow crops other than cotton. Indirectly, however, the diversification of agriculture has been a boon to the South which, with a one-crop economy, had a very unbalanced development.

White butterflies on cabbages arrived in New Zealand in 1930 from some cabbages which drifted ashore to Napier Harbour. Now it is a pest in New Zealand.

In 1865 the Phyloxera attacked the vineyards of Europe. The leaf disease of coffee in Ceylon wiped out half the coffee plantations in 1869. The potato famine of 1846-47 in Ireland was the work of a small fungus *Phytophthora infesitans* which came from America. It had a disastrous effect on Irish peasants whose main food is potato. Nearly two and a half million people died of starvation or migrated.

The rust fungi which live in barbary bushes attack wheat in spring and spread very rapidly destroying miles of wheat land, The red and black rusts of wheat are two forms of the same fungus, Puccina Craminio, and they are problems to the wheat cultivators of the world. In 1916-17 Puccina destroyed 200 million bushels of wheat in the USA and 100 million in Canada. The pest had to be controlled at great expense by spraying fungicide. In 1940 a rust-resistant spring wheat 'Thatcher' was introduced into the US.

There are also pests like locusts peculiar to one crop or a small range of crops. Bugs which affect the the cocoa plant in Gold Coast, have even changed the farming practices in the Gold Coast.

The pest factor operates not only during cultivation but also between harvest and consumption and in warehouses. Control of pests costs money which puts up the overhead costs.

All these pests and diseases in plants and animals (and men) are of importance to an intelligent analysis of the economic patterns and types in a region. They cause a great deal of loss, undependability in production and sometimes have a great impact on agriculture, as well as on industry and housing conditions.

2

THE HISTORICAL FACTOR

SINCE Ritter expounded his theme 'the historical factor in Geography', it has been recognised that geography must use historical matter 'to understand the presence and character of existing things'. But, in spite of Ritter's emphasis on the time factor in understanding present patterns, many geographers continued to believe that Geography could explain existing phenomena in terms of contemporary conditions. Even today there are geographers, particularly in this country, who look askance at those who emphasise the historical factor in Geography and summarily dismiss them as unscientific. But the past is the key to the present in all aspects of Geography whether physical or human. While the physical geographical element changes slowly and more often has to maintain a geological time scale, the human element is subject to comparatively rapid changes. There may have been long periods in history when a society remained almost static for want of an impetus to change the existing patterns. On the other hand, there have been periods in history when violent revolutionary changes have taken place and in a short time changed the face of earth. Even a war can be a great stimulant to technical and socio-cultural advancement.

Geographical factors are not static. They do change in time. The human aspects of geography are most unpredictable. In some cases the existing geographic patterns cannot be explained in terms of current processes but only in terms of the past. Geography was never merely a descriptive subject but one which sought the causes of existing patterns of phenomena in an area. The time factor and what happened in the past in that area are an integral part of geography. The economic geographer who is investigating the present economic patterns in an area, therefore, must dig into the past to fully comprehend the cause of such patterns.

But how far back in time should he go. This depends on the problem and the region he is investigating. He turns historian only insofar as it explains the present.

Historical Geography, is the reconstruction of a past geography and is now accepted as one of the branches of this discipline. The methodology the historical geographer uses, when he delves into the past patterns is the same as that of the geographer who attempts to comprehend present patterns in an area. The synthesis, the causal relationship of phenomena, the impact of both the human and physical phenomena on an area, all these are common to the study of a past period and an analysis of the present. Both studies use the time factor to understand geography.

To grasp the full significance of economic patterns, a search into the past happenings in the area is necessary to understand their impact on the present areal patterns and types of economy. Many characterstic features of an economic system, their distribution patterns, their rate of growth, their regression and decay, all are in some way or other related to the past happenings in that area. New discoveries, new technical developments, increased knowledge of plant and animal, and of human societies and their organizations, awareness of regional variations, government legislation from time to time, international controls and policies are 'happenings' during the course of time which may or may not have left their mark on the ground. It is for the economic geographer to sift out what is relevant in the past to explain or even forecast patterns.

Physical conditions in an area may be the initial forces that dominated economy but man is still the most important factor that makes use of the physical resources to create an economic pattern. The motives for developing a particular economic system change from time to time and from place to place. Diagrammatically the relationship between space and time may be presented as (Fig. 2.1):

During the course of time, man gets certain impulses or impetus to work the physical environment and put it to his use. The cause and intensity of this impulse or impetus may vary due to specialized needs and technical skills available. Generally, 'necessity is the mother of invention'. But the force which drives man to meet his needs is a 'human resource' and like any other resource of the world is unevenly distributed. An increase in demand, attractive returns for the effort put in, a desire to better conditions, the

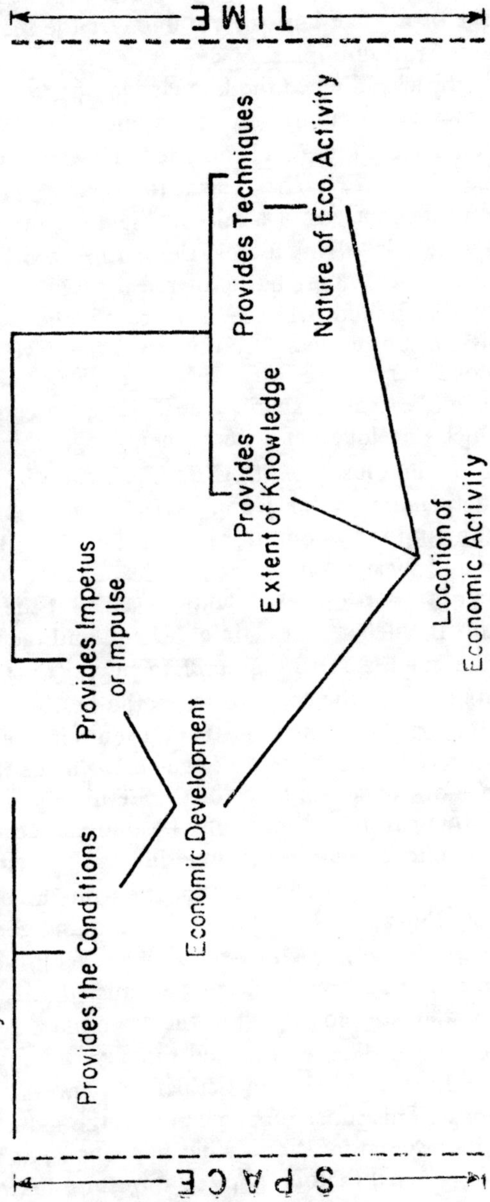

FIG : 2.1. *The relationship between space and time.*

emergence of institutions or Governments which provide the directive force or a sheer curiosity to uncover the secrets of nature may be the motivating impulse.

Man has been adding to the knowledge of the earth ever since he came on the scene some six thousand years ago. He has developed better techniques and tools to bring nature's resources to the service of man. He has learnt to organise production and distribution from the needs of a self-sufficient society to that of a commercial society involving almost the entire world. This skill and knowledge which man has gathered through experience are also unevenly distributed over the surface of the earth so that today there is a clear-cut distinction between the developed and the developing countries.

History alone can explain the present location of some industries which developed at a time when geographical conditions were different from those existing today. The Iron and steel industry of Bethlehem (Pennsylvania, USA) may be explained in terms of contemporary conditions, such as availability of coal in Pennsylvania and West Virginia, iron in the Lake Superior region and the ports of import on the Atlantic coast. But the industry was established in Bethlehem at a time when anthracite coal was available in the north-eastern region. Except for a slight shift of the new plants towards the coast to make the best use of the port facilities for imported ore, the industry continues in the same region although anthracite coal is no longer used in the industry. The full significance of the continuance of the Bethlehem steel works in East Pennsylvania can be grasped only by understanding the role of geographical phenomena in the area during the past.

The same is true of the location of the iron and steel industry in north-eastern England. Originally, both iron and good coal were available here within easy reach of each other. With the continued expansion of the industry, iron got exhausted, necessitating its import. But the industry continued in the same place because of a relationship established between it and the physical environment in the past. The industry, like that of Bethlehem, shows a slight shift towards the coast. This does not mean that the industry is pulled away from the original location. What happens is, as the industry grows and geographical factors and relationship between phenomena change, the new plants that spring up are located to the old plants to take advantage of the established location, and also at places which make use of the changing geographical factors influencing the industry. There is never a wholsale shift of any industry to a completely new location unless the profits at the new place are greater than the losses incurred in the shift. It is far more economic to continue the industry in the same place at a marginal profit than shift wholly to a new place or close down the works. Shifting an industry involves shifting towns and the services connected with them. This tardy response of old industries to new environmental conditions is called geographical inertia. The development of techniques, the inventions and discoveries of new fuels and metals during the period of the Industrial Revolution (the eighteenth century) developed the characteristics and location of the industries in England. Much of the iron and steel industries of England do not have the same physical advantages they had when they were first established in particular areas. The iron and steel regions of South Wales, Midlands, the North East and the Edinborough-Glasgow rift valley are now considered problem areas economically. But the works continue in the same place regardless of the deteriorating geographical environment effected by time.

The same is true of British farming. New techniques introduced after the agricultural revolutions of the fourteenth century and later in the seventeenth and eighteenth centuries called for large farms. But the response to the new techniques was slow. British agricultural methods did not change. There is usually a gap between technical inventions and the implementation of these in practice, either due to the cost factor or because of the reluctance of man to take the risk of moving from the known to the unknown. Such lack of response to new environmental conditions are seen today also.

On the other hand Communist Russia's response to the great October Revolution of 1917 was almost immediate and brought with it a tremendous change in industry, agriculture, transport and other economic activities. The five year planned developments beginning with 1927 changed the face of the USSR within a few years.

The Industrial Revolution which reached Germany in the nineteenth century also effected many changes. France, after World War II, has entered a period of significant econ changes but lagged behind Germany and England in the eight and nineteenth centuries.

It was also due to certain factors in history that the American economic pattern evolved as a contrast to the patterns in Europe. The same racial stock that inhabited Europe came to the USA in the seventeenth century. The physical conditions in the north-eastern regions of the USA, which were settled first, were somewhat similar to that of Europe. There was plenty of fertile land to be cultivated and industrial resources were also considerable. Yet the economy of USA and Europe developed along different lines. History alone can give a clue to this differential development.

Europe was settled long before the railway age. In the context of the slow transport available at that time, each region and community had to develop a certain amount of self-sufficiency in economy. Europe also went through a period when canals were the major form of inland transport. Industrial and commercial centres cropped up on the canals to take advantage of the cheap and convenient waterways. All these developments of a period prior to the industrial revolution left their mark on the ground. In Europe, therefore, the post revolution industries are a superimposition on the past patterns and their impact can be seen in the present factory industries. On the other hand, till the eighteenth century there was no great development in America. Only its Atlantic fringes were settled at the time when Europe went through a major industrial revolution. The great penetration into the interior of America came after the railway age. The USA rapidly absorbed the techniques of industrial Europe both in agriculture and industry. The trans-continental railways were built. The railways offered free land in the empty west to anyone willing to move in and develop it in order to ensure the economic running of the railways. America began her life with the modern period with a heavy export-import economy. Its present economy, therefore, is different from that of Europe.

The industrial revolution in England had also an impact on the economy of Argentina. Argentina had to increase its food supply to feed the growing industrial population of England in the nineteenth century. Two-thirds of the population of Argentina today live in large towns of more than a million, distributed generally along the coast, while the interior is comparatively empty. This imbalance in the rural-urban population of Argentina can be comprehended only in its historical context.

The physical environment of Argentina does not give any clue to this peculiar feature in population distribution. This country is an open grassland with environmental opportunities even for a people lacking in advanced technology. Except for the northern section which is rather mountainous, the land is flat and quite favourable for cultivation and for the construction of rails and roads. Lack of accessibility is not a problem for human settlement. The climate on the whole is also good with mild winters and hot summers. The vegetation is grass, the soil deep, composed of sand, clay, silt and wind-blown loess, eminently suited for crop raising. Even though surface water is not plenty, there is enough subsoil water for crops. The open plains and fertile soil call for a fair distribution of population over the entire area.

The region has none of the industrial resources which demand concentration of econonmic activity at particular places. It has very little coal and no iron for heavy iron and steel industries which normally give rise to a concentration of population in small areas. Yet the population of Argentina lives in very large urban settlements.

Argentina was first settled by the Spanish colonials who were a non-agricultural people rearing scrubby half wild cattle. The great transformation of the humid Pampas, which now has distinct regional subdivisions, came between 1850 and 1870. In 1853 the new Federal Constitution was introduced and a degree of political stability was achieved in Argentina. When she stepped into the modern period, her characteristic features were a sparse population, a people only interested in horses, cattle and sheep and not in agriculture, an abundance of first quality grazing land and land for farming and the tradition of large private estates (*Estencias*).

The impulse which changed the face of the humid Pampas came not from Argentina but from England. Britain had by this time gone through the industrial revolution and had become the workshop of the world. She had to raise more and more food for her growing industrial population. The small size of the country and the limitation in arable land did not permit expansion of agriculture. Moreover, there was no incentive to invest in agriculture when huge profits were accruing from industry and commerce. It was more economic to invest the accumulated capital in other countries with suitable land and excl industrial products for the food necessary for her increasing urban population. Britain began to depend on imported food. Most of the world's humid grasslands were still scantily populated. The conversion of these grasslands into food producing areas, a characteristic feature of the latter half of the nineteenth century, was achieved through a series of technical developments.

The industrial revolution in England had already ushered in the railway age. Knowledge of plants and animals, their relationship with the environment and knowledge of the hitherto unknown parts of the world had accumulated. Argentina's humid Pampas offered favourable conditions for the investment of the surplus capital of industrial Britain, to produce the food necessary for its population. Britain decided to open up Argentina with rails and roads. Between 1880 and 1886 the flow of British capital to Argentina was very strong. Most of the railroads were built by British Companies.

The flat land was conducive to the building of a transport system and there was rapid development of roads and rails.

The railroads brought huge profits to the *estencias* and the stock holders. The land being already partitioned into large units by the Spanish colonists, whose prestige rested on ownership of land, life in the *estencias* did not change. They still had a pastoral base. In the beginning, only Argentinian cattle were raised. They were good only for the production of salted beef, hides and tallow. But the salted meat had no market in Europe. In 1877 the refrigerator ship was invented which made it possible to send frozen meat to England. But British taste would not accept Argentinian meat. High grade beef cattle was then imported from England to meet the market demands of a British population. These animals needed careful breeding and could not be reared on the grass and scrub of Argentina. The shift to fenced pastures from scrubland pasture came between 1880 and 1900. The new animal needed better feed. Alfalfa was grown as cattle feed and in the humid Pampas it grew exceptionally well.

The whole economy being geared to an export market, the transport lines converged on the ports which transported the frozen meat to Europe. There was no need for small collecting centres on the routes as there was no market in the interior. A concentration of urban activity in the port-cum-large collecting centres induced them to grow further. There was demand for services such as water, electricity, transport, entertainment, brewery, and so on. They also developed consumer industries such as the textile industry and the canning industry. The ports and collecting centres became also industrial centres attracting to them more population and more services.

The Spanish colonials who owned the *estencias* being urban people, this culture was transferred to Argentina without great difficulty. The Spaniards, in spite of the fact that their prestige depended on land, were at home only in an urban environment.

Finally much of Argentina was opened up after mechanisation was introduced into agriculture. When Britain decided to open up Argentina with roads and railways she also introduced mechanized farming. There was very little necessity to increase rural population. Labour was needed in the large collecting centres rather than at the farms. The methods of farming introduced into Argentina also necessitated the growth of an urban population. People migrated from Europe. As a result of all these historical happenings Argentina today has about two-third of her population concentrated in very large towns. The emptiness of rural Argentina is still one of her greatest economic problems. With the introduction of wheat cultivation in the Pampas, this rural emptiness is creating even more problems. The economic instability of Argentina is reflected in her political instability. In this manner Argentina's economy was influenced by forces outside the country.

The location of the cotton textile industry in Ahmedabad in India is also the result of certain factors in history and the policies followed by a colonial Government in the nineteenth century. England decided to develop the textile industry in Lancashire by importing ginned cotton and yarn from India. Bombay became the major export port of cotton and cotton yarn. Gradually it also became a centre of a British-owned textile industry. Indian indigenous textiles were debarred from entering the British market even as early as the eighteenth century and there was no possibility of reviving its trade after Britain acquired territorial control over India and introduced new policies. Lancashire protected her industries by tariffs which prevented Indian calicoes entering England. Next, the Lancashire cottons began to invade India. No protection was given to the Indian industries by the foreign Government. With competition from mill cloth and the policies of an alien

Government, the indigenous industry declined. During World War I, Japanese competition with Lancashire cottons in the Indian market, proved a blow to the British textile industry. It also stimulated the revival of the Indian cotton textile industry under Indian managerial control. But the Indian entrepreneurs of the new factory industry, finding land prices in Bombay very high preferred up-country locations where land was cheap. The choice of Ahmedabad was mainly due to the fact that it was the home-town of one of the pioneers of the new factory-based textile industry.

Ahmedabad had also longstanding experience in the manufacture of handlooms. Her skill in spinning and weaving the finest cottons had been achieved long before it became a factory industry. Economic geographers are often tempted to explain the location of the textile industry in Ahmedabad in terms of the existing conditions namely that it is situated in the midst of a rather rich cotton area, that its transport links with the interior and with the ports are adequate, that it has enterprising industrialists with the necessary capital and that its market has a comparatively high purchasing capacity. But the location of the industry in Ahmedabad can be fully explained only with reference to the history of the factory-based cotton textile industry in India and the hostile policies followed by the British Government. The industry was not established in Ahmedabad because the pioneers found cotton growing in abundance in the region. On the contrary the loamy sandy soils were not as suited to the growing of cotton as the black soils of the Deccan. But the enterprising Gujarat peasant finding a ready market for cotton was induced to cultivate cotton in place of subsistence crops for better profits. He could grow cotton in the loamy dry soils of central north Gujarat only with the help of irrigation and fertilizer. Cotton cultivation as it exists, therefore, followed the location of the industry in Ahmedabad. It did not generate it.

Ahmedabad was also not particularly endowed with transport links with the interior. The'nodality' of an industrial centre which gives it access to the market and the raw materials, was not one of the attributes of Ahmedabad when the industry was established there. Most of the broadgauge railway lines of British India bypassed Ahmedabad and focussed on Bombay through Baroda-Surat and Indore-Mhow. Even today one of the problems of industrial Ahmedabad is its inadequate transport. Its links with much of the rest of the country are mainly by metre-gauge railway, some of which are quite circuitous. With independence some broad-gauge lines have been opened but the breakthrough in transport is still to come.

Government legislations also can halt or develop industry at a given time. The capacity of the Pittsburg steel to compete with the steel centres of the Lake ports was because of the Basing Point (abolished in 1948) which decreed that no steel could be sold at a lesser price than Pittsburg steel. It was a protection given to a particular steel company because it served the greatest needs of the nation at the time. It halted the shift of the industry westwards to the iron region and the coasts of the lakes for some time although these locations would have been more economic.

Examples of government legislation hindering the course and pattern of a country's economy were innumerable in the colonial period when the mother-country often decided to curb indigenous industries to boost up their own industry.

3

HUMAN RESOURCES

THE physical resources of the earth gain an economic value only when they are of use to man. Natural resources are bestowed with commercial value by man. Man is the beneficiary as well as an agent of production. Human resources, therefore, are quite distinct from natural resources. So far as the economic geographer is concerned, it is the working population, which comprises the labour force of a country which is of significance. It is this section of the population which contributes to production in the country. Besides, supplying the labour force, the population also serves as a market for the products which are generated by labour. Man contributes his labour, directs the production processes, discovers new ways of utilising his environment, and invents new arts. It is his capacity to work and think, his ability to direct and organize the forces of Nature, his technical skills and his determination to better himself that makes him economically useful. Man is outside the environment and yet a part of it. Without him a natural resource cannot become an economic resource.

If man is so vital to the production and the market, the size and density of the population, its rate of growth, age and sex composition, the population's efficiency as a labour force and its capacity to function as a market and so on in a given region are factors which have a vital bearing on the economic development of the region.

SIZE AND DENSITY OF POPULATION AND ITS RELATION TO LAND

A world map of population density shows that density is higher in the coastal plains and river valleys of south-east Asia, where the soils are fertile and the economy is agricultural. Huntington sees a connection between the monsoon lands and the concentration of population in asiatic countries. In Europe and N. America he discovered a link between the cyclonic storm-belt and population density. In Europe and N.E. America a great concentration of population occurs near coalfields and more recently where petroleum, natural gas and water power are available. The development of heavy industries and consumer industries based on power resources has given rise to the concentration of population in these areas. Large crowds of people also flock to the crossroads of commerce, be they nodes on the sea routes. Several regions of the world which have natural resources, an early start in life and advanced economies have also attracted people.

The size and density of population are only of statistical value. The 'quantity' of people in an area has to be critically assessed in relation to the availability of resources. A high density of population may indicate over-population but even a low density of population can cause problems of over-population. All densely populated regions of the world are not regions of squalor and poverty. Some of them maintain very high standards of living. On the other hand, there are regions which are sparsely populated and whose inhabitants only just eke out an existence. Population density and numbers, therefore, are to be related to the carrying capacity of land to understand its economic significance. This "carrying capacity of land" cannot be measured in terms of acreage but has to be evaluated in terms of its productive capacity which is reflective of its ability to support human life and satisfy human wants. The more advanced a society, the more complicated is the assessment of the carrying capacity of land. In simple societies the measurement of land capacity is more easily achieved than in societies with complex economic and social organizations. Every new technique, every new way of life and new use of land, every discovery of a new resource, any change in the relationship between man and land, require a reassessment of the carrying capacity of land.

Further, the " carrying capacity of land" is not confined only to the region one is investigating. Commercial activities and the capacity to invest capital in distant lands have broken down the economy of self-sufficiency, creating a gap between the place of production and the place of consumption. In modern times, therefore, the carrying capacity of land does not mean the internal carrying capacity but also its external capacity. England, during her imperial days was exchanging her industrial products for food. She invested her savings accumulated through an industrial economy in foreign lands and she collected the interest in foodstuffs and raw material. She established territorial claims over much of the underdeveloped world, thousands of miles away. The carrying capacity of land in England of the imperial days had to be assessed in terms of the products she could command from regions over which she claimed territorial sovereignty and other administrative rights. She could not have supported the population of her top heavy industrial economy but for her "external carrying capacity" derived from the colonies, Empire and the Commonwealth countries. Holland had an internal capacity of land to support a population of 120 per square mile. When she had her colonies to depend upon, she could support about 540 people per square mile and was still not considered overpopulated. The political changes in Indonesia (former Netherlands, East Indies) affected the man-land ratio in Holland. The relationship between the number of people and the acreage of land they live in, lost its significance during the colonial period. This was a common feature of most of the colonial countries till World War II shattered the hold partly. Today some of these countries still have huge investments in the mines and in the agricultural and industrial resources of the backward countries which can benefit them in terms of their land capacity. New industrial countries like the US are also exploiting such primary resources in the developing world, because of its capacity to invest capital.

Trends in population and its effect on the carrying capacity of land

When population increases in an area, the internal capacity of land to support the population becomes inadequate. There is more and more pressure on land. If no force, (such as improved technology, extensive and intensive cultivation or an industrial break-through), improves the capacity of land to meet the challenge of an increasing population, it becomes 'pent-up' in area and the standard of living gradually declines as in China, India and some of the south-east Asian countries. In other words, it becomes an overpopulated country with increasing pressure on land. According to Malthus, whose 'Essay on Population' was first published in 1798, such a region would lose its population through malnutrition, disease, death and natural calamities so that nature's balance is restored. Malthus wrote before the industrial revolution when the capacity of land was confined to agricultural production and its internal resources.

Most regions of the West, when faced with overpopulation, met the challenge with industrialization, commercial expansion, territorial acquisition and migration. England went through the industrial revolution in the eighteenth century and Germany in the nineteenth century. The lack of incentive to industrialization in France, when other European countries stepped up their activities, is attributed partly to its slow growth of population. France's industrial achievements came only after World War II. Commercial expansion of a region which could not support its people (atleast till the eighteenth and nineteenth centuries) led to territorial acquisition. The Empire builders of the eighteenth and nineteenth centuries were merchants.

An increase in population in a region must be viewed in relation to the resources. It is usually an accepted theory that when means of sustenance increase, numbers also increase. But this has been disproved in the industrially developed regions of the West. Man has greatly increased his capacity to produce more food and more industrial products through technical revolutions of immense significance since Malthus wrote his Essay. But it is in these very highly developed regions where production is at a maximum that population is tending to level-off or even decline.

A region with an agricultural economy seems to have a higher birthrate than a region with an industrial economy. The attitude towards raising large families seems to have changed with the mechanical revolution. The crowded industrial cities of the world do not have the facilities for housing large families. The need for technical skills to support oneself has made education a necessary attribute of city life. Urban people now look to a higher standard of living, better environment, better education and better facilities for their families. In an undeveloped agricultural and handicraft economy, prevalent in many parts of Afro-Asia a large family is an asset. Even children can be gainfully employed in the field or be taught to handle simple tools of a handicraft industry. Besides food of some kind is not a big problem in a village-based economy as it is, amongst the city population. Whatever the reason for this disparity in the population growth in the agricultural and the highly developed industrial countries, it is atleast proof that numbers do not increase when means of sustenance increase. While there is a tendency to increase the population in the early stages of industrialization, the US and several countries of Europe in the west, and Japan in the east, have levelled off their population after a few decades of development. Some of these countries even show a decline in population which is alarming the white nations of the world. Worse still, the new preventive measures against diseases, better care of the sick, better drugs and so on are giving these people an extended life so that the death rate is falling. The large number of people in the age group of above 50 (above efficient working age) is proving to be an economic drag.

Standards of living

The standard of living of a people is directly connected with the resources available and the number of people that have to be supported with a given resource. Since natural resource is converted into an economic resource only through human effort and technical skills, the total resource of a region is reflective of its human efficiency.

$$\text{Standard of living is therefore : } \frac{\text{Resources} \times \text{Technique}}{\text{Population numbers}}$$

Mechanization is the one single factor that has changed the standard of living in the developed countries. Agriculture can rarely bring in the profits that a successful industry can. Hence, the capacity of an agricultural community to accumulate capital and reinvest it in new enterprises is much less than that of an industrial community. Land which used to produce the necessities of life is now producing commodities which enable man to live in comfort and luxury. The market for such products is elastic and the commerce of the world has expanded from a trickle to a flood with improved techniques in transport. Industry and commerce have raised the standard of living in the world in the last two centuries to a great extent.

It is clear that if population increases without any increase in production, the standard of living will go down, the purchasing capacity of the people will decrease, and the markets for the products of economic activity will shrink. The underdeveloped countries of the world have a low standard of living and low purchasing capacity partly because of lack of technical skill and partly due to the exploitative economy which is a characteristic feature of most of these regions. In an exploitative economy, the profits of industry and agriculture are appropriated by the mother country or investing country, whose entrepreneurs own most of the industries. The choice of area for the reinvestment of the capital accrued as profits is left to these capitalists so that the region in question does not necessarily benefit by the increased production.

At the rate of the present production and the financial commitments to the lending countries, therefore, the underdeveloped regions of the world are facing problems of over-population. A formula given by H.W. Singer, based on the work of Harrod Damar and Hicks, gives the position in one of these countries (Egypt) which, more or less, is applicable to all the countries which are backward, if not in actual statistics, atleast in principle.

The rate of growth of per capita income (D) (Standard of living), says Hicks, is equal to the rate of net savings (S), multiplied by the productivity of new investments per unit of capital investment (P), minus the annual rate of growth of population (R). Singer gives the following formula, $D=SP-R$ and the figures corresponding to these in his area of investigation, as follows:

$S=6$ Per cent of the national income
$P=0.2$
$R=1.25$
$D=SP-R$, that is, $6\times0.2-1.25=-.05$

Hence the rate of growth of the per capita income is less than zero. In other words, where production does not catch up with the increasing population there is no improvement in the standard of living. It might remain steady or even decline depending on the capacity to increase production or check the growth rate of population. The standard of living is of great significance to the economic geographer. Changes in population trends vitally affect the resource appraisal of a country and the standard of living.

Some countries are considered overpopulated and some, underpopulated but an overpopulated country can reach an optimum population by increasing production or by decreasing population by birth control. Which of the two policies is followed depends on the wisdom of its Government or its people.

Optimum level

An intermediary position between extreme overpopulation and extreme underpopulation is considered an ideal man-land ratio. The ratio is referred to as the 'optimum population density'. The word optimum means 'best' and is thus subjective. People differ in their opinion of what is best. Hence there is no statistical measurement or even estimates for the optimum level. But an acquaintance with the "concept of optimum level" is worthwhile. Zimmerman says "To a painter who sees beauty only in nature the optimum level may be zero. To the sociologist who believes in Summer's dictum that 'civilisation is a function of numbers in contact', the optimum may be higher. But to the economist the optimum level is of purely material and untilitarian value". According to Woolfe, "Population optimum is that man-land ratio which yields the largest amount of final consumer goods in return for a given energy output". But given the same energy output, the yield and output of man differ from place to place, depending on his skill, knowledge, the will to work and many other factors. So the optimum level of population differs from society to society, from place to place and from time to time.

To reach the optimum level in population, a country or region does not have to depend on an increase or decrease in population. Space handicap can be overcome by improved transport. Technical improvements can increase production and bring the population near to the optimum level.

Apart from the size and density of population, trends in population, its relation to land and standards of living, there are various other aspects of population which have a vital impact on economic development. The distribution of population within an economic unit, the average expectation of life, age group and sex ratio, all affect labour and market.

DISTRIBUTION OF POPULATION

The distribution of population within an economic unit may be unbalanced. Natural resources such as good suitable land, good location for industries and trade, availability of minerals and such environmental factors may first attract population to a particular area. But the existing population and the sheer fact that an area is settled earlier, may draw to it more and more population during course of time. Economic factors such as intense use of land, industrial development, trade and commerce and the capacity to draw resources from outside (for example colonies), demand for labour, service functions and transport facilities in turn induce further influx of population. The availability of natural, historical and economic facilities tend to give a pattern to the distribution of population within an economic unit. There is overcrowding in one place and lack of population in another, even in an area as small as a city or town. Populations also migrate from rural to urban areas in search of jobs thereby causing an urban-rural imbalance, giving rise to many economic problems such as the depletion of rural areas and the consequent deterioration of agriculture, and problems of housing, sanitation, unemployment, and slums in the towns.

Distribution of population within a given economic unit is affected also by certain human factors. People choose to live in certain places and once they are established somewhere they resent change. This leads to overpopulation in certain areas within the unit and underpopulation in other areas in the same unit. In certain areas colour prejudices affect the distribution pattern of population. In the US the Negroes are forced to live in certain areas. The same is true in South Africa. In the latter, the area reserved for the Negroes increased its population without any increase in resources as they were generally only hired labourers in the British mines. This led to congestion, poverty and squalor in the Negro areas. Hence, Africa which is considered an underpopulated country has problems of overpopulation because of certain prejudices on the part of the ruling community.

In Egypt 99 per cent of the people live jammed in 4 per cent of its land. The rest of the country is uninhabited. Egypt has all the challenges of overpopulation and underpopulation. China's teeming population is more or less crammed in the eastern provinces (proper China) partly due to its fertility and partly due to its historical significance. An unbalanced distribution of population can create acute economic problems. Whatever unit the economic geographer is investigating, such factors in population distribution are of significance to his final analysis of population problems.

Expectation of life

The average expectation of life in a country or region is important to the economic geographer because it gives a clue to the working life of a man or the efficiency of the labour force of a country. Some of the European countries have an expectation of life of about 60 to 65. New Zealand, Australia and the US also come very close to Europe in the average expectation of life. Indian expectation of life has increased from 27 in the 1930s to about 47 and more at present.

It is the working population that supports the whole population. The training period of a worker lasts upto 14 years in some countries and upto 20 to 22 years in special techniques. The average expectation of life suggests the length of period a man can contribute to production after his training period.

Age group

The age groups of population is significant to the economic geographer for the same reason. A worker is virile and healthy normally from the age of 20 to 50. If the average expectation of life in an area is high and the number in the 50 to 60 (and more) group is large it can be a liability to the country or region. On the other hand, if the average expectation of life is low (27 or 30) the country may be deprived of its working force after having invested its capital in the training of the population for over 20 years. This is a great economic loss to the country. The group represented by the 20 to 50 age (roughly the working force, other things being the same) will show a declining trend. The young age group represented by 0 to 14 or 0 to 20 age can be recognized as the group that contributes to the future labour force of the region. A region with a high rate of infant mortality loses much of its potential labour force. The average expectation of life, the age group in the population and the rate of mortality in the different age groups are to be considered while analysing the impact of population on the economic development of a region.

Sex ratio

Sex ratio of the population ascertain the future labour supplies of a region as well as its present labour supplies. Women generally do not work in heavy industries. In certain countries there are legislations preventing women from working in such industries. In an agricultural country, on the other hand, women do form a substantial labour force. In the tribal villages of India women work shoulder to shoulder with men. The sex ratio of the population has to be viewed in the context of the requirements of labour in a region.

Sex ratio of the population also has an effect on the social life of the people in a region, which in turn affects its economy.

Occupational Classification

The occupational classification of population is significant to the economic geographer because on it is based the functional groupings of population. A region with a high proportion of its population working in tertiary activities is considered a developed region while one with a high proportion in primary activities (generally an agricultural or mining region) is considered backward. The economic characteristics of a region can be assessed from the occupational structure of the population. The validity and reliability of such an assessment will, however, depend largely on the detailed data available regarding the functions the people are engaged in.

Caste, Language, others

Other factors in population which may have a bearing on the economy of a region are racial differences, language differences, marriage age, education, urban-rural composition and mobility. In India the caste differences have a great impact on its economy particularly in the rural areas. In South Africa there is the problem of apartheid. Language differences exist in many countries such as Bulgaria, other east European countries and the USSR, creating problems in economic cohesion. In India, each language group has its own state and the different states are entitled to a certain amount of autonomy in economic development so much so that the language areas are rapidly becoming economic units. This prevents a national outlook, and a national economic plan taking force, which is so necessary for a developing country.

Literacy

Education of the population is an absolute necessity for economic advancement. The census usually records the population of literate and illiterate people in a country. But literacy alone does not ensure economic progress. It merely provides the foundation on which economic skills can be developed. The high percentage of illiteracy found in many of the undeveloped countries is reflective of the quality of its potential and present labour force. Many social and political problems also arise out of illiteracy which have an impact on the economy of the region.

All aspects of population are to be viewed by the economic geographer with the purpose of ascertaining its quality and quantity in terms of labour and market and the impact it has made on areal patterns.

4

THE LABOUR FORCE

To the economic geographer the quantity and quality of labour in a given region is of the utmost significance because it is the labour force of a country or region that is responsible for the quantity and quality of the production of the region. It is the labour force of the country that converts its natural resources into commodities for man's use. It is the link between the physical world of raw material and the economic world of vendible commodities.

Hence the quantity of labour available in the region, its quality, its distribution, its relation to the requirements of labour in the region, its outlook, mobility etc. have all a bearing on economic development.

THE QUANTITY OF LABOUR

The quantity of labour in a given region has to be measured against the requirements of the particular region it serves. A region which is considered underpopulated may still have problems of unemployment and underemployment because its economy is not advanced enough to provide work for its population. Unemployment occurs when supply of labour is greater than the requirement (demand) for labour. Even in countries like the US, which is not considered overpopulated, there are problems of unemployment partly because mechanization has reduced the need for human labour. But in Asiatic countries unemployment is mainly the consequence of retarded economic growth. Where supply of labour is in excess of demand, wages tend to be low, trade unions lack strength and the purchasing capacity of the people is below par.

DISTRIBUTION AND REGIONAL CONCENTRATIONS OF LABOUR

The distribution of labour depends on the facilities available in particular centres or regions and on the distribution of population in general. The attraction of better jobs, better wages, better housing, better living conditions, better services, better facilities for education, wider opportunities, bonuses, pull the labour force to areas where such facilities are available. Usually it is the cities and towns that have the maximum of such facilities. Migration of labour from the rural to the urban areas is a common feature in almost all parts of the world. But the force of this migration varies from place to place depending on the dynamism of the town to attract labour and the power of land and agriculture to stem the tide. The concentration of population in towns is because of their capacity to satisfy human wants, ambitions and desires. The rural-urban migration is a characteristic feature particularly in the early stages of industrial development. It wears off gradually when growth in the town ceases or levels off.

Further, the concentration of skilled labour in particular areas can create regional variations in its economy. The quality of labour required by an industrial country is different from that of an agricultural country. Specialised skills, industrial morale, output per man, hours of work and so on have changed the type of labour required for economic activity. Such skills may be concentrated regionally. A particular kind of skill required by the region may not be available in that region. The heavy industries, for example, do not employ women, leaving a large section of the population (female) unemployed. Sometimes, traditional and cultural factors debar women from working as in the Muslim countries or in some Asian communities. Such features create shortage of labour as well as problems of unemployment.

Skills of a specialised nature were also required in the pre-industrial age, which resulted in clear-cut regions of industrial activity. The woollen industry (carpets and shawls) of Kashmir, the metal and brocade industry of Varanasi (Banaras), the tie-and-dye industry of Rajasthan and Gujarat, the Patolas of Patan, the Kinkhab of the Punjab, were all localized in particular areas during the handicraft period, because of the availability of skilled labourers in that area. Even now they show regional concentrations for the same reason.

In some cases, the availability of such skills during the pre-mechanized period had an impact on the location of an industry when it moved into the factories. In the nineteenth century cotton weaving in England came to be located in Rossendale, East Lancashire and in the districts north of these, partly because of the reserve of handloom weavers at that time in the area. Spinning, on the other hand, was localized in South East Lancashire. The separation of the weaving sector of the industry from the spinning sector was due to the concentration of a particular kind of skilled labour, a hangover from pre-industrial days. Spinning was mechanized earlier than weaving and even when weaving was mechanized, both continued to be located in the two separate regions for some time. There was also a well marked distinction in the location of the coarse spinning of Oldham and the fine spinning of Bolton. The Oldham districts of coarse spinning included Oldham, Rochdale and Bury while the Bolton districts of fine spinning included Bolton, Leigh, Stockport and Manchester. The coarse spinners used the short stapled cotton from India while the fine spinners imported long stapled cotton from America. The distinction had far-reaching consequences on the location of the industry, trade of England and the economic policies she imposed on her colonies and the Empire, particularly after she lost her American colonies.

The same distinction was seen also in the location of the weaving sector of the industry. The tropical markets were generally for coarse cloth, and these were woven in the Blackburn districts. The labour force in the cotton factories consisted mainly of women who could make coarse cloth. On the other hand, the weavers of Nelson and Colne were specialized in fine weaving. The weavers were mainly men. Such distinctions in the location and type of industry were largely a hangover from the pre-industrial period when labour was less mobile. The factory industries, however, gave a certain kind of spatial mobility to labour. The building of the Manchester Canal which made the town a suitable port for the import of cotton, gradually drew both weaving and spinning into the Manchester region. It was more economic to locate the spinning and weaving in the same factories.

MECHANIZATION AND ITS IMPACT ON LABOUR

The immediate effect of mechanization is generally unemployment. A ton of coal can produce more mechanical energy than a thousand men and a large scale use of the fuel can displace many human beings. But industries are capable of generating more profit and more capital than agriculture ever can. The capital is generally ploughed back into the industries inducing further growth. The demand for labour from the new plants increases, depending on the rate of growth of the industry or other economic activity. Once the growth rate slows down the demand for labour will also decline. The peak demand for labour in a mechanized economy, therefore, will be when an industry shows maximum rate of growth.

Mechanization of industry and agriculture has not been a strong force in India. During the British period, industries were actually curbed or discouraged because Britain wanted India to produce the raw material for her industries and food for her growing industrial population. The handicraft and cottage industries were wiped out as new fashions were introduced and western dress made compulsory for offices and institutions. The policy of independent India also wavered between full industrialization and the maintenance of the old crafts. The handloom industry, despite all discouragement, survived the British period and now gives employment to a large number of people. The products have also a very wide market. As such it is protected by the present government with special rates in cotton yarn and so on. But the handloom industries have tended to be located in small places as before. Other heavy industries also have not shown any spectacular development to catch up with the growth of population. The rural-urban migration of labour, therefore, is not as much due to the opportunities presented by industry and commerce but more due to the services for the large population of the towns, particularly menial services. It has often created the problem of slums in big cities.

Mechanization results in speedy production. The investment cost for factory industries is much greater compared to handicraft industries and the smooth running of these factories to ensure a steady output is an absolute necessity for their success. Hence only large scale production can really make factory industries economic. A factory must be able to run at full capacity or else the loss is great. Strikes, delays in supply of raw material, power cuts, labour problems and so on can ruin a factory industry more quickly than a handicraft cottage industry. The setting up of factory industries can succeed only if there is a wide enough market for their commodities, an adequate transport system to reach the goods to the market, and a disciplined labour force.

LITERACY

Specialization of skills in a mechanized age is based on literacy. But literacy alone does not ensure the availability of skills. As mentioned earlier, it is only the foundation on which skills can be built. Unless the general standard of education is high, specialization in skills cannot be achieved. So, the economic geographer must assess the opportunities available for higher education and technical education and the quality and purpose of education before he judges the quality and quantity of the potential labour force in a region In the planned economy of USSR, eductional institutions work in close collaboration with the labour requirements of the country or a particular region at a given time. When that requirement is met, the institutions are flexible enough to change over to other specializations. If education has no goal, the quality of labour will be poor. In some developing countries like India and Egypt, there are still no adequate facilities in educational institutions to meet the economic needs of the country. The accusation usually levelled against its people is that the educated class prefers a secure government job against the risks of industries. But this is a hangover from the imperial days when the British Government required only clerks in their offices to run the country's administration successfully. Independent India's requirements of labour are different from those of colonial India. A developing country needs technicians, engineers and highly skilled labourers as well as pioneers in industry, entrepreneurs, organizers and directors who can force breakthrough and set the country on the path of progress. It is the educational institutions that should undertake the responsibility of supplying the labour required by the country. Industrial morale, integrity, the will to work, knowledge, the incentive to increase production, all these are qualities which a labour force must possess to make the economy of a region capable of competing or cooperating with other regions. No amount of planning at government level can solve this problem of labour, unless labour itself understands its responsibility. And this responsibility comes through a purposeful and sound education.

COST OF LABOUR

The cost of labour is part of the cost of production. The market price of a commodity includes the cost of labour. High cost of labour increases the cost of production. Producers sometimes seek an area where labour is cheap, to locate their industry. The drive of some developed countries to invest their capital in the industries and primary activities of the developing world is because labour is cheap in these areas. Japan was able to compete in the world market before the first World War with British commodities because of her cheap labour. Even today the cost of labour in Japan is much less than in some other highly developed industrial countries. Japan's competitive capacity in the world market, therefore, is high.

It is because of the competition in the market that producers try to keep the cost of labour at a minimum level. This is possible particularly when the supply of labour is greater than the requirement. In such a situation the producers have the upper hand and labour is in a weak position. Trade unions are not a success. Demand for high wages are often turned down and labour continues to be poorly paid. But in the long run low wages of labour have a disastrous effect on the economy of a country. Labour with a high purchasing capacity can be a stable market for the products of industry and agriculture. A developing country which is still unable to compete in the world market, can look to a stable market at home if the people have a higher purchasing capacity. An overwhelming dependence on a foreign market can be detrimental to the country's progress. Producers must realize that they can function only with the cooperation of labour. High wages ensure a high purchasing capacity which in turn can create a market for their goods. But wages of labour must be proportionate to the price at which the commodity can sell in the market.

IMPORTED LABOUR

Labour is imported usually to meet the special requirements of a region. It can be either an importation of very highly skilled labour or that of semi-skilled and unskilled labour. The importation of highly skilled labour from the developed countries to the undeveloped countries is to meet the requirements of specialized skills. The cost of such labour is very high and sometimes leads the country to indebtedness or to the control of its industrial policies by foreign bodies. The difference in the wages of indigenous labour and foreign labour causes great economic dissatisfaction which may impede the development of the country. But at certain stages of industrial development in the backward countries, an import of highly skilled technicians may be necessary. The economic geographer must understand the govenment policies under which skilled labour is imported, because it can have an impact on the nature and type of industry developed, its foreign connections and control.

On the other hand, there has been a flow of unskilled and semi-skilled labourers from country to country. During the imperial days, Britain imported labour from India and Ceylon to work in the rubber estates of Malaya and the mines in Africa, because indigenous labour was either unsatisfactory or unwilling. Since Britain had territorial control over India and Ceylon, she could direct the migration policies and keep the wages of imported labour at a minimum. The discrepancy in the wages of white labour, Indian labour and native labour had a deep impact on the economy of Malaya and South Africa. The apartheid in Africa, the Indian problem in Malaya, the problem of Tamilians in Ceylon are all the consequences of the labour policies adopted by Britain in their colonies and the Empire. The same is also true of negro labour in the cotton estates of southern US. The negroes were imported as slaves to work in the cotton fields because there was a dearth of white labour for cotton cultivation and cotton picking. Cheap labour was required to meet the demands for cotton in the market. It developed a particular kind of economy in the south, with the white American as the owner of huge cotton estates, worked with slave labour. The cotton magnates of the south had full control of the raw material which the industrialists of the north required. The Civil War in the US was not fought so much to free the negroes from slavery but to give the growing industries of the north control over the raw material, by breaking through the closed economy of the feudal lords of the South. Had the war been really fought to free the slaves and to give the negroes equality under the constitution, their position would have been far better than it is today. Colour prejudices are not absent in US. The negro areas are overpopulated regions of squalor, poverty and unemployment even though the South still has an inadequacy of labour. Colour bar and social discrimination against imported labour create several economic problems, which often explode as political problems.

MOBILITY OF LABOUR

Mobility of labour is an important aspect of economic geography. In a traditionally skilled agricultural economy the mobility of labour from place to place is very little unless there is a famine or some such calamity. Agriculturists are considered to be more conservative and resentful of change. The agriculturist is less mobile because the land requires his constant attention. Industry also requires the constant attention of the director. But the agriculturists, except where cultivation is highly mechanized and organized, generally work on their own lands, whereas the industrial labourer may more often be a hired one, who can seek opportunities elsewhere. Labour is, therefore, considered to be more spatially mobile in an industrial than an agricultural economy. Higher wages and better prospects make industrial labour mobile.

But mobility of labour does not only mean the inclination to move from one place to another (spatial mobility) but from one occupation or function to another. This type of mobility has been greatly reduced with the advent of the machine age and the high specialization required of present day skilled labour. In the very highly developed countries where specialization has reached the zenith there is extreme immobility of labour from one occupation to another. A man who spends all his life making screws or fixing them to their sockets may be highly technically skilled but may not be able to adjust to any other occupation. He may not even know the use of the machine he is working on. On the other hand, where specialization of an extreme nature has not made labour rigid and a man knows something of everything, mobility from one activity to another can be achieved with greater ease. He may not be very efficient but he will be capable of doing something. Extreme specialization therefore, can be a handicap and it generates problems of skilled unemployment.

5

THE MARKET FACTOR

PRODUCTION is in response to market demand. It is not the availability of resources in a given area or the technical skill of man to exploit the raw material and make it into an economic resource that generates production, although the lack of these may be a serious handicap to economic development. Production depends on the availability of a market. Man produces goods with an eye on profit. He is not likely to put his efforts or expend his capital on production unless he is sure of a profit. The expectation of profits varies from area to area, from people to people and from one economic activity to another.

If other things remain the same (a phrase usually used in economic theories) there will be a free movement of goods from the supply area to the market area. But other things never remain the same in reality. A free and simple movement of goods is hedged in by high price centres. Goods are generally pulled to a market which offers the highest prices provided inadequacy and high cost of transport, government regulations, international controls, social, cultural, traditional and historical factors and a lot of other things do not interfere.

Theories in economic geography give the 'supply and demand curve' with which everybody is familiar. Prices are high when demand exceeds supply. But how many considerations come into a nation's life other than price ? Does price dictate man's desires ? Are his tastes and fashions, his way of living, controlled only by price ? Similarly, a nation which has self-sufficiency as its goal or desires to protect its own economic activities from foreign competition, may prefer to produce goods herself at a high cost even if she can import them at a lower price from lands better endowed with human and natural resources. Russia after the Bolshevik Revolution opened up much of the difficult lands of the Arctic and

Siberia at a very heavy cost. She aimed at self-sufficiency, not only for the country as a whole, but for each of the planning regions to a certain extent, to ease the strain on her poor transport system. National policies, government actions, transport, social and historical factors, reliability and dependability of the commodity, tastes, fashions and other things direct the course of trade apart from high prices. The geographer who is concerned with 'reality in area' must be aware of the limitations of economic theories when analysing economic patterns in an area. Truth can never be confined within the bounds of a theory. Geography is a field science and what is important to it is the existing pattern in an area in all its ramifications. The interpretation of economic theories in terms of the actual facts existing in an area and in a community, is what distinguishes an economic geographer from an economist. Applied Economics, which subject comes nearest to economic geography, and is now becoming very popular amongst economists, also does not consider the total phenomena, both natural and human, and the interrelated and combined impact on the ground. The economic geographer focuses his attention on the ground patterns and uses theories and processes as tools to understand the causes of existing patterns. The economist's emphasis, on the other hand, is on the development processes. He may ignore the ground altogether and sometimes certain aspects of human nature, when he expounds theories.

'Supply' in economic geography has also to be viewed from a particular angle. 'Supply' does not mean estimates, nor does it mean what can be made available to man through his technical skills. It means the amount a producer is willing to put out into the market at a particular price at a given time. The supply of coal at a given time, in a given area, in economic terms, does not mean all the coal that is lying underground, nor the amount that can be mined with the skills available, but the amount that the owner of the mine is willing to supply at a particular price. "Demand" again does not mean the amount that a people would like to have, which is only a desire, and of no economic value. It means the amount that people are willing to buy at a particular price. While the goal of the producer is to get the maximum returns for his investment, the goal of the consumer is to get his goods at the minimum price possible. It is the interaction of these two goals which fixes the price of goods in the market. The quantity of supply from the producer depends upon his expectation of profits. The 'effective demand' in the market depends on the price and a host of other things.

TYPES OF MARKETS

The economic geographer, when dealing with the market in a given area, must understand the nature, characteristics and the type of the market available.

Local Market

The local market is generally a small one. It is temporary or permanent depending upon the stability of the demand. It serves usually a population within limited bounds. The commodities that enter a local market are generally perishable goods which cannot travel very far. The prices in a local market are not fixed. Each vendor may charge his own price and try to make a profit. Fluctuations in the prices in the local market have seldom any impact on the economy of the nation or even the region.

Local markets sometimes crop up to perform a particular function for a given period. Sometimes, if a dealer does not find it profitable to continue in an area, he may seek a new market. In the early days of the exploitation of nitrates in Chile, there was a demand for meat to feed the miners. When the miners moved, the meat vendors also moved to a new market. In most of the pioneer mining settlements in Australia and the US such local markets made their appearance and disappeared with the disappearing market. Local markets for a number of commodities are very common in India. They have mobility because the establishment costs are very little. But they lack reliability which is required for economic stability.

Regional Market

The characteristic features of a regional market, are more or less the same as those of the local market and its functions along the same lines. But it serves a wider area and may express itself on the ground in the form of a departmental store. The prices in regional market may or may not be fixed.

National Markets

These are usually affected by the policies of the government of the country. The government may protect the national market by import duties and subsidies. The size of the national market depends on the prosperity of the country, the purchasing capacity of the people, transportation facilities and the effective demand. Mere size of the population of a country does not by itself provide a large national market. The national markets are wholesale markets. They do not engage themselves in retail selling like the local and the regional markets. The prices are fixed. The trade patterns of different commodities are different in the national market.

National markets give rise to the growth of towns. The specialization of the functions of these towns depends on the facilities available, the size of the market, the type of commodity sold and its space relationship with the rest of the country. (In China and India, however, towns have grown round even local and regional markets. This is because a 'town' in India is categorised as one mainly because of the size of its population and not by its functions. Many of the small towns of India are not functionally towns. They are only large villages).

The collapse of the national market may have lasting effects on the country's economy. Fluctuations in prices in the national market and undependability of supply and demand, will have an impact on the nation as a whole resulting in nation-wide regression in trade and economy.

International Markets

International markets are outside the control of a country's government. Once a country enters its products into the world market it is influenced by world production and world demand. It has to meet the challenge of competition from different countries with perhaps better organizations, better techniques and better know-how. If the production of wheat in countries that are engaged in the international trade of wheat, fluctuates, the prices in the world market for wheat will also be unstable. The farmer in the Murray-Darling Basin of Australia may be hit hard if there is a bumper crop in the prairies of America. The fluctuations in the world prices of wheat will affect all the producers of wheat who have put their commodity (wheat) in the world market.

The wider the market the greater is the incentive to increase production and expand trade. But the risk of the producer who seeks a world market is also great. The impact on the nation's economy when world markets fail is great enough to cause serious depressions. It may even cause world depressions as many of the economically developed and undeveloped countries are involved in such a trade as either producers or consumers. However, since the economic calamities of fluctuation in prices in the world market are great, international organizations are set up by the member countries to maintain a steady supply and demand and stabilize prices to prevent world depressions.

Certain countries, like Argentina, Brazil, the Gold Coast etc., which depend mainly on an outside market, have unstable economies because they deal with markets outside the control of their own policy-making bodies. The importing country might even deliberately put the exporting country's economy into a jumble to curb its development, and further its own interests. Such pressures can be brought upon the exporting countries by many subtle ways like changing the value of the currency of one country against that of the other, keeping a close watch on the export-import patterns and so on. The same was true of colonial countries. Political independence is absolutely necessary to follow an independent economic policy. Colonies and Empires (when they existed) had no say in the matters of trade or other policies. The mother country decided its economic policies and it was usually to the detriment of the dependent country.

USES OF COMMODITIES

To understand the nature of a market and the factors that control it, the economic geographer must know the uses of commodities. There are certain commodities in the world which are used for more than one purpose. Food grains are used both as animal feed as well as human feed. Soya bean is used as food, in the plastic industry, paint industry and in the making of soaps. Timber is used for the paper industry, for furniture and for building. At one time, before the steel age, it was extensively used for ship-building. Coal is used for metallurgical industry, for producing thermal electricity, for the chemical industry and for transport. The more the uses of a commodity, the steadier the market. But the prices of the commodity will depend on the interplay of each demand. An expansion in the chemical industry will put up the price of coal for the metallurgical industry. The prices of steel might go up in the market although there is no apparent connection between the chemical and the metallurgical industry. An increased use of Soya beans as food could affect the soap, plastic and paint industry. An increased publication of books might affect the furniture industry. It is essential, therefore, that the economic geographer must view products in the light of their uses and their impact on the different consumers. The use to which commodities are put to, also change from time to time with technical advances and tastes of people.

In contrast to products which are put to various uses there are others which have very few uses. The main use of jute is for the handling of grains in bulk in gunny bags. The prices of jute in the market will, therefore, depend on one factor, that is the quantity of grain that needs to be moved in bulk in the world. If the demand for gunny bags declines the jute producers may find themselves in a sorry plight.

Commodities of component industries

There are some commodities like cars which are the result of component industries. The finished product of one industry is the raw material for another industry. A car requires the assistance of the iron and steel industry, engineering industry, rubber, paint, textile, glass and other industries. In such cases the market for the component parts will depend on the market for the finished product. Each industry can benefit greatly by linkage of industries.

Competitive products

There are many products which are competitive in the sense that two or more raw materials can produce the same commodity. Sugar can be produced from beet as well as from cane. One is a product of the temperate regions and the other, a product of the tropical regions. The clothing industry makes use of cotton, silk, wool and synthetic cloth. In such cases it is necessary to investigate into the extent of the production of all the raw materials and their prices to understand the trends and characteristics of the market for the final product. An increase in beet output in the temperate regions will affect the cane growers of the tropical and subtropical world.

Substitute products

Certain products of the world have substitutes. Synthetic products which are appearing in the market now can have an impact on the production of the natural product. Synthetic rubber has affected the production of, and the market for, natural rubber. It is only the policies of Great Britain, whose planters have a great stake in the Malayan rubber plantations, that permit them to continue cultivating rubber in the face of competition from synthetic rubber. One of the advantages of the natural product is that it is cheaper to produce. But the prices of the synthetic products may be reduced in the future either by large scale production or through improved technology enabling them to compete more effectively with the natural products. Nylon and rayon can be substitutes for silk. The expansion of this industry in Japan (and also India) has had a disastrous effect on the silk industry. In 1940 silk supplied more than 75 per cent of the material for the hosiery industry in Japan. By 1948 it was reduced to 4 per cent. Plastics are ousting copper, brass and China ware from many homes. The market for fresh limes are affected by squashes and syrups. The use of substitutes, however will depend upon tastes, fashions, the purchasing capacity of the people and the competitive prices in the market for the different substitutes.

Related products

Some products are related products in the sense that they are produced at one and the same time from the same commodity. Beef and hide are produced when cattle are slaughtered. Lamb and wool, gas and coke are other examples of related products. In cases of related products the market for one will have an impact on the prices of the other. Supposing the demand for beef increases, the production of beef will be expanded to meet the market requirement. But while producing the beef, hides are also produced. If the market for hide has not expanded, the supply will exceed demand and there will be a slump in the prices of hide. To understand the conditions in the hide market, the economic geographer would also have to enquire into the market for beef. So also in the case of gas and coke. In the early days when the demand was only for coke, the by-product gas was allowed to be wasted. Today gas from coal has its uses. But the extent of the production of gas depended earlier, on the demand for coke. Gas has now become one of the major fuels and it is produced for its own sake from low grade coals which cannot be used for coking. The gas industry, therefore, is somewhat independent of coking coal. The entry of petroleum and natural gas has also relieved the dependence of gas on the coking industry.

Seasonal markets

Certain products have only a seasonal market. The market for soft fruits and milk expand particularly in summer in Europe. Woollen products find a market just before the winter sets in. Very often producers take advantage of such seasonal markets.

Elasticity of market

A market is considered to be elastic when response to supply is quick. Necessary goods such as wheat, rice and bread have an inelastic market because the requirement of the people for necessary articles remains more or less the same whether the supply or the price increases or decreases. For the luxury goods and those commodities which make life a little more comfortable, the market is said to be elastic. But the necessary goods, goods of comfort and luxury goods depend very much on the purchasing capacity of the people, their tastes and perhaps, their traditions. In the villages of India and other developing countries, where even the necessities of life are a luxury, the markets for goods such as cereals may show some elasticity. Subject to the above conditions, a producer has chances of expansion where markets are elastic although it may not be true in all cases because of the difficulty of defining luxury goods. Elasticity of market does not depend on one factor. It is related to the purchasing capacity and the standards of living of a people.

Creation of a market

A market can be created by the ingenuity of a producer. He may attract a market by offering low prices ; discovering new areas for his commodity ; or by improving techniques ; and by advertisement.

Low prices can attract a market. But to permanently retain the low prices, a producer will have to resort to large-scale production. If the market for the commodity is not an expanding one, the producer will have to restrict his production at some stage and increase his price when the market is stabilized. Forde was able to put out his cars into the market at a cheap rate by mass production. Low prices can, therefore, be a temporary or a permanent feature depending on the demand in the market and the capacity to supply.

A producer might seek new areas to vend his commodities. Prior to 1914 there were many untouched markets in the world. But now the markets of the world are already crammed with producers and there is keen competition amongst them to 'capture a market'. The largest markets in the world are the developing countries, that is Afro-Asia and Latin America in general. But a successful trade can be carried on only between countries of equal standards of living. A Bantu or a pigmy living in the African forests or a peasant of an Indian village who cannot afford a square meal a day, has no use for the products of the industrial world. Unless their purchasing capacity is improved and their ways of living changed, the Afro-Asian people cannot be an effective market for the industrial nations of the world. The anxiety of the developed nations to raise the standards of living of these people and change their ways of living through missionary work, social and cultural organizations, education, aids and so on is not entirely due to humanitarian motives, but also because they want the teeming populations of Afro-Asia to be a demanding market for their goods. The US is one of the most developed countries today. She has a surplus of both industrial and farm products and can produce more if necessary. Her problem is finding new markets for her ever-increasing production, or else, resort to forceful cutting down of production to maintain prices. She does not have the territorial control over Afro-Asia which Britain enjoyed during the imperial days. Britain could dump her manufactured goods on her colonies and Empire and exploit their raw materials to advance her own industrial economy. She could, through Government action, force these countries to produce the food and industrial raw material to feed her population and her industries. But this kind of exploitative economy collapsed with the Second World War. Most of the countries of Afro-Asia, how so ever weak they are economically, are now politically independent and have a chance to frame their own policies. The US can penetrate into these markets only through collaboration, aids, trade agreements, loans, and such devices. In this she has to compete with the West European nations who are equally anxious to capture the vast market.

Alternatively, these new markets can be captured by bringing down the cost of production which is rather high in the industrial world. They can invest in the industries, transport, shipping, agriculture and mines in the developing world, and make use of the cheap labour available in these countries. Foreign investments in the various economic activities of the developing world are considerable today. The automobile industry, petroleum, mining, transport and chemical industry, and plantations are financially slipping into the hands of foreign companies. If the developed countries own the industries and control the economic activities of the developing world, they can open up a new market in Afro-Asia and Latin America for their goods by keeping the cost of production at a low level suited to the purchasing capacity of their people.

New techniques can also create a market. When the refrigerator ship was invented and frozen meat could be sent over a long distance from Argentina to Europe, it opened up the European market for Argentinan meat. Vegetables and fruits are now finding distant markets with the invention of the canning process on the one hand and the speed and dependability achieved in transport on the other. A long list of commodities has come out of the electrical industry such as household gadgets, radios, radiograms and televisions, precision instruments, transport which has escalated the demand for electricity.

Advertising in order to capture a market is an art by itself and a weapon used by all producers. The US and the West European countries excel in this art. To make advertising a success, the producers must understand the psychology of the people, in other words, the Achilles' heel of the consumer. The aim of advertisement is to induce or persuade people into believing that they are getting what they want. It must appeal to the people. An investigation into the national character, tastes, traditions may be necessary to make advertisement successful. In England where the people take great pride in their own production, advertisements will emphasise the 'wholly English' character of the commodity. Ham from English pigs, raised in English farms, with English know-how may appeal to the people more than 'imported goods'. In India, on the other hand, advertisements usually emphasize the imported nature of goods, however despicable it may sound, because the people, particularly the rich, take pride in possessing imported commodities. There is a lack of national consciousness. The nature of the advertisement must, therefore, change with the outlook of the people.

Industrial research is necessary to find new uses for materials, to maintain the quality of goods, to discover new techniques, for conservation of materials, and for reducing costs. Any modern industry will have a research cell and laboratories attached to it. Independent consulting units are also available to assist the producers in their entrepreneurial work. Some economic units collaborate with universities to get the services required. Organization and quality control are today the best methods of stabilising a market.

Marketing research is also one of the features of modern industry. Highly advanced economic units maintain close contacts with the consumer. Market research institutions go into the details of the requirements and tastes of the consumer. When General Motors made a bid to capture the European market for automobiles after the Second World War, it set up agencies to study the width of roads, parking facilities, the size and shape of the car most liked the by Europeans and the like. Many such foreign agencies are operating in this country also to ascertain the extent of the market for particular commodities.

In the long run, however, it is the quality of the goods that matter to the consumer. It must be durable, dependable and reliable. A product of good quality may sell at a price of some 10 per cent to 20 per cent higher than others and still be able to stand up to competition from low priced goods of lesser quality. Low prices may capture the markets temporarily but if the quality is not good the demand will fall off. Palm oil in Africa never reached peak production because the quality was bad. On the other hand Philips radios, Swiss watches, German precision instruments and cameras have a market regardless of prices because of their quality. Japan's manufactures, which were considered of poor quality before World War II, are now some of the best in the world. Nearer home, although not of such gigantic order, are the Godrej and the Tata products. Consumers are vigilant. High integrity and honesty are required to win the confidence of the consumer and establish a stable market.

Market and its relation to distance

'Distance' is important both to production and market but distance in economic geography refers to the cost factor and not to the distance on the ground. The dictum that 'New York is nearer to Tokyo than California' is related to the cost of transport. Ocean transport is cheaper than land transport. New York may thus find it cheaper to sell her goods to or buy from Japan rather than from California. World markets are now accessible to most countries with a surplus to sell because of the revolutions in transport. Distances to the market have, therefore, to be considered in relation to cost. This aspect is dealt with in Chapter 6.

6

TRANSPORT

MODERN transport has changed the whole concept of space relationship on the surface of the earth. The advent of the rails after the discovery of cheap steel in the nineteenth century and the automobile and the macadamised roads in the twentieth century have revolutionized world transport. Further inventions such as the jet plane and the commercial pipelines of the latter half of the twentieth century ushered in an era of speed and convenience in transport never known before. In the context of the slow transport available to the people of the ancient and medieval world, a great degree of self-sufficiency was necessary for regions, towns and villages. Large economic units of the type found in the US would not have been possible when transport was cumbersome and slow. The multinational political units such as the USSR could not have emerged but for the availability of closer and quicker contacts. Speed in transport has made large-scale exchange possible and the economy of self-sufficiency has given way to an economy of large-scale exchange.

Speedy transport has enabled man to specialize in production and exchange his goods for the goods of other regions. Specialization and exchange, of a kind, did exist since the dawn of history, but transport being slow, only goods of a non-perishable nature and of high value could enter world commerce. Today huge regions can specialize in particular products whether agricultural or industrial, and draw to them other necessary products, by exchange. This has given rise to large areas having a certain kind of uniformity in economic development so that the geographers, attention is turning increasingly from 'natural regions' to manmade 'economic regions' or other similar regions based on human activity.

Transport enables products to be made at a place where the cost of production is low. It also allows the producer to take advantage of the high-price markets in distant areas. It has encouraged not only commerce on a large scale but many cultural and social activities. We now have access to better schools, better medical services and a better way of life. Speed in transport has created a certain amount of leisure which can be utilized for other gainful occupations. Modern cities are dependent on transport. The destruction of transport lines can paralyse a country's economy. It is for this reason that transport becomes the target of attack in times of war. Transport has also helped to decentralize the city. The garden cities of the world, the dormitory towns, the extensive suburbs and satellite towns would not have been possible but for the transport links. It has also helped to link up the rural and urban areas and to make a whole country into one single economic unit. The self-sufficient isolated village of the ancient and medieval period is fast disappearing even in the so-called developing world.

HISTORY OF TRANSPORT AND THE CHANGING ECONOMIC PATTERNS

The early period
(upto the fourteenth century)

Land transport

On land man has been using man power and animals to move his goods since ancient times. Originally, the wheels of the cart wagons and chariots were solidly fixed to the axle and the axle was allowed to rotate with the wheel. The wheels were made of stone or wood and were quite heavy. A cart with a wheel which was heavy and rotated with the axle was adequate enough on straight roads but while turning, one of the wheels had to be shed, which was a serious handicap. Even four-wheeled wagons were known but since all were attached to the axle they were even more cumbersome than the two-wheeled carts.

The Animals were hitched on to these carts by means of yokes and various kinds of yokes were known. But the yokes that were suitable for oxen would not work with horses and mules. The full strength of the horses could not be used on carts because the yokes hurt their shoulders. The pulling-power of the animals was limited to the weakness of the yoke and the harness. The two-wheeled carts drawn by oxen were the most popular mode of vehicular traffic in the early days.

Another serious handicap of land transport was that vehicles had no breaks. While going downhill, a heavy object was dragged along with the cart to limit the speed. In the hilly countries it became easier to use the animals themselves. Roads, even in the plains, were not paved or made hard with concrete. They were deep with silt and dust in certain parts and could be used only in fair weather. Distances covered by animals and carts were small and moving goods from one place to another took months and years.

River transport

During the same period transport by river was easier for certain commodities. Anything that could float could be sent downstream with the current but getting the boat upstream against the current was difficult. Sailships of one, two and three sails were known but the art of tacking or going zigzag at an angle to the wind, was not possible. With the winding river courses it was difficult to find a wind which would carry the boat upstream. The oar was mainly used to go upstream but this meant that more men had to be accommodated in the boat leaving less space for commodities. A pole could be used where the rivers were shallow and the boat punted upstream but this also meant extra labour. Boats were also pulled upstream from the banks of the river by animals or human beings. But not all rivers were] suitable for pulling the boats from the shore. The rivers had to be reasonably narrow and roads had to follow the rivers to make use of animal and human power for upstream traffic. Light boats with little cargo alone could go up the river and it was much more expensive than downstream traffic. Upstream traffic was therefore, negligible at this time. The development of commercial centres downstream was a feature of the civilizations of the ancient and early medieval period.

Ocean Transport

In ocean traffic the sailship was used. The design and pattern of the sailship differed from place to place. The sail and the oar provided the motive power. Sails were common in freight ships while oars were used in battleships. Oars were not popular in freightships because the oarsmen took too much space, cutting down the space for cargo. On the other hand, extra men were quite an asset in battleships as they could be used in war.

The greatest handicap of the sailship was its inability to tack, that is sailing at an angle to the wind. This meant that a sailship could move only with a favourable wind or a tail-wind. The ships had to wait for months at ports for a favourable wind. Sailing was easy in the partially enclosed seas, endowed with winds which blew in one direction part of the year and in another direction the rest of the year as in the eastern Mediterranean and in the tributary seas of the Indian Ocean. But not all parts of the world had such convenient winds which could be used by mariners for a to-and-fro journey seasonally. Such winds like the monsoons and the Etesian permitted sailing in the open sea even in the ancient days. But sailing 'out of sight of land' was limited because of the lack of navigation instruments. The north star and the sun were the only guidance for the mariners. The north star was not visible beyond a certain latitude. The use of the sun as a guide was also limited in certain latitudes. But with the sun and the north star to guide them, mariners of some parts of the world were able to go to a limited distance out into the sea. Otherwise they sailed hugging the coasts. This too was possible only in the seas which were flanked with land masses as in the tributaries of the Indian Ocean and the Mediterranean. It is not surprising therefore, that the cradles of civilization were in the countries flanking these oceans and exchange of goods between the Mediterranean lands and the lands of the Indian Ocean gained an impetus for the same reason.

The economic system that emerged out of this slow and cumbersome transport system was one of self-sufficiency on the one hand and of taxation and exploitation of the rural areas on the other. The ancient Indian and east Asian towns and villages had of necessity to be self-sufficient. Both towns and villages produced the same kind of goods. But the towns were generally the seats of royalty or aristocracy and as such had a higher purchasing capacity and superior administrative authority. The urban people could command industries producing quality goods, to be located in the towns. Many of the factories were owned by the royalty and the aristocracy. But on the whole the economy of self-sufficiency permitted little exchange between town and country. The town had very little command over the rural products (such as food) which were necessary to support an urban population. The townpeople could only persuade the villagers to surrender their goods as the village was not dependent on the town for the necessities of life. In the context of such an economy the towns could not grow to any great size. Indian town planners limited the population of the towns and maintained it at a certain level. The industries of the towns were not allowed to grow beyond the requirements of the townpeople. They also planned the town in such a way that a certain area around the town was set aside to produce the food necessary for the limited population of the town. The present 'revenue area' of the town in India is reflective of the garden land of the ancient town, which supported the urban people with the necessities of life. It was an indirect form of taxation on the rural area.

In the countries of the west, on the other hand, cities were sustained by taxation imposed in the rural areas. The authority to tax was established by force and conquest. If the cities and the ruling class overtaxed the rural areas, the villagers had only what was left after taxation. The administrative class living in the cities were the ruling class and the rural areas were the ruled. The administrative class came to be considered the highest in the society and the military class, which assisted in the conquests of the ruling class and maintained their authority in the rural areas, by force or by fear, was considered second dominant class.

Besides the seats of administration, there were the commercial cities on the major trade routes. Generally trade were high in value and low in bulk and so complemented the cost and delay of a cumbersome transport. Transport to the interior rural areas being difficult, very little of the bulky cereals and low value commodities of the farm entered the trade of the commercial cities. It was largely a trade on barter and high value commodities like gold, silver, precious stones, spices, aromatic roots, ivory, and so on. This trade was conducted over great distances across the seas to the river ports of most of the countries which entered commerce. Sea transport proved to be the most efficient transport available to to the Ancients. It gave rise to coastal and river-mouth commercial centres with a substantial overseas trade. But their contacts with the interior was limited. There were a few well-known commercial cities also on the great trunk roads in countries where land transport was somewhat adequate. The commercial city brought in the high revenues for the ruling and the military class. It was they who brought the goods from overseas as well as from the interior and arranged to get the luxury products for the rural people. The rich merchant princes had a high social status and they were ranked third after the ruling and the military class. The cultivators of land were considered the lowest class and were valued only as potential manpower for military purposes, although they comprised the class which sustained the ruling, the military and the commercial class.

As the cities grew and wars increased taxation of the rural people became heavy. Raiding, robbery, piracy, subjugation and conquest of the rural people were all considered legal particularly in the west, where taxation of the rural people was the only means of sustaining the urban rich. The relationship between urban and rural people was often strained under such a system.

The medieval period
(fourteenth to the nineteenth century)

Land Transport
Around the tenth century the horse collar and the horse-shoe which were perhaps a Chinese or a Scythian invention reached Europe. These inventions enabled horses to be used more efficiently on land. The horse collar increased the pulling power of the horse and the shoe prevented injury to the hoof. The horse could now carry more load. But hitching the horse to the wagon was a problem because the carts were very high and cumbersome to be load. Its centre of gravity being high, it was likely to overturn. The horses had to be tied one behind the other to maintain the stability of the cart. Further, the carts had no breaks. The front axles continued to be stationary and it was difficult to steer. The wheels had to be dragged sideways at turning points. Heavy loading upset the cart. The carts could be used only because the roads were so thick with dust and mud that the wheels could not move freely. The thick mud acted as a break. On a hard smooth surface such wheeled carts were in danger of turning over or skidding. The speed of land transport was still limited to about 30 km. a day. It was not till the nineteenth century that a change came about in land transport.

River Transport

In river transport also there was no great change upto the nineteenth century. The only invention of note was that tacking came to be known and the sailing ships could be used on rivers more efficiently. But the rivers had to be wide enough to give the boat room for zigzaging and there had to be a favourable wind. A tacking ship could go upstream against the current. The coastal plains through which rivers flowed into the sea being an area of land and sea breezes could come into the service of man through the use of the tacking ship. Many inland towns which were within the limits of land and sea breezes and situated on wide enough rivers such as London and New Orleans came into focus economically with the tacking ship.

Ocean Transport

It was in Ocean traffic that significant changes were made after the fourteenth century. The struggle of the European people with the seapower of the Arabs brought about a fusion in ship architecture. The western European ships had only one large square sail mounted on a mast midship. The Mediterranean ships, since ancient times, had a large sail as well as a small one which was mounted on a mast in front of the ship (foremast). The Europeans borrowed this idea but hitched the small sail at the stem of the boat. Eventually ships began to carry three sails which increased their efficiency.

The second invention in ocean-going ships was the improvement of the rudder. Draining water by pumps was introduced and the ships could now get rid of the water from time to time which made longer journeys in the ocean possible.

In the field of navigation, the compass, a chinese invention, came into wider use. The cross and the Astralabe for measuring the latitudes were also developed. A ship could now go east or west along a known latitude, sail by compass and take the latitude readings periodically when the weather permitted and repeat the journey whenever required. If the ship strayed from its course it could be brought back with the aid of the compass and the latitude readings. Much of the knowledge of the Arabs and the Indians passed into Europe through the Majorcan and Italian mapmakers. It is this knowledge that made history during the next few centuries. Tables of latitude were carefully worked out or borrowed from Arab itineraries by the European traders and preserved for use by others. It made it possible for mariners to go out of sight of land anywhere. It was no longer the privilege of a people endowed with partially enclosed seas with favourable seasonal winds to propel their ships to and fro. With the increasing motive power of the sails, and the accurate knowledge of latitudes, long journeys could be undertaken. Larger and larger ships were built to accommodate the rich merchandise of the East. The merchants of the West began to travel round the world.

But it was not till the seventeenth century that longitudes could be measured. Sailing from north to south or vice versa was difficult till the invention of the Hugyens pendulum clock. It was adapted for marine use sometime in the seventeenth century. But till longitudes could be measured with some accuracy only east-west sailing was possible in the open sea.

It was the tacking ship, the knowledge of the latitudes, the wider use of the compass and the invention of the rudder that ushered in the Age of Discovery in Europe. Portugal under the leadership of Henry the Navigator (1394-1460) took the lead. Spain and Portugal had close contacts with the Arabs and were in a position to imbibe the knowledge of the Arabs. Venice (Italy), which was also feeling the impact of Arab supremacy in the Mediterranean and the East, was making an effort to gain knowledge of the sea routes to the East. The round the world voyages of Bartholomew Diaz (1487) Vasco da Gama (1497) and Columbus (1497) were made possible because of the inventions of this period. Had Columbus actually sailed from Gibralter to the west he would have been caught in the 'Horse Latitudes' and vanished off what was known then as the "edge of the Earth'. Between the two zones of Calms, the Doldrums (near the equator between 50 to100 miles on either side) and the Horse Latitudes (North of the Tropic of Cancer and Capricorn which latter was not yet a frequented area) is the belt of the trade winds; (the area which in the Indian Ocean enjoy the seasonal Monsoon winds). Columbus, in order to avoid the region of Calms sailed to the Canary Islands situated at 28° Latitude and came within the trade wind belt. But since the trade winds here blow towards the south west, he was blown westwards instead of to the east. He expected to reach the East by sailing west following the revolutionary idea prevalent at the time in Europe that the earth was round and not flat.

With the Age of Discovery came colonization by European countries, first of America and then the subjugation of the producers of wealth in the East. The struggle for a monopoly of trade with the East lasted several centuries. Following Portugal came Holland, England and France. Their East India Companies were established with a view to gaining control of the trade of the East. The Merchant Companies became Empire builders to control their trade by subjugating the producers of wealth. Great Britain finally succeeded in establishing a world-wide empire by the nineteenth century.

It was the capture of trade that enabled the commercial cities of the medieval and early modern period to develop into gigantic trading cities with world-wide contacts. The rebuilding of European cities started with the colonization of America and with the 'Crusade' against the Arab monopoly of trade in the Mediterranean and the Indian Ocean between the eleventh and the thirteenth centuries. But transport of goods was not easy with the sailship. Europeans anxious to get hold of the immense wealth of the East and New World introduced new norms of behaviour in the East, hitherto unknown to its people. Piracy, smuggling, capture of ships in the open seas, holding ships by force in return for surrender of their goods or for payment of ransom, threat, bluff and blackmail, all became legalised with the advent of the Europeans in the eastern seas. Elizabeth I of England legalised piracy and secretly assisted free booters and bandits.

Many of the European towns began to depend on trade. Gradually trade in precious metals, spices and precious stones was replaced by bulky raw material as England began to acquire territory in America and the East and went through the industrial revolution. England's towns began to manufacture goods. On the other hand France was not able to establish close commercial contact with her overseas territories. Her towns continued to grow on taxation of the rural areas and not on commerce and industry. It was heavy taxation of the rural areas that sparked off the French Revolution in the latter part of the eighteenth century.

The standard of living in the commercial towns was much higher than in towns dependent on taxation. The trading city was in a position to buy food with the luxuries she commanded through commerce. The commercial city had a variety of goods which came from America and the East to tempt the rural people to surrender the necessities of life. The rural areas also developed with the trade. The feudal landlords (manorial lords) of Medieval England, who were rich farmers, had no means of getting the luxuries of the East in the interior except through the merchants. Transport to the interior being difficult, the manorial lords were dependent on the merchant adventurers for luxuries. But the commercial city had no great control over the rural farmers. If the farmer decided to keep his goods and had no great desire to accumulate the luxuries of the commercial city, there was nothing that the merchants could do.

The merchants and manufacturers became important in society. Life centred round trade but the commercial city had no hold on the rural areas. The desire of the merchants to establish their rights over the producers of wealth and control trade led to the merchants becoming empire-builders. In the eighteenth century, England also went through the industrial revolution which by the nineteenth century gradually revolutionized transport.

The modern period
(nineteenth century and after)

Land transport

The railroad was established in the nineteenth century and in the twentieth century the motor truck came into use, both of which speeded up transport on land from the bullock cart speed to about 950 kms. an hour.

The railroad was the result of a combination of several ideas which came in during the industrial revolution. In the mining areas of England, wheels were already running on tracks and various arrangements were in vogue to hold the wheel on to the track, such as putting the flange on the wheel. The steam Engine was also invented in 1770 but it was not put on the rail. Railroads were run by horsepower till 1800. Steel was also known but it was costly.

The steam engine could not be put on the rail because a rail had yet to be invented which would carry the weight of the engine. This depended on the development of the iron and steel industry. So far only three forms of iron were in use namely cast iron, wrought iron and steel. Cast iron contained 2½ to 4 per cent of carbon and was therefore, brittle. In the past it was the cheapest of the three, and it was extensively used. Wrought iron contained no carbon. It was malleable and had high tensile strength but it was more costly than cast iron. It was produced by heating cast iron in a forge and as the iron was worked to the surface, the carbon exposed to the air was allowed to burn out. Both labour and fuel were consumed in the process, making it more costly. Steel contained ½ per cent to 1½ per cent of carbon. It had most of the tensile strength of wrought iron combined with the hardness of cast iron. But at the time it was very costly to produce. In early nineteenth century all these irons were produced by the Basic process. The iron ore was smelted in a furnace to produce cast iron. The cast iron was further heated in a forge to get rid of all the carbon to produce wrought iron. Small quantities of wrought iron were again heated and the right amount of carbon added to make steel. The fuel consumption was thus high in the making of steel. At the time when the railroad was invented there were only cast iron and wrought iron which could be produced at a reasonable cost and neither was ideal for powerful steam engines. Wrought iron was malleable although it had tensile strength. Neither the track nor the wheels could carry much weight. As a result the weight of the locomotive and its load capacity had to be kept down. The first locomotives were very small and crude. The limitation of the wheel load is important in a locomotive. The power of the locomotive is limited to the friction of the drive wheels on the track and this is proportionate to the weight pressing on the wheels against the track. The pulling power of the locomotive is ¼ to half of the weight on the drive wheels. If the cylinders put out more power, the wheels would spin on the track. But light small locomotives could make amazing speeds.

What was required to perfect the railroad was a suitable iron which could take the weight of a powerful steam engine. For half a century after the railroad was invented, the development of locomotives and railways was retarded for want of a cheap metal. It was the Bessamer process (1856) which revolutionised the process of making both wrought iron and steel. Bessamer introduced a process by which the hot molten iron from the furnace could directly be transferred to a vat, and air pumped up through it to burn out the carbon. Bessamer thought that he could produce steel by simply stopping the air from flowing into it before all the carbon was burnt out. But in practice it was difficult to cut off the air at the right moment and the carbon required for steel had to be added afterwards. The Bessamer process was a great step in the conservation of fuel and labour. It also enabled all the processes to be located in the same place. The separation of the furnace and the forge from the steel centre was no longer economic and there was a saving on transport costs as well. It took some time after the Bessamer process was discovered to make cheap steel. In some countries the process was delayed because Bessamer could not handle phosphorus iron ores like the ores of Lorraine. These had to await the Gilchrist-Thomas process (1873-75) which revolutionised the iron and steel industry of Germany and gave the regional individuality to the Ruhr iron and steel belt.

Cheap steel made possible bigger wagons, heavier locomotives, high steam pressures and bigger rails which could carry even heavier locomotives and wagons. Today one can produce special kinds of steel for different purposes by adding the required amount of any metal like vanadium, nickel, manganese, chromium, and so on. The open hearth and the electric process have further perfected the steel industry. Trucks, automobiles and macadum roads gave a further fillip to land transport.

River transportation

The steamboat made its appearance earlier solving the problem of upriver traffic. For half a century after its invention its chief use was in inland water transport.

The steamboat, like the railroad and the locomotive, was the result of a combination of ideas even though Fulton is regarded as its inventor and its first use was in the Hudson river in 1807. The development of the steam boat was delayed also because of lack of cheap steel. Watts' combustion type of engine could use 12-15 pounds of steam pressure and derived its power mostly from air pressure. Low pressures meant that most of the heat was consumed by vaporisation. Hence it was not economic in the use of fuel. It took very large cylinders and piston to produce power and they took a lot of space. The Mississipi boat-builders soon abandoned the condensing principle and engines were designed to use the steam to push the piston and then to release it as exhaust. With this engine the steam pressures could be raised to 40-60 pounds.

But for such pressures steel boilers were required. Ships were overloaded and the engines and boilers were also overloaded. There was no danger of skidding in ships as in the case of railroads boiler explosion was a constant threat.

Cast iron and wrought iron were the only metals available for steamships till cheap steel came on the market. The steam-boat had two mechanical defects, one the possibility of a boiler explosion and the other inefficiency in the use of fuel. But in case of failure, the river steamboat was near land. In the open seas this was a great handicap. Secondly, the long journeys on the sea required a large quantity of fuel so that there was little space for cargo. River steamers were close to land and could be refuelled. It was for these reasons that the steamboat came to be used on rivers much earlier than on the sea.

Ocean transport

Though the steamship was the most important invention of this era, due to mechanical deficiencies it could not be used in the ocean for some time. It was only after the Bessamer steel came into the market that ocean-going steamers could be perfected mechanically. In the 1860s steel was used in place of wood in the making of the hulls of the ships. This added strength and gave greater cargo capacity without increasing the motive power.

While ships were being improved, the increased use of steel for all machines was going on. Boilers in ships were made of steel and boiler pressure was increased to 100 pounds in 1850 and 225 pounds in 1890. These high pressures gave greater fuel efficiency. The invention of the multiple expansion cylinders also increased fuel efficiency. Compound expansion was introduced in 1854 and triple expansion in 1894. Each of these reduced the amount of coal necessary for a given trip. More cargo space was made available in the ship. In 1870 the condensor was developed, greatly reducing the amount of fresh water that a sea-going ship had to carry.

All these inventions resulted in larger ships, and stronger engines which consumed less fuel. The steamship became a success in the ocean in the latter part of the nineteenth century. The sail-ships continued to be used for some time after the steamship came into the ocean. Sails were also kept as a reserve in case of emergency.

The railways, the truck and the steamship completely

changed space relationships. The railroad was first a substitute for canals particularly in Europe where there was an extensive canal system. Later the railways proved to be superior and became competitive. Rails were quicker and could adapt to a greater range in relief. With the railways on land and the steamship on the sea, a two-way traffic was established at all seasons both on land and sea. Inland waterways also used the steamships. There was a rapid growth of ports and inland lake ports (particularly in the US). There was now no need to trade in luxuries. America introduced the railways before the interior was settled so that she started her life with a heavy export-import economy. Her agriculture was mechanised and there was scope for specialization in crops from the beginning. Clear-cut crop regions came into existence with specialization and mechanization. The South East produced cotton, the North Central, corn and pork, the South West beef, mutton and wool. Europe at this time produced manufacturing goods and a trade between America and Europe took place. Towns began to handle merchandise and transport goods. Later when the manufacturing cities claimed these goods, big business was already established in the agricultural areas of the US.

In Europe the manufacturing cities grew. Food and raw material came first from America and later from other countries of the Empire, the colonies and the Commonwealth. Bulk goods could now be carried to distant lands cheaply.

The farmer in the rural areas, like the man in the city, had now to depend on his purchasing capacity to buy goods. If the city depended on manufactures, the rural areas depended on big business in agriculture. Specialization and exchange became the rule in the developed countries. But the rural areas perhaps did not have all the facilities that the big city had, such as underground drainage, electricity, and so on because it was cheaper to install these facilities in the thickly populated cities.

Transportation made urban-rural contacts easier and economic interdependence possible. Both rural and urban people depended on each other because of specialization (as in the US). In such a society all occupations were accepted as long as there was demand. Big business became the core of economic values. Money played an important role in the equal trade economy not only in the cities but also in the rural areas.

However, the spread of modern transport and the consequent impact of its on trade and big business was unevenly spread in the different parts of the world. In the underdeveloped world transport is still inadequate and many countries of Asia and Africa have not yet emerged from the bullock cart and the pack animal stage of civilization. Each region, therefore, has to be investigated in the context of the transport available to it to assess the nature of its economy, its commerce and its industry.

FUNCTIONS OF TRANSPORT

One of the main functions of transport is to assemble the raw material and semi-finished goods to the centre of production and to disperse the finished goods to the market centres. Industries and other economic activities require several commodities which may have to be hauled over great distances to an accessible central place. The greater the efficiency of transport the quicker can the materials be assembled. The size of an industrial complex or an agricultural region in the modern world depends upon the efficiency with which large quantities of raw material can be moved over greater and greater distances in the shortest possible time. A quick efficient transport system is also necessary to disperse the finished products to the markets. Production is not complete unless the goods reach the consumer. Transport costs are included in the cost of production and the price of a commodity in the market is inclusive of the transport cost from the centres of production to the market. Hence the availability of a cheap and efficient system of transport adds to the competitive capacity of a producer in the market. It affects the location of economic activity and the emergence of markets.

Both in the assembling of raw material and in the dispersal of goods to the market, transport plays an important role in the economy of a country. Paucity of efficient and cheap transport is one of main causes of a retarded and underdeveloped economy.

COST OF TRANSPORT

The cost of transport, although very important in production and distribution is not easy to assess. It depends on the type of transport used, differential freight charges, the quantities transported per trip, cut-throat competition, differences in charge on trunk lines and branch lines, alignments, government controls and other factors. The assessment of the cost of transport in the modern economic system is a complicated matter. 'Geographic distances' (usually understood as mileage on the ground) are distorted by the cost factor which in turn is controlled by so many factors. In terms of transport costs 'New York is nearer to Tokyo than to San Franscisco'. There is, therefore, only a vague relationship between distances on the ground (geographic distance) and the economic distance (dependent on the cost factor).

TYPES OF TRANSPORT AND THE COST FACTOR

For all commercial purposes the types of transport that are available today are roads, railways and shipways. Air planes have still to become cheaper and to increase their freight capacity before they can be used for transporting the world's goods on a large scale. They can be used now only for high priced, low weight goods which can bear the cost of transport, or for quick specialised services where time means money. In highly developed countries the airoplane is used for commercial purposes because it is extremely efficient and quick. Pipeline is another type of transport which is used for moving liquid material underground, particularly the world's petroleum. But its use is limited in the commercial world because it can carry only liquids. For purposes of the commerce of the world, in general, therefore, the transport that is available are roads, railways and shipways. The differences in the efficiency and the cost of these transport systems have a bearing on the location of economic activity.

Roads

Roads have become efficient for commercial purposes in the modern world with the coming of the trucks and motors. Road transport has certain advantages. They can handle small units for local needs such as grocery, milk, laundry, etc. Trucks, vans and motors can give door to door service which is a great convenience in modern society. Sometimes transporting goods by road saves time because delays at stations can be avoided. Of all the transport systems roads have the greatest flexibility and it is often more convenient than rail or ship. It is safer also to transport goods by road as loading them in smaller bulk than in railway, makes it possible to give them more care and attention.

But roads are very costly for long distance cartage.

While analysing the cost of moving goods on the different types of transport, two factors have to be considered namely the initial cost or overhead costs and the moving cost of transport.

In road transport, the initial cost, compared to railways and shipways, is low. The initial cost includes the laying out of the roads, the building of the stopping places or terminu, cost of maintenance etc., while the moving cost is the actual cost incurred in moving the goods.

The problems of distance and standard charges did engage the attention of the European countries for a long time. It was found that standard charges could not be the same throughout a long route because the initial charges on a line remained the same whether the distance is short or long. Hence, the block and tapering systems were introduced. In the first, the track is divided into blocks and the cost varies with the blocks. In the second, the cost of transport increases at a decreasing rate as the distance (mileage) on the ground increases. Some countries follow the block system but most countries of the world have adopted the tapering system. The moving cost on road is comparatively high, that is, as one goes further in geographic distance, the increase in the proportionate cost is higher than in railways and shipways. Hence roads become costlier than rails and ships as distances increase. Roads are therefore, more economic for short distance hauls while rails and ships are cheaper for long distances. The geographic distance is, therefore, distorted by the cost factor (economic distance). Where there is cut throat competition between roads and rails the cost becomes even more complicated and a thorough survey of differential costs will have to be made before analysing the impact of transport on the location of economic activity in a given area.

There is no simple solution to the problems of distance and cost and each country has evolved its own pattern to fix the rate of progression. The rate charged may depend on the revenue required by the country or the profits aimed at by the owners of transport on the one hand and the ability of goods to move under high rates, on the other.

Railways

The cost of railways is more difficult to assess. In many countries railways are nationalised unlike the vehicular traffic on roads where private companies still operate. If the railways are owned by the Government the standard charges are the same throughout the country except where relief factors, (railways to hill stations) speed and care available on the different trains etc., influence the cost. In countries like USA where the railways are owned by private companies (often by individual families), differential freightage charges are imposed to increase the competitive capacity and the 'cost of transport' is extremely complicated. But it has a bearing on the location of the industry and as such, a study of freight charges on commodities in a given region in USA would be revealing to the economic geographer.

The principle on which railways operate is the same as in roads, that is the block system or the tapering system. But the more prevalent system is the tapering system. In the railways however, the rate of decrease as distance increases is greater than in roadways. In other words as distance increases the cost on railways decreases more rapidly than in roads. Hence for longer distance, railways are cheaper than roadways.

On the other hand, the initial cost (overhead costs) in railways is very much higher than in roadways. The building of railway lines, wagons, engines, stations and the maintenance of these are more costly for a railway complex than that for roadways. Nearly 2/3 of the total cost of railways is on account of the overhead costs while only 1/3 is accounted for by moving cost. The initial cost remaining the same whatever the distance travelled, railways are more costly for short distances but it can easily compete with roads over long distances. A railway can make profits in a short time.

RAILWAY GAUGES AND COST

There are several gauges used in the world. The standard gauge is 4'-8½" and it is used in USA and all over Europe except Spain and the USSR. Spain uses a 5'-5¾" gauge and the USSR, 5 feet gauge. Australia uses the standard gauge in New South Wales, and a 5'-8" gauge in Victoria The rest of the country has a 3'-6" gauge There are several gauges in Africa. India uses three gauges, the Broad Gauge (5′-6″), the Meter gauge (3′-6″) and the Narrow gauge (2′-6″). The differences in gauge affect the cost of transport.

The gauge (width between the rails) conditions the size of the wagons and the quantity carried in one trip. In the case of roads also the size of vehicles affects the quantity carried. But carriers of goods on roads are generally of a standard size or it is left to the operators to choose the size of the vehicle. However, narrow roads do limit the size of the vehicle that can be put into function. In the railways once the line is put down, only a certain size engine and wagon can ply on it. Narrow gauge railways will have to make several trips to move the same quantity that a broad or standard gauge railway can take in one trip. The small size of the engine in a narrow gauge railway, also limits its pulling capacity so that the number of wagons that can be attached to a narrow gauge engine is limited. In the long-run therefore, a broad gauge line is more economic than a narrow or meter gauge line.

But narrow and meter gauge lines have been laid down in some parts of the world because the initial cost of laying down the line, building the wagons etc. is lower than that of a broad gauge line. In the early stages of economic development when a country or region has very little goods to move, the narrow gauge and meter gauge are naturally more economic. This was particularly so in the mining regions of South Africa and in certain parts of India where exploitation economy was prevalent. The initial cost of laying down rails being 2/3 of the total cost, a reduction in this cost greatly brought down the total transport cost. But the railways themselves (or any transport) usually generate economic activity and the region develops other activities as time goes on. The pressure on the railways increases as more and more commodities demand to be moved. Passenger traffic also increases as population increases with economic development. Gradually the narrow and meter gauge lines are unable to cope with the increased traffic and these railways become an economic liability. The conversion of a narrow or meter gauge into broad gauge is costly. India is also facing the problem of differences in gauge with the rapid economic development of the country. With independence and a spurt in economic activity, goods are demanding to be moved quickly and in bulk. The earlier railways on narrow and meter gauges are proving to be inadequate. Many broad gauge lines have been introduced in the once meter gauge and narrow gauge regions, but many more are proving a liability.

Differences in gauge also prevent through traffic. Break of bulk is inevitable where gauges are mixed. It increases the cost of transport and may cause damage to goods. It is also time consuming and risky.

CHARGING WHAT THE TRAFFIC CAN BEAR

All transport, whether railways, roads or shipways, try to make up atleast part of the initial cost and all of the moving cost unless national policies or policies of the private transport companies have other guidelines for special reasons. But individual items need not pay for themselves. The total traffic on the line must cover total cost as well as make a profit. Railways and other types of transport, therefore, are able to take certain goods at a lower rate than other goods. The principle on which goods are classified and different charges are made on different goods is based on 'what the traffic can bear'. A commodity which fetches a high price in the market can bear a high cost of transport. Gold can bear a high cost of transport. Coal on the other hand cannot be charged the same because it is a low value commodity. Coal may also be moved at a special subsidised cost because it is a necessary item for the industrial welfare of the nation. Goods are, therefore, classified by the railways according to their value in the market, their bulk etc. and charged accordingly. "Charging what the traffic can bear" is difficult to define because it depends on so many factors. But the differential cost of movement of goods is of importance to the economic geographer because it affects the location of economic activity.

Break of bulk

The cost of transporting goods also increases with break of bulk. A through line is less costly for transporting goods than a line with break of bulk or a destination which is on a branch line even if the distance is the same. The distance from A to B on the main line may be 200 km. and that of A to C on a branch line from the main line, may also be 200 km. But the cost of transport from A to C will be greater than the cost from A to B. This is because the initial cost of two lines have to be met and because of the cost of loading, unloading, delay etc. caused by the break of bulk.

Cutting losses

The user of a transport system, as has already been mentioned, has to pay two costs (i) something towards the initial cost and (ii) the full moving cost. Individual users pay only a small percentage of the overhead costs of the railway or any transport line but every user has to pay the full moving cost. The maximum possible amount towards the initial cost is normally taken from every user. But this cost can be reduced to the minimum, 'just to cut the losses'. Railways and all other forms of transport earn only when they are moving goods or passengers. The overhead costs have to be met anyway, even when they are idle. So it is more economic to cart something and contribute at least a minimum towards the overhead or initial cost than leave the wagons idle. Hence the full moving cost and 'something' towards the initial cost should be more acceptable to the transport authorities than keeping the wagons in the yard. This is the economics behind concession rates given by rails, roads and ships. The motive in giving concession is not to make a profit but to cut the losses. It is not easy to make a distinction between material carried at a profit and that which is carried just to cut losses. Not all goods can be carried on the basis of cutting the losses. Some goods have to pay more to enable others to be carried at lesser cost. If the transport system on the whole makes a profit it should suffice.

Thatcher gives an example of how complicated the cost of transport can be. The London Railways were told that Canadian cattle were being taken from Birkenhead to London more cheaply than Midland cattle to London, although the Midlands was much nearer to London. But the railways argued that they had to agree to the Canadian cattle being taken from Birkenhead to London by rail at a cheaper rate because the cattle otherwise had the choice of going all the way to London by water, which would be cheaper and more convenient. If the railways refused to take the cattle, for a price which would only 'cut losses' and not cover the full cost, the Midland cattle would have to pay more to make up the loss of the railway. The agreement with the Canadian cattle actually earned something for the railway, so that it was in a position to offer less for the Midland cattle, because it was sharing the cost with the Canadian cattle. Even though the analysis of cost is extremely complicated it has to be tackled for a full understanding of the location of economic activity in any region.

FULL CAPACITY LOAD AND ITS EFFECT ON COST

The cost of transport is affected by the way commodities are packed and sent and the regularity with which they are despatched. If the commodities are packed well, and the full space in the wagons utilised, more commodities can be carried in one trip, which will reduce the cost. Thatcher gives an example to prove this point. The farmers in Hull complained that they paid more to reach their butter to London than the Danes did. The Danish butter came in compact wooden boxes and it was despatched regularly. The butter was unloaded at London Terminal and sent by train whose capacity could be fully and regularly used. The Hull farmers on the other hand sent their butter in odd lots packed in such a way that the railway wagons from the London terminal could not be used to full capacity. The cost of transporting Hull butter from the London terminal was, therefore, high.

SHIPWAYS : INTERNAL WATER TRANSPORT AND OCEAN TRANSPORT

The initial cost of building ships (the size of tankers and ships is now 250,000 tonnes and more) providing port facilities, harbours and maintaining them is very high compared to rails and roads. But the running cost is comparatively low. For very long distances, therefore, waterways are the cheapest.

But ships lack flexibility. Sandbars and silting at the ports can be a grave handicap making dredging, which is very costly, necessary to keep the navigation channels open. In Inland water transport, freezing of the rivers and lakes, winding courses, seasonal fluctuations, waterfalls, silting etc. limit the use of ships.

The use of ships is limited to water and port facilities. Modern ships can use only highly fitted harbours. The carrying capacity of a ship depends on port facilities and the route it takes. If the route is through narrow canals or straits, like the Suez and the Panama Canals and the Malacca Straits, only ships of small tonnage can ply through. Like railways on narrow gauge limiting the size of the wagons, these narrow channels and straits limit the tonnage of the ships. Many of the narrow channels of the world like the Malacca Straits, the Red Sea, the Persian Gulf, Gibralter, the Waist of the Mediterranean, the Panama canal etc. are natural bottlenecks on sea highways which limit the size of the ships and their carrying capacity per trip. In the modern world very large ships ranging from 100,000 to 300,000 tonnes are used in world commerce making the hitherto much used sea routes through Gibralter, Suez, the Red Sea, Aden and Malacca to Hongkong of doubtful value. Ships of bigger size can go on the Atlantic and round the Cape of Good Hope to the Indian Ocean and from thence to the Pacific via the Timor Sea, Arafura Sea and the Torres Straits which are wider than the Malacca Straits. But the Mediterranean and Red Sea route has the advantage of being the shortest route to the east and of going through heavily populated regions. The Cape of Good Hope route traverses through empty seas and underpopulated regions most of the way, unless it makes long detours in the Indian Ocean. The demand for widening and deepening the Suez Canal and developing and peopling tropical north Australia is partly because of the American entry into, and the use of the extra large ships in world commerce.

Sometimes the ports themselves become industrial centres to avoid the cost of break of bulk from sea transport to land transport and haulage on land. Often navigable rivers may connect the sea port to the interior. The St. Lawrence Sea Highway (built by Canada) has made the lake ports of USA into sea ports, as goods can now go up to the Lake ports from the Atlantic Sea without break of bulk. The St. Lawrence Sea Highway is now crowded with traffic that it needs widening and deepening. But Canada is not enthusiastic about the project because the greater benefits would be to USA. Sometimes the change from sea traffic to river or lake traffic is achieved only with a break of bulk. Canals are often built to connect the port with the interior. Such canals, if wide enough, can be used by sea-going ships. But most of the canals of the European countries, which were built in the seventeenth and eighteenth centuries, are narrow and shallow for the present day ocean going ships. Canals also have to compete with railways and roads.

In ship transport nature provides the way and the companies or the Government provide the terminals. The ships are supplied by other companies engaged in ship building. Competition is very great in such cases. Ocean highways can be used by all nations and, therefore the problems arising out of competition is international unlike in railways and roadways. Railways and roadways are, in a sense, protected industries and their problems are internal and can be settled internally upto a point. Coasting steamers can compete with railways to a certain extent. In USA, the Panama Canal route from east to west competes with the transcontinental railways.

Shipways' main handicap is their slow speed and delays caused by certain factors. Its earning power is measured by the number of trips it makes and the amount of goods it carries. In case there are no good port facilities ships have to anchor at a distance and lighters have to transfer the goods to land. This causes delay and inconvenience. In the Plate river in South America, only small ocean going ships can ply. Most of the Indian rivers are not suitable for ocean going ships because of the low water level in the non-rainy season. In summer (rainy season) waters have to be regulated and the navigation channels constantly dredged to make the ports an efficient connecting link between land and sea. Massive dredging have to be undertaken to keep the channels to Calcutta clear. Ships have to wait at three places for the high tide, to cross the shallows between Calcutta and the estuary.

The fact that ships are designed to suit the facilities of particular ports and the ports are equipped often to handle particular cargo, make them less flexible than railways and roads. Ports are usually equipped with mechanised hauling of a specialised nature and it is not possible to re-design the ships or ports except at a very high cost. Further, shipways are dependent on railways and roadways. The ships unload the cargo at the ports. But the efficient functioning of the port depends on its connection with the interior. The railways are not dependent on the ships for their cargo although they may carry a large quantity of the cargo unloaded by ships at the ports. They can have a freight independent of the ship.

AIRWAYS

Air transport, at present, is important on a large scale only for passenger traffic. The initial cost of setting up the terminals, building the airplanes, their maintenance, etc. are much higher than for any other transport system. Air terminals require a considerable amount of land for the drive in. Therefore, they have to be situated far away from the towns. There is, therefore, a break of bulk at the airport itself.

PIPELINES

The pipelines carry oil, gas or water generally. They require flat or gently sloping land because the flow depends on gravity. The diameter of the pipe conditions the quantity of oil or water that flows through it. Once a pipeline of a certain diameter is laid down it is difficult to change it. The pipelines, therefore, cannot adjust themselves to a fluctuation in flow. The maintenance of the pipelines is also difficult. Being underground usually, it is difficult to detect flaws immediately. Break of bulk is inevitable at the refinery which is usually situated away from the oil wells and connected to them by pipelines. The world ownership of oil wells and the pattern of trade in petroleum have created some of the oil ports of the world, with facilities for refineries and transfer of the refined petroleum into tanker ships. A further defect of pipelines is that they cannot be constructed across oceans although attempts are being made to take pipelines across seas like the Mediterranean, which are comparatively small.

The cost factor in transport, the different types of transport with differential costs, the principles on which those function have all distorted the geographic distances in the world. But these complicated transport costs have a bearing on the location of the industries and markets. The difference in the cost of the three major types of transport used in world commerce can be graphically represented as follows :

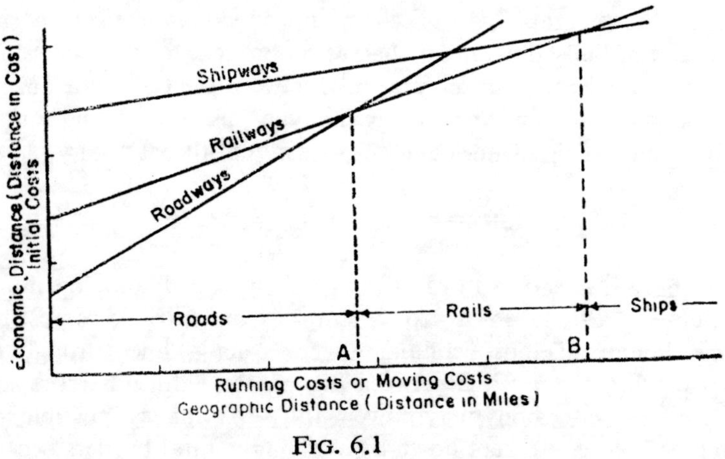

FIG. 6.1

As far possible all transport will try to make up the overhead cost (initial cost) as well as the moving cost and also make a profit. No transport earns when it is idle. The overhead costs have to be anyway met whether the transport is in use or not. But the overhead cost is a constant factor while the moving costs vary with mileage and other factors already mentioned. In the case of roads the initial costs are very low but the running costs are high. Hence after a distance at point *A* on the ground, roads become costlier than railways. In the case of railways, the initial costs are much higher than in roads but the running costs are proportionately lower with increasing distance. At point *A* and onwards therefore, railways can easily compete with roads in cost. In the case of ships the initial costs are very high, higher than both railways and roads, but the moving cost is very low. Hence for very great distances, shipways are cheaper if facilities are available. At point *B* on the diagram a ship can compete with railways in cost. These differences in cost have arisen because of the differences in the initial cost and running cost in the three types of transport. The initial cost (overhead costs or terminal costs) remain the same whether a railway or ship moves 20 km. or 2000 km. Since these initial costs are higher in rail than in roads and highest in the case of ships they are not suited for short distances. However, theories and graphs are to be used with caution by the economic geographer. Every traffic will have to be viewed individually as other factors may be operating to distort further the geographic distance in terms of economic distance, such as break of bulk, differential charges on branch lines, concessions, and above all competition, not only between the types of transport but between different lines in each type, usually arising out of private ownership of lines and consequent cut-throat rivalry.

ALIGNMENT AND THE COST FACTOR

Transport always tries to run through economically developed and populated regions so as to capture as much traffic as possible. Even though it is most economic to construct a line through the shortest distance possible between two points, natural barriers such as a hill or water body may prevent this. As far as possible the overhead costs are kept down by avoiding natural barriers because bridges, tunnels, cuttings, embankments and so on raise the cost of the line. But in avoiding these it would not be economic to pass through empty country where there is no traffic. A transport line must pass through areas where it can obtain maximum traffic. Empty countries like Argentina, Brazil, Western China, Siberia and even Western USA (particularly during the days of settlement of the prairies) present problems in transport. A line becomes more costly when it cannot pick up maximum traffic on the way and this can be done only when it passes through an economically developed region.

COMPETITION ON ROUTES

Rival lines can compete with each other for traffic between terminals which they both serve. This happens when transport is owned privately as in USA In India most of the vehicular traffic on roads are owned privately. In such cases the routes taken may be quite parallel or they may divert to such an extent that they may serve two different regions altogether though their terminals are the same. Circuitous all rail routes in USA are sometimes quite wasteful. The Canadian Pacific Railway, for example, used to take business for San Franscisco from points as far South as Tennessee and Arakansas when there was a more direct route via Kansas. But this was a time when only trunklines served parts of the mid-west. Atleast 50 per cent of the traffic from Pennsylvania toPittsburg even now is diverted from the direct route due to competition.

COMPETITION OF TRANSPORT AND THE MARKET FACTOR

Transport is an agent for the distribution of goods. The cost of the goods in the market includes the transport cost. Competition in the market is the competition between rival producing countries or organisations selling in the same market. Production includes both from utilities (commodities) as well as place utilities (a particular place becomes a node). It is transport that creates place utilities and its costs are more elastic than factory costs. The Pittsburg district in USA used to enjoy preferential treatment by the Basing Point system. Pittsburg is situated in a gulch or in the junction of gulches. Walls were built to keep the shales from falling on the Pennsylvanian track as it enters the city. Transport charges to and from Pittsburg were therefore, high. The Basing Point decreed that no steel could be sold at lesser price than Pittsburg steel plus its transport charges. Special freight rates were allowed for Pittsburg Steel. This was abolished only in 1948 with competition from the Lake Superior iron and the steel companies which were established later. Pittsburg lost its artificial advantage in the market.

Under normal conditions markets will have some reference to geographic distances, that is, markets will be near to the production area. But because the transport cost is included in the production cost, the location of markets, like the location of industries, is influenced by the cost of transport. When a producer's cost of production is very high already, he cannot afford to pay much on transport of goods to the market. He may ask the railways for concession rates. The railways may agree to cart his goods when they are not operating to full capacity in order to 'cut losses'. It is not easy to draw a line between traffic carried just to cut losses, the traffic that is carried at normal rates for profit and traffic that just meets the cost. While surveying the markets however, the economic geographer has to recognise these variations in cost in his area of study. Even a seasonal markets can be created by variations in traffic costs.

Least cost transport analysis and its impact on location of industry

It has been already noted that the cost of transport is an important factor in the location of economic activity. Producers seek an area for the location of their enterprise where the cost of transport to assemble raw material for an industry and to distribute the finished commodity to the market, is the least. Under normal conditions industries should be located either in the raw material area or in the market area. The orientation of the industry to the raw material or market area is based on the principle of the least cost of transport. If it is more costly to transport the raw material than the finished goods then, the industry will be located in the raw material area. The pull of the raw material is great if it is used in bulk or it is energy consuming or weight losing in transport. The pull of the market is great where the finished goods are costly to be transported. Iron and steel industry for example is a raw material oriented industry normally, although it is showing a tendency to move to the market in certain parts of the world because of increased efficiency in transport and technology. Iron and steel industry requires three main raw materials namely coal, iron and manganese (or for special steels, vanadium, nickel, chromium etc.). Manganese, vanadium and such other minerals used for special steels are required only in small quantities and therefore, have no great pull on the industry. Iron and coal, on the other hand, are used in large quantities and therefore are in a position to determine the location of the industry. Between iron and coal, coal had the greater pull because, in the early days of the iron and steel industry in Europe, about 2½ tons of coal were required to smelt one tonne of iron. Hence it was cheaper to move iron to coal provided other things remained the same. The dictum that 'iron moves to coal' was established under European conditions. But actually iron moves to coal because it is cheaper to move one tonne of iron to coal than 2½ tonnes of coal to iron. But conditions can alter if the ratio of coal to iron changes due to changes in the quality of the two. If the coal is of good quality less of it is required in smelting. If the iron content in the ore is very high more coal may be required to smelt the iron but the quantity of pure iron that can be obtained by expending the extra energy, is high. The cost of transporting coal to iron is compensated for by the extra quantity of pure iron from a good quality ore. For all practical purposes the ratio of coal to iron is changed. As the iron and steel industry spread over the world many types of coal and iron ores were found in the different parts of the world. The Lake Superior iron ores of USA contain about 60 to 80 per cent iron. Hankow in China and Bastar in India have also high quality iron. Hence it is economic to locate the industry in the iron area. Technology has further improved the heating capacity of coal. In the form of coke, coal has a higher heating capacity. Technology has also discovered ways and means of conserving fuel so that the ratio of coal to iron has changed. The rule of the thumb that iron moves to coal has been disproved in USA and the USSR and even in India. But whether the industry is located in the iron or coal region it is based on the same principle of 'least cost of transport'. If it is cheaper to move iron to coal then coal has the greater pull on the industry. But if it is cheaper to move coal to iron, the iron area will become the site of a steel industry.

The location of the steel industry is also affected by other factors but once again it is based on the same principle of 'least cost of transport'. The iron and steel industry of Kuznetsk in Siberia has to depend largely on the Magnitogorsk iron some thousands of miles west. The Siberian railway is about the only railway line that runs through the territory to link up the coal with the iron. When the Communist Government decided to develop the heavy industries of the USSR to catch up with European outputs and ushered in the Five Year Plans in 1927, the problems of distance, isolation, empty interior and the backward economy of Siberia were even greater than today. The Siberian railway was virtually running through empty country with not much traffic to pick up on the way. The wagons which took the iron from Magnitogorsk had either to return empty or bring back coal from Kuznetsk. The reverse flow of coal from Kuznetsk made transport cheaper as the cost could be shared by the two commodities. A two way traffic being cheaper, iron and steel industries were located at the iron and the coal end of the great planned region of the 'Kuznetsk—Magnitogorsk Combine'. Later the USSR discovered the Karaganda coal which was nearer to Magnitogorsk. But the Kuznetsk coal far excels the Karaganda coal in quantity and quality. Efforts are also being made to discover iron near the Kuznetsk area. But nothing of the magnitude of the Magnitogorsk iron has been located. A reverse flow, makes transport cheap and explains the location of the iron and steel industry in the Magnitogorsk and Kuznetsk regions in the USSR.

The movement of iron and coal to a midway area is also based on the principle of least costs. In the Lakes Region of USA and the Black Sea Region of the USSR the industry is located neither in the coal area nor the iron area but midway between the two. This is because of the facilities available to transport the iron by water and the cheapness of transport by water. The main coal area which had an early start in USA was the Pittsburg coal region. The coal was of very high quality and iron was available to some extent in the vicinity. But when the high quality Lake Superior iron was discovered the major source of USA's iron shifted westwards across the Lakes The Great Lakes provided the cheap transport necessary to link up the two resources. But the market was in the thickly populated eastern region where as the west was still comparatively an empty country.

As time passed and Pittsburg ceased to enjoy preferential treatment of the Basing Point, she could not compete with the iron and steel industries of other regions. Situated in a saucerlike Basin its transport costs were high. The Lake Superior iron could come by an all water route to the shores of any of the Lakes and if a reverse flow of coal from Pittsburg was made possible it was more economic to locate the industry on the shores of the lakes. Pittsburg coal began to move to the lake shores to meet the iron of Lake Superior. Break of bulk could be avoided if the plants were situated on the shores of the Lakes. The discovery of the Illinois coal has moved the industry further west along the shores of the Lakes although Pittsburg coal is still used at these sites for certain stages of the industry. But the heavily populated market continues to be in the east. This checks the movement of the industry too far to the west, despite the presence of the high quality Lake Superior Iron. The new location is therefore, actually a movement of the iron and steel industry to the iron ore as well to the developing markets of the Midwest.

The same features are seen along the coasts of the Black Sea the USSR. The Donetz coal and the Krivoyrog iron were responsible for the early start of the iron and steel industry in Ukraine. But the industry is gradually moving towards the shores of the Black Sea, taking advantage of the water transport. The finished product can also be transported by water to some of the central Asian markets and across to the Mediterranean. Like in USA it is a move towards the market. The same is true of the iron and steel industry of China.

The location of any industry is therefore controlled by transport costs and the theory of least cost. But the assessment of the cost of transport is very complicated and needs to be surveyed in individual areas. The data has to be collected by field work keeping the above considerations in mind.

LEAST COST ANALYSIS AND THE ORIENTATION OF INDUSTRY TO THE MARKET

The movement of industries to the market is also based on the least cost theory. It is usually the lighter and the consumer industries that get located in the market area. Such industries generally use raw material which are not very costly to be assembled. But the finished products of such industries are very costly to be transported. Often duties on the finished product, increase the cost. Such industries are therefore, best located in the market area, provided facilities are available, for example the numerous service industries in the urban areas. With the advent of electricity the pull of the market in economic activity is greater than before. Electricity can be transported (transmitted) over long distances without much cost and difficulty.

The well known Van Thunen's theory published in 1826 determining the land use patterns about a city is based on transport costs. Thunen recognised that the pattern of agricultural land use depended on competition between various types of crops for a particular piece of land. According to him the controlling factor in this competition is economic rent that is "return from investment in the land". Briefly the form of land use providing the greatest economic rent would make the highest bid for land and displace all others. Transport costs were a primary factor determining Economic Rent. Transport costs, says Thunen, increase with distance. Therefore, Economic Rent from any one land use is a function of distance from the market (which is the urban area in Thunen's theory). The relationship of Thunen's economic rent and the distance from the market is generally explained graphically as follows:

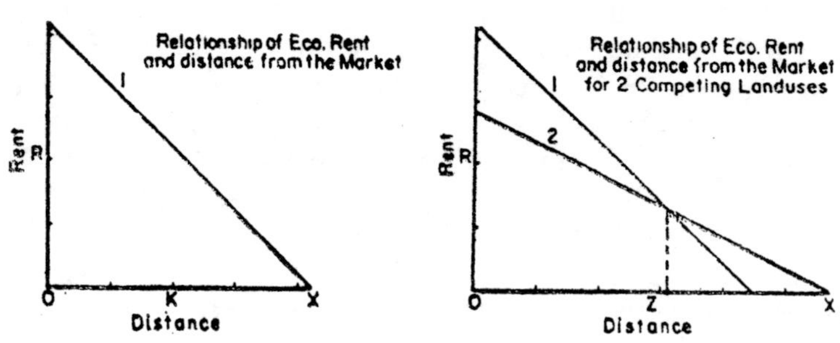

FIG. 6.2

O is the market. The increasing distance from the market and the consequent increasing transport costs cause the rent per unit of land (R) to be diminished. In other words economic rent declines with distance from the market. At point *X* in Figure 2.1, it is completely absorbed.

But this one land use in Figure 2.1 is competing with other

land uses, which, depending on their type and production, have different R slopes. In Figure 6 1 land use (1) yields a higher economic rent R close to the market O but because its slope is steeper than for land use (2), its advantage ceases at point Z at a distance of OZ from the market. From this point onwards land use 2 yields a higher rent until this is entirely absorbed at X at a distance of OX from the market. The fundamental factor which controls the steepness of the R slope is the relative ease with which the total production of a unit area can be transported to the market. Commodities which yield a large quantity per hectare like potatoes or firewood yield a high rent close to the market but because the transport cost per hectare is high the rent diminishes rapidly with distance from the market. Commodities which yield a lower bulk per hectare, (for example, grain) do not fetch such a high rent, close to the market. However transport cost per hectare for grain is relatively low and the actual value per unit of weight is relatively high. Economic rent therefore, diminishes much more slowly with distance from the market. One other factor influencing the steepness of the R slope is the perishable nature of the product. Because of the degree of perishability being higher in certain commodities like milk, fresh vegetables etc., they can be produced only close to the market.

Figure 6.1 can represent not only the competition between two crops (may be potatoes and grains) but also competition between two systems of growing the same crops. The per hectare production of any crop can be increased with intensive cultivation, application of more labour, more fertilisers and better techniques. At the market an extremely intensive use of land is desirable because the resulting increased production pays off in higher economic rent. With greater distance from the market such intensive land use becomes less practicable because the advantage of increased production per hectare is offset by increasing transport costs. So at greater distance from the market, a less intensive system of land use becomes more desirble. Land use (1) Figure 6.1 may be an intensive crop rotation whereas, Land use (2) may be a rotation system with considerable fallow land. However, if a non-intensive rotation produces a high yield per acre but of low value like firewood, a less intensive land use can exist near the market. Secondly, if intensive land use results in products of low bulk, but high value like cheese, this land use can exist far away from the market according to Thunen.

The principle of declining intensity of land use away from the market is generally attributed to Von Thunen although he has qualified it by certain observations.

The competition between two land uses shown in Figure 6.1 can be expanded to include a number of land uses. In this case land use 1 yields a greater economic rent in zone OZ, land use 2 in zone OX, land use 3 in zone OW and so on. Because O is the market it is easy to take O as the centre and OZ, OX, OW etc. as radius and construct the famous Thunen's circles. Such rings are the framework of the well known pattern of the land use of Thunen round a market area (city). It is based on transport costs.

The nearest to the market, Zone 1 will be devoted to vegetables, milk and items producing high yields per acre and perishable goods. The next three zones are crop farming zones of gradually decreasing intensity. The decline in economic rent owing to increasing transport costs make it necessary to apply less and less capital and labour until only the most extensive rotation system is possible. Thus in Zone 3 rye is the most valuable crop. In Zone 4 rye is mixed with pasture and fallow. In Zone 5 the three field system prevails with 1/3 land under crops, pasture and fallow respectively. In Zone 6, the distance from the market is so great that only the most extensive grazing activities can be carried out profitably.

Van Thunen wrote in 1826. The situation has changed now with the development of technology, organisation and the living habits of people. Development of transportation has had the greatest effect on production and market. Cost of all types of transport has declined in relation to most agricultural production costs. More over transport costs are not directly proportionate to distance and bulk. Because of refrigeration and air conditioning techniques, perishable commodities can be carried over great distance without spoiling. An increasing amount of agricultural produce is processed before shipment. These new developments have tended to change the tastes of the city dweller. Van Thunen's work was based on actual observation. He identified the basic forces determining the pattern of land use about a city by his own findings. These basic forces became the key to his theory. The applicability of a theory depends upon the correct identification of the basic forces. Where these forces are operating the theory provides a way of understanding the patterns. But where the forces are not operating the theory has to be sacrificed for reality. The basic forces which Thunen identified no longer exist under modern transport conditions and transport costs. In other words the basic factors which created a particular pattern of land-use have changed but they still are closely linked with transport and transport costs. What has changed is not the principle of least cost but the type of, transport, cost of transport, type of agricuture, organisation, facilities, tastes etc , of the people. The economic geographer has to be very cautious while using theories.

Branch lines

In certain cases industries are located on transport lines, particularly the main lines where break of bulk is least. In such case the effect of transport on industry or economic activity is direct. In Northern Rhodesia the 'Farming Corridor' is the creation of railways. The extension of wheat cultivation in the Siberian steppes is very much conditioned by the Siberian railway. The brickworks of Oxford are situated on the main railway line. Nearer home the ribbon like development of industries from Surat to Ahmedabad through Baroda is mainly the creation of the broadgauge railway. Baroda itself owes much to the broadgauge Bombay-Delhi and Bombay-Ahmedabad railway lines for its development into an industrial centre. In the early days of railway development, the British Government was willing to give concession rates in transport for industries in Baroda to feed the Baroda railway and make it profitable. As a suitable place for industry has few facilities except through Bombay-Delhi railway and the concessions if any made available to its industries. Its main defects are lack of water, interior location and lack of markets.

Staggering of load

In many of the underdeveloped countries where the transport system is inadequate staggering of load becomes necessary This is a feature not absent in developed countries. The capacity of the Canadian railways is inadequate to move its wheat. Hence the load is staggered. The trans-Siberian Railway of USSR has a staggering load. The broad guage railway recently constructed between Kandla and Ahmedabad is so inadequate to move commodities to and fro from the port that the load has to be staggered. Railways also resort to staggering of load during seasons. In such cases facilities for storage of goods have to be made for a regular flow of goods. Railways and other transport system can function efficiently only when there is a regular flow of goods. Staggering of load at particular seasons is uneconomical because artificial regularity of flow must be resorted to by building store houses which increases the overhead costs. It also reduces the speed in transaction. Delays are uneconomic.

Decay of small ports

Transport complexes of the modern age have put may ports of the sailing ship period out of function. It is cheaper to concentrate the facilities required in a modern port at particular places Mechanical devices for loading and unloading, special docks for particular commodities, maintenance of navigation channels and deep water at the harbours, adequate transport to the interior, all these require a heavy outlay of capital. Hence a concentration of it at a suitable port is more economic than scattering ports all over the coast of a country. The sailing boat on the other hand could anchor anywhere if there was enough water. But the river port of the sailing ship period was not costly to set up. They had very few of the facilities found in the modern ports Most of these river ports gradually decayed. But some caught up with the new requirements of the steamship like Antwerp, London, New Orleans and so on.

Linkage of industries

In the modern times the finished product of one industry may be the raw material of another industry. If the industries are linked the transport cost would be less and the producer can bring down the cost of production. The nucleus of all industries is Power (coal, petroleum and electricity of which coal has the least mobility) and metal (of which iron is the most widely used for machines today). Coal and iron roughly therefore, forms the nucleus of an industrial region. The finished product of the iron and steel industry and the wastes from coal permit other industries to be set up in the region economically. The linkage of industries further induces the growth of the region The region becomes a region of concentrated population with a high purchasing capacity and therefore, also provides the market for the industries Industries being one of the critical factors which make a country power ful politically, the region becomes politically important with many leaders having a say in policy matters. It is efficient transport which makes such large industrial complexes possible. It also makes regional specialisation possible.

Transport capacity is an index to national economic development. Industrialisation cannot be achieved without an adequate transport system. Industrial economy requires quick assembling of raw material and quick disposal of the goods to the increasingly widening market. Large scale production is necessary for bringing down cost and modern factory industries cannot function economically except at full capacity. If the assembling of raw material or the disposal of goods to the market is delayed, the loss is considerable. As such, efficiency in transport is fundamental to economic advancement.

7

ENERGY RESOURCES AND ECONOMIC STRENGTH

POWER or energy is today significant to all modern economic activity. Energy is the capacity to work and it is ultimately measured in terms of work. 'Nature reveals itself to Man through energy' says Ostwald.

> The warmth of a summer's day, sunlight, the movement of the earth, winds, waves, water-falls, tides, plants and animal life... all matter in motion reveal to us energy at work.

Energy at work ably illustrates the unitary nature of Science, for it embraces so many fields of science "The dynamic characteristics of all bodies of the Universe, such as the sun which is the principal source of energy, falls within the field of Astronomy; the restoration of our energy supplies through photosynthesis is the field of Botany; the production of heat in the animal body is the field of Zoology; the release of heat energy through chemical changes is the field of Chemistry; the distribution of the various forms of energy falls within the field of Topography; the accumulation of available energy in the form of coal, petroleum and natural gas is the field of Geology; the laws of thermodynamics, energy transfer and conservation is the field of Physics, the study of cost and efficiency of fuel is the field of economics". Other social sciences are also involved in explaining the energy patterns and the effect of energy on man and society. In analysing the interaction of man in society to his varying environment, the geographer has to draw upon the physical, the biological and the social sciences. The economic geographer, as noted, confines himself to the economic interaction of man to his varying environment and the resulting regional variations in economy on the surface of the earth. This environment is not static. It changes with man's knowledge, his technical skills, his attitudes and tastes from time to time.

The beginnings of man's efforts to control energy other than his own muscle power is lost in antiquity. When man learnt to light a fire to cook his food and keep himself warm he had harnessed and discovered the use of energy. As the patterns of living changed and became more complex and as man's numbers increased, his energy demands grew and they were met by ingenious inventions. He domesticated animals to get more power for work. Slavery, a vital factor in history, was a means to acquire power for work. Much of the famous works of man in the ancient and medieval days were achieved by his own and animal power. Later he learnt to use inanimate energy. He invented gunpowder, a devastating source of energy, which made and remade the maps of the world and decided the fate of many nations. He then discovered the windmill and the waterwheel and harnessed the energy of wind and water. Sometime during the course of history man looked into the bowels of the earth for energy resources and discovered coal, petroleum and natural gas. The industrial revolution was mainly due to his ability and inequity in using coal on a very large scale.

Animal power could not have exploited the energy resources of the earth to the extent that mechanical power made possible in the eighteenth century. Even though man knew the use of coal as a source of heat long before the industrial revolution, he could use only that coal found on or near the surface of the earth. But steam power permitted deep mining and large scale exploitation of energy and metal resources. The use of inanimate energy has also made transportation easy. The locomotive and the truck by-passed the limitation placed on animal-driven transport. The mobility of metal and conventional energy resources has increased with the mechanical upgrading and added to the efficiency in transport so that industries have spread all over the world. It has also made the population of the world more mobile. However, the use of mechanical energy has its defects. Some of its sources are exhaustible like coal and petroleum so that a civilization built on mechanical energy would be unstable. Coal, petroleum and natural gas are renewable but it takes millions of years. The outlay of capital, further improvement in technology and man's attitudes in favour of conservation can also make the use of mechanical energy more efficient and dynamic. This would require a uniformly powerful stimulant for society to move in this direction.

Man's craving for energy after discovering coal and petroleum expressed itself in the damming of rivers and in the generation of electricity. There is a further move to develop electricity from other unconventional sources. The deadly explosives blasted rocks and cities alike and he realised his dream of converting matter into energy with the release of atomic energy This discovery is having a profound effect on the economic, cultural, social and political patterns of the world. One is apt to agree with Fairgrieve that :

> in its widest sense, on its material side, history is the story of mans' increasing ability to control energy Any means by which man can get more energy and waste less of it, marks an advance.

Progress in the field of controlling and conserving energy may lead to war One nation may have more control over energy than another and disturb the political equilibrium of the world.

Forms and sources of energy

There are different forms of energy—mechanical, electrical, chemical and so on. Energy transformations can also be carried out, for example, mechanical energy can be converted into electrical energy as in the case of the dynamo. Chemical energy can be converted into mechanical energy as in the case of the internal combustion engine. Electrical energy can be converted into heat as in an ordinary electric stove.

The various sources of energy are the sun, wind, tides, wood, vegetable oils, alcohol, coal, petroleum, natural gas, thermal and hydro-electricity and atomic energy. Of these coal, petroleum and natural gas are fossil fuels and their stocks are limited. Hydro-electricity is derived from running water while thermal electricity is derived from coal, mineral oil and so on. The radioactive minerals used for atomic energy are mainly uranium minerals. The sun, although the source of all energy in the world, is little used by man directly for industrial purposes although great strides have been made in the use of solar energy recently. Wood, tides, wind, vegetable oils and alcohol are only minor sources of energy in the modern world The main sources of power which influence the location of economic activity on a large scale are coal, petroleum, natural gas and electricity in the present world, and as such are dealt with in detail and a brief survey of other sources of energy is also made.

Solar Energy

Solar energy at present is of little importance to industry and cannot replace other sources of energy which are more concentrated, but it may supplement these on the domestic front. In time to come when other sources of energy like coal and petroleum get depleted, it may contribute to a large extent to the supply of energy. The high initial cost of generating solar energy, the difficulties in storing the energy; the relative low intensity of the sun's heat in the present industrial regions of the world, the changing position of the planets in relation to the sun and consequent atmospheric effects, all these limit the use of solar energy. In recent years, however, the work on the utilization of solar energy has received a very great impetus. Several solar heated houses have been put into function in the US. Many designs of water heaters using solar energy are available and a large number of simple appliances using the sun's energy are in use in Japan, India, and other parts of the world. A number of solar furnaces for the production of very high temperatures by concentrating the sun's rays through the use of mirrors, have been constructed and they are being tried out in Algiers, USSR and the US. They are still at an experimental stage. Solar radiation may be converted into electricity by photo-electric devices and thermo-couples, but the cost is considerable and their efficiencies low with the technology available at present.

While the direct utilization of solar energy has not yet been economically and commercially feasible, the bagic dependence on the sun for energy cannot be denied. It is the sun which helps the plants to build up vegetable matter from carbon dioxide and water, a process known as photosynthesis. It is through this process in nature that we get the food we eat and the wood we burn. It is vegetable and animal matter that once existed that is today found in the form of coal and petroleum. Further, the sun evaporates water and gives us rain. This water forms rivers and sometimes waterfalls, which are sources of hydroelectricity. The sun, therefore, is the ultimate source of all energy although its direct use in industries is almost insignificant at present.

Wind

The wind has been historically important as a source of energy. In the ancient and medieval times when the seas were traversed by sailing ships, it was the wind that provided the motive power. To the Dutch the windmills literally meant their land because it was these slow-moving wind mills that enabled them to push back the waters of the sea from their land. The commercial development of wind at present, however, is almost nil. Here and there, power generators working on wind may be in operation. In the rural parts of the developed countries like the US, Great Britain, Germany and USSR one might still come across a windmill generating power but they are there more for their antique value and quaintness than as a source of energy for industry. There is energy in the wind but the utilization of wind for generating power for modern industries has its problems.

The first of its problems is its variability. The speed of the wind varies from season to season and from day to day. Any source of energy for modern industry must have some stability of supply. The necessity for speed in production, achieved through mechanization, requires also speed and regularity in the supply of raw materials and power resources, to make the industry a success. Wind lacks this stability and regularity.

Secondly, windmills of a strong construction which can withstand high winds are not capable of yielding power from moderate winds. Low velocity of under 20 miles per hour (mph) is not considered practical and a velocity above 30 mph is unmanageable. A steady wind of between 20 and 30 mph throughout the year is a rare phenomenon in any part of the world.

Thirdly, the only part of the wind accessible for use is that which is close to the earth. But to use this space for generating wind power on a commercial scale would require the earth's entire land to be covered with windmills of high efficiency leaving no space for the growing of food crops or for utilising the power generated. The presence of such high towers would also prove dangerous to air traffic. Energy from winds, therefore, is not likely to supply more than a trifling part of the world's future energy stock.

Tides

The total amount of energy from tides is large. If it were accessible, it could supply one half of the world's present energy needs. The energy is there, one can see it, hear it, it is perpetual, it is free and very close at hand, but for all practical purposes it is of little economic use. Numerous schemes have been deviced to capture energy from tides but none of them is practicable except the basin method. In this method huge basins are filled during high tides taking advantage of the differences in the levels of the high and low tides. A successful basin scheme requires two things, a large mean difference between high and low tide and a shore-line of suitable physical configuration for the establishment of one or more storage basins. Atleast a three metre tide is required for an economic installation of a basin and very likely few installations of less than six metre tide would really be practical. Places about the earth where tides average six metres are not many. In the search for new energy sources, therefore, tides do not offer much.

Vegetation and alcohol

The world's total consumption of wood fuel is about 7 per cent of the total energy requirements. Agricultural wastes, such as corn, stalks, cobs, straw and so on are also used as fuel by certain communities of people the world over. All these have a low calorific value, compared to the more concentrated fuels like coal and petroleum. Larger quantities of wood and wastes have to be transported to get the same amount of energy as coal or petroleum. The transport and heat efficiencies of such fuels, therefore, are much less than that of coal or petroleum.

Vegetation can also be converted into liquid fuels like alcohol which is prepared from starch or sugar-bearing materials like potatoes, cereals and molasses. But alcohol will supply only a fraction of the world's total energy requirements.

Atomic energy

The development of atomic energy has made great strides in recent years. The utilization of this energy for industrial purposes has already become a feasible proposition as can be seen from the Calder Hall Power Generating Station in Great Britain and several other plants round the world. India also has atomic power stations at Tarapore and Kalpakkam. Atomic energy is more powerful than any of the known sources of energy and in the future can play a decisive role in the location of economic activity.

The basic radio-active materials used for atomic energy are mainly uranium minerals. The chief rock sources of these uranium minerals are (1) pegmatites of granite composition and (2) hypothermal mineral veins, (these are products of crystallization from hot igneous solutions), and (3) sediments.

Uranium minerals are distributed over wide areas but mining of the mineral is confined to a few places at present. There is no doubt however that the distribution of uranium minerals will have an impact on the future world patterns of economic activity and future world politics, just as oil has today. Already the scramble for obtaining these mineral-rich areas of the world is directing the economic and political policies of the developed world. The use of this energy for industrial purposes is limited.

Each country has its own energy patterns determined by the availability of the sources of energy, degree of industrialization, habits of life, distribution of wealth, character of the national economy and the like. Countries like Norway, Sweden, Japan and Switzerland have turned rapidly to electricity because of their high hydroelectric potentialities and inadequacy of other sources of energy. In the US the demand for liquid and gaseous fuels increased when output of petroleum became abundant. Petroleum in the US is found in areas where coal is scarce. Recently, with the need for conservation of oil resources the US is making efforts to tap other sources of energy. In Great Britain, Germany and some other countries of Europe, the use of coal for industry was known as early as the eighteenth and nineteenth centuries because of the abundance of coal deposits and the use of coal as the earliest of the industrial fuels. The USSR uses all the three sources of energy because her energy demands, after the introduction of the planned development of economy, are increasing rapidly and her resources of energy are distributed widely over space. India also uses all three sources of energy. The use of coal, petroleum, natural gas and electricity has increased considerably since independence.

At present the main sources of energy for industry and agriculture are coal, petroleum, natural gas and electricity. These are widely used and mined or worked on a large scale. The present pattern of economic activity in the world, therefore, is more or less controlled by these energy sources.

COAL AS ENERGY SOURCE

Of the energy resources mentioned, coal, petroleum and electricity form the main sources of energy for modern industry. The technical developments in the use of various fuels and the increasing knowledge of existing resources have made necessary the reassessment of the fuel resources. Coal became useful in the modern sense only after the discovery of the steam engine in the last quarter of the eighteenth century and technical developments which took place during the period of the industrial revolution in England. The utilization of energy in modern industries is very complex and engineers and scientists are constantly making efforts to improve the methods of conversion of the raw material into energy resource and to adapt energy to the requirements of specific industries.

> The availability of energy does not depend on the number of forms of energy tapped nor on the amounts of energy resources which are being utilised, but it depends even more on the care and efficiency with which these available supplies are being utilised. The greatest progress may be expected, not from the country which possesses large coal deposits, but from the country which used its coal most efficiently and most wisely.

Under modern conditions of easy transportation and interchange of ideas, developments in technique usually become available to the whole industrial world, provided the people are vigilant, educated and enterprising enough to make use of the knowledge.

There are certain facts about coal that are important to the economic geographer. There is a tendency to assume that a geographer's function is only to know the distribution patterns of the resources of the earth. The broad distribution of most of the resources of the earth are now available in atlases and needs little further elaboration. The energy patterns of the world are a little affected by topographical distribution of energy resources but the properly planned use, control and conservation of resources depends on man's initiative and greatly affects the distribution of economic activity. The economic geographer has to find out the causes of the distribution patterns of economic activity on the surface of the earth and not merely describe its location. Man has discovered the fuel resources, he has learnt the technique of converting it into energy and has built his industrial world. The physical resources perhaps gave him the incentive to start his ventures in a particular area but the continuation of it as an industrial complex depends on man's technical knowledge, his demands and the facilities he has at his disposal in that area. It is the combined impact of these forces that create an industrial or agricultural region.

Ranks and types of coal

There are different ranks of coal such as anthracite, bituminous, semi-bituminous, lignite and so on. The difference in the rank of coal arises out of the geological forces such as consolidation (compaction) and condensation. Compaction is respnosible for the varying density in coal while the heat value of coal is dependent on condensation. High rank coals are found in folded rocks in contact with igneous rocks. The coking quality of coal which is important to metallurgical industries is also the result of geological forces. Coal further is categorised into types. The differences in the type of coal is due to the original differences in the composition of the organic matter that went into the making of coal. To the laymen such differences in rank, type and quality are superfluous but to the industrialist such details are of great significance. The decision to locate an industry in a particular place may often depend on such facts.

The fixed carbon content in coal gives coal its heating capacity. This is the result of condensation. Upto a certain point the heating capacity of coal is related to the carbon content. Lignite has a carbon content of 38 per cent and its heating capacity is only 7,400 British thermal units (ash free). Semi-bituminous coal has a carbon content of 79 per cent and its heating capacity is the highest amongst all ranks of coals being 15,400 BTU. But anthracite which has a carbon content of 96 per cent has only a heating capacity of 14,400 BTU. The most sought-after coal for industry is therefore semi-bituminous or bituminous.

Secondly, coal contains volatile matter. Anthracite contains only 1 per cent volatile matter, semi-anthracite 10 per cent, bituminous 17 per cent, bituminous medium 40 per cent, sub-bitumious 34 per cent and lignite 19 per cent. Volatile matter in coal increases accidents and risks in mining and industry. Mining a high volatile coal can be costly as labour might demand more. Anthracite coal is the safest to mine while bituminous coals which are used for industries have a comparatively high volatile matter. The moisture in lignite and consequent low volatile matter reduces its risks in mining. But it cannot be used for industries unless its heating capacity is increased by technology, or by conversion into other forms of energy like electricity.

A third quality in coal which has some economic impact is its moisture content. Anthracite has only 3 per cent of moisture, semi-bituminous 4 per cent (less than semi-anthracite). In lignite the moisture content is 43 per cent. A large percentage of moisture in coal makes it soft and friable so that it wears away in storage. While burning, it gives out smoke. If found in large quantities, moisture reduces the heating capacity of coal.

The ash content in coal is due to the various organic and inorganic sediments which went into the making of coal. A high content of ash in coal reduces its value for industries.

Some of the physical qualities of coal are also of interest to the industrialist. A black lustrous coal will fetch a high price in the market than a woody, dull and claylike coal. (Clay and slate in coal are the result of inundations of washes while coal was being formed. They greatly reduce the value of coal and make mining costly). A hard coal is adaptable to storage and will be considered more valuable by the industrialist than a friable soft coal which deteriorates on storing.

The length of the flame and the smokiness of the coal are other qualities important to the industrialist. Bituminous medium and bituminous coal burn with a medium to long, and long flame respectively; while anthracite and semi-anthracite burn with very short flames. Anthracite on the other hand is smokeless, semi-anthracite and semi-bituminous nearly smokeless while bituminous medium, sub-bituminous and lignite, are smoky.

There are other facts also about coal mines which are of significance to the industrialist The average depth of the mine affects the accessibility of coal and the cost of mining. In England where coal has been mined for two centuries the average depth is about 312 metres while in the US, where the mining industry is comparatively young, the average depth of mines is about 61 metres. Some of the old coalfields of Europe are getting exhausted while certain parts of America are only skimming the top seams.

The average thickness of the seams also varies from country to country. The better seams being worked first, some of the old coalfields of Europe are now forced to exploit thin seams. The quantity of coal that can be recovered from such mines, given the same output of work, is much less. The average thickness of seams in Britain is less than in the US. Coal mining in USA is also much more highly mechanised than in Great Britain or Europe. The average output per man in USA is more than that in Great Britain.

The nature of the roofs and floors in the mines, folds and faults, inclination of the seams, inflammable gases, water seepage in the mines, all affect cost of mining. If the roofs and floors are collapsible it causes a great deal of risk to the miners. The mines will have to be cleared of the debris before they can be worked again. Faults and overthrusts in the rocks also make it difficult to put down the shafts. The direction of the seams change with rock fractures and faults. Inclination of the bed also has its effects. If the seam is vertically down, the depth of the mine increases soon. If the seam is more or less horizontal the mine would remain at the same depth for a considerable time. Conditions of drainage also have a detrimental effect. Pumping water from the mines is a problem in some of the leading coal producing countries. Fire in mines, due to the volatile matter in cool, and such other accidents put back the country's productive capacity.

The economic geographer must also concern himself with some of the peculiarities of a coal mine. Coal mining establishments have no alternate use. It can only produce coal. An agricultural farm producing cotton or coffee can be put to other uses, if these crops fail. But if the price of coal slumps, the coal miners have no other alternative but to slow down production and work below capacity. This characteristic feature of a coal mine brings about considerable depression amongst the labour force particularly in areas where mining coal is the sole source of income. To maintain a coal mine idle is more costly than to run it at a slow pace. This fact breaks down the law of supply and demand and affects the prices of coal in the market. Coal mines further get exhausted after a time. Techniques in fuel conservation have been introduced which give these coal mines an extended life. But all mines are liable to be worked out some time and they are also subject to the law of diminishing returns.

The seasonal demand for coal, particularly when used in house heating, makes it difficult to adjust mining (supply of coal) to demand. It makes storing necessary to meet the seasonal peak demand, thereby putting up the price of coal. Some coals do not lend themselves to storage, being friable and soft.

Coal production has not kept pace with the energy requirements of the world. There may be particular areas where supply of coal exceeds demand partly due to lack of development, or due to the economic availability of other sources of energy like petroleum, natural gas and electricity, or due to technical developments in the conservation and efficient use of fuel.

The value of coal relates to the needs of a particular region. Usually industries evolve in a region because some raw materials are suited for a particular industry. But if the region's coal is not suited to the industry it has evolved, then it is as good as having no coal. The rapid strides made by the British coal mining industry is due to the fact that the type of coal found was suited to her industries and market. Coal from South Wales is suited for use in steamships. It is easily accessible to the British Channel and to the British Navy and the Merchant fleet. Durham coal is excellent gas coal and it could be readily sold to the Scottish and British gas works as well as to the continent. It also went to Germany via Hamburg, Le Harve, Paris and then up the Rhine to Cologne and Manheim. The New Castle coal is suited for metallurgical coke and being in the vicinity of iron and limestone, soon developed a metallurgical industry. In the case of Britain the distribution of specific types and ranks of coal has been rather favourable. Also coal is found in the vicinity of iron here.

The US on the other hand is less fortunate in the distribution of its different ranks and types of coal, but this is compensated for by its immense deposits. The Pittsburg coal is easy to work, good in quality, large in size and it is coking coal. The average thickness of the coal seems is about 2 metres and they are accessible. But it is situated comparatively at a distance from the markets of Eastern US. Further, iron lies hundreds of miles away although it is connected to the coal by a water route. The efficient transport system and the comparatively cheap waterways make the

Pittsburg coal economically viable.

Such variations in the value and use of coal make statistical assessments of coal distribution irrelevant to the economic geographer. Statistics do not give the details of the quality of coal and local entrepreneurial ability to use it. These have a significant bearing on its utility as an industrial resource, and thereby the distribution pattern of industries.

Characteristic features of Indian coal

Coal is one of the most valuable mineral products of India. Since electrical energy is still not very highly advanced to meet the requirements of industry, and the production of oil is still below needs, the importance of coal as an energy resource is great. In the British days the railways consumed most of India's best coals. But since independence and the advance of metallurgical industries, attempts are being made to conserve the limited quantity of good coking coal. New techniques are also used to convert low grade coal for use in industries. Iron and steel industries now consume a large portion of the coal. The rest is used by mills and factories of every description. Most of the Indian coal is concentrated in the Lower Gondavana series of rocks, that is in Bengal, Bihar, Orissa, eastern Madhya Pradesh and in scattered fields in Maharashtra and Andhra Pradesh. Some Tertiary coals are found in Assam and Kashmir and lignites in North Arcot. The Lower Gondvanas are geologically divided into Panchet, (upper) Damuda (middle) and Talcher (lower) series. Most of the coal is found in the Damuda series.

A large portion of the Gondavana coal is non-coking and unsuited for metallurgical industry. Good coking coal in India is estimated to be 700 to 750 million tons and at the present rate of consumption, may not last for more than fifty years or so. Technical improvements have resulted in fuel efficiency. The well known West German Krupps-Reun process enable the non-coking Korba coal of Madhya Pradesh to be utilised in the Rourkela Steel Plant. A thermo-electric plant in Korba transmits coal in the form of electricity to the Bhilai plant in Madhya Pradesh. Lower grade coals are also being converted into electricity and used in industries to conserve coking coal for metallurgical industries. On the other hand India has enormous reserves of iron which she cannot use without an adequate amount of coking coal.

The coal in India is found mainly preserved by faulting which makes mining difficult. Some are found in overthrust structures which are also difficult to mine. Few are in anticlinal structures, which are easy to mine.

The coal seams in India are thick, in some cases about 30 metres. The average depth of the mines is about 61 metres. Mining has been improved and mechanised to a great extent but seepage of water, roof collapse, collapse of coal pillars and so on are not absent.

The Damuda Series of the Gondvana are divided into the Raniganj (Upper), Barren (Middle) and Barakar Measures (Lower). Coal is found in the Raniganj and Barakar Measures. The Raniganj Coal Measures are non-coking or poorly coking and range from bituminous to sub-bituminous. It burns with a long flame. The Barakar Coal Measures have relatively low moisture content and low volatile content and a high proportion of fixed carbon content (52 per cent to 64 per cent). The Barakar coal is good coking coal but it has a high percentage of ash content (13 per cent to 15 per cent). It is possible to improve this coal by suitable cleansing methods.

TABLE 7.1 : **Qualities of some of the coals of the Raniganj and Barakar measures**

Seam	*Moisture*	*Volatile matter*	*Fixed carbon*	*Ash*	*Fuel ratio*
Raniganj Upper measures					
Dishargarh	1.83	35.95	50.54	11.68	1,41
Sanetona	2.31	34.78	51.07	11.84	1.47
Ghusick	4.10	33.80	53.50	12.70	1.58
Raniganj	5.81	33.14	45.90	15.15	1.39
Jambad	5.19	36.98	45.59	12.24	1.23
Barakar Lower Measures					
Chanch	1.63	28.96	56.02	13.39	1.93
Ramnagar	1.61	27.99	58.15	12.25	2.08
Laikdih	1.58	28.74	60.27	9.41	2.10
Laikdih*	1.40	26.00	62.00	11.40	2.41
Damangarea	1.24	23.00	62.00	15.00	2.70

* Bottom 17 feet of the seam.

Source : Coggin Brown & Dey, *India's Mineral Wealth.*

The Raniganj Coal Measures are absent in most of the Gondwana Coals, as in the case of the coalfields of East and West Bokaro, Giridih, Rajmahal Hills, Rampur and so on. While the coals of both the Raniganj and Barakar Measures are found in the coal fields of Raniganj, Jharia, North and South Karanpura. The two Measures are separated by the Barren Measures which contain no coal but are represented by sandstone and shales and sometimes iron stone.

PETROLEUM AS ENERGY SOURCE

Petroleum has been known for as long as gold and silver. Many petroleum-bearing vessels have been found dating from the time of Abraham. More than 7000 years ago the Egyptians used petroleum in their embalming process. The bricks in the wall around old Babylon was held together with an oil composition. The Phoenicians caulked their boats with an oil preparation. Drilling for oil as a fuel, even as we do today, was known in China in 200 B.C Constantinople was defended from the Crusaders by the Arabs with the help of flame throwers who made use of oil. In the thirteenth century A D. Marco Polo reported that a pool of oil in Armenia was considered good for 'burning and for the cure of distemper in man and cattle'. Three centuries ago there was an extensive oil industry at Baku on the Caspian Sea and it still continues to be one of the major sources of petroleum in the USSR.

However, the phenomenal progress of the petroleum industry has been due to the development of the internal combustion engine and its use in industry, automobiles and air planes, all of which are products of the latter part of the nineteenth century or the twentieth century. In USA where great strides have been made in the petroleum industry, the first oilwell was drilled only in 1859 and 630 gallons of oil per day was produced. It was predicted that if USA continued to take oil at that rate from the ground her petroleum would be exhausted in five years. But today, after more than 100 years of exploitation, she still remains one of the major producers and consumers of oil.

Origin of Petroleum

The origin of petroleum is supposed to be organic. Probably

both animal and vegetable matter have gone into the making of petroleum. It is believed that only rocks of marine origin, sedimentary rocks like sandstone, shales and limestone, contain oil. It is never found in igneous rocks or in metamorphic rocks derived from igneous or sedimentary rocks. It was first deposited in clays and sands along the coasts, or in swamps and lakes and preserved from being oxidised by a covering of other materials. The organic matter was converted into petroleum through heat, pressure and bacterial action. A good oil reservoir rock has much the same characteristics as a good water-bearing rock. Sandstone and shales with sufficient pore space and dolomite and limestone which are fissured enough for the free movement of oil to form into a pool within limited bounds, are the most suitable rocks. New techniques are now available to open up the existing fissures and create new ones by injecting a chemical solution of graded sands in the oilwells. This technique is used in India in the Digboi fields of Assam where the sands have a low permeability. There must also be a cap rock to seal the oil underground without which the oil will escape to the surface and be lost. Lastly a suitable rock structure is necessary to contain the oil. Such geological structures are found in anticlines. During earth movements folding and faulting take place and anticlines and breakes are formed respectively in the rocks. Sometimes breaks in rocks allow the oil to seep through or the oil pools are formed at different depths than found in an anticlinal structure, making drilling difficult or more costly Anticlinal structures are the most suitable for drilling oil. Folding and faulting of the rocks, permit also a natural separation of oil, water and gas. The gas which is light comes to the top and water, which is heavier than oil, accumulates at the bottom. Since drilling for oil is very costly an operator must have some knowledge of the oil-bearing rocks and rock structures. He must be able to detect the places where there is evidence of marine organic deposits in the remote geologic age.

Search for oil

Both geochemical and geophysical methods are used but the former is now almost defunct. In the geochemical method the gases extracted from soils, a few feet below the surface, are analysed for hydrocarbons or samples of the soil are analysed. In geographical prospecting instruments such as the gravimeter, the magnetometer and the seismograph are used. Electrical methods are also being perfected. A good deal of progress has been made in the past quarter of a century and it is now possible to determine the nature of the underground rock layers by observations made on the surface.

The gravimeter measures the gravitational pull of rocks and this is slightly different at different places depending on the density of the layers of rocks underneath.

The magnetometer has a magnetic needle, the dip of which at different places gives an idea of the density of the underground layers of rock. This is also used in aerial survey for oil.

The seismograph is an instrument for detecting earthquakes. When an explosion takes place the earthquake waves travel at different speeds through rocks of different densities. For example, they travel through soft layers of rock at 1220 metres per second whereas in dense rocks the speed may be as much as 7,010 metres per second. Thus by artificial explosions underground, the density of rock layers can be determined by the seismogragh.

After finding out by these methods, the places where the oil-bearing rocks are present, test wells are bored. All wells bored will not yield oil. Even with the modern technological advances, one well out of five, on an average, may yield oil but with luck even the first well dug may strike oil. In 1950, of the 5,290 wells dug in USA, only one in nine was successful, but better knowledge of the geological structures make mining less uncertain. In India even the first oilwell dug has yielded oil in many places. Again oil may be found at a great depth or almost at a few hundred metres from the surface just like coal, making drilling efforts expensive and difficult or cheap and easy respectively. Petroleum exploration therefore is still a gamble in spite of the highly technical skills which have been developed in detecting oil-bearing rocks.

Classification of crude oil

Oil is a mixture of hydrocarbons. The proportion of hydrogen to carbon remains more or less the same being about 85 per cent carbon (in weight) and 15 per cent hydrogen. When recovered from the ground it also contains small quantities of sulphur, nitrogen and oxygen and varying quantities of natural gas, water and dirt. The physical properties of oil also vary from gasoline to pitch or asphalt. The physical properties of oil have an economic bearing because it affects not only its accumulation and migration underground, its detection and recovery from wells, but also gives a rough idea of its chemical composition and probable behaviour. Amongst the physical properties of oil the important are colour, specific gravity, setting point, flash point, vapour pressure, viscosity, wax content and calorific value.

The colour of crude oil may vary from colourless or pale yellow to black. The commoner oils are brownish red. India's heavier oils are almost black. Colour is important in refined products such as kerosene and paraffin wax.

The specific gravity of crude oil is important because it is often used as basis for fixing the prices. The lighter oil contains a a higher percentage of the petrol forming hydrocarbons. The specific gravities of crude oil vary from 0.65 to 1.0. Medium gravities are the commonest.

The setting point of crude oil is derived by cooling it. Some of the constituents begin to solidify and eventually the oil 'sets' or ceases to flow. This gives the temperature of the set point. The pour point is 5°F or 3°C above the set point. Crude oils with a high wax content have high pour points. Waxy oils do not flow easily through pipelines.

The lowest temperature at which vapours are given off by the crude oil or one of its volatile products ignite on application of fiame is termed as the flash point. Flash points are used to measure the inflammability of oil and prevent fires and risks.

The viscosity of crude oil is a matter of great economic importance because it is a measure of its resistance to flow. It has an impact on its transport, the mode of handling and the use of petroleum products. Some crude oils are so viscous that they cannot be pumped or transported without heating. Some oils become viscous under low temperature conditions of cold weather.

Instruments are now available to measure the physical properties of oil such as the chromometers and tintometers for assessing colour; the API (American Petroleum Institute) hydrometer for determining the specific gravity; viscosimeters for measuring viscosity and others for measuring vapour pressure, flash point and so on.

But oil is classified not on the basis of its physical properties, although these are important from the economic point of view. It is based on its chemical composition. The relative quantities and combinations of the natural hydrocarbons vary greatly in the different crudes. Crude oils are thus usually divided into paraffin-based and asphaltic-based. Most of the common varieties are combinations of these. As the name indicates paraffin-based crude oil consists mainly hydrocarbons of the paraffin series. It has good yields of paraffin wax and lubricating oils. The asphaltic-based crude oils have high proportions of naphthenic compounds but contain little or no paraffin wax. Some of these are rich in petrol and kerosene. It is only possible to make broad generalization of the different crudes. Their composition vary greatly from one field to another in a small area and with the changes in depth. But the chemist has to plan his refining methods according to the physical and chemical properties of the crude oil. Even though with technical advancement in oil refining, it is now possible to get almost any product from any crude oil, processing is carried to the best advantages by adopting the best refining methods suited to each class and type of crude oil.

Refining of petroleum

The refineries are usually situated miles away from the oilfields and petroleum is carried through pipelines or oil tankers to these refineries. The refining of petroleum is accomplished by fractional distillation. Fractional distillation means the separation of a liquid mixture into fractions or portions by distilling, and collecting the different fractions as the temperature rises. The vapours from boiling oil are allowed to pass through pipes for cooling and condensing. As the vapour condenses into liquids at different temperatures it is possible to separate the 'fractions' from the crude oil. Although the process is theoretically very simple, it is extremely complicated in practice. The composition of the fractions will depend on the crude oil but new techniques are available to change the composition of the crude. Table 7.2 will give an idea of the fractions that are collected from crude oil at different temperatures.

The constituents of gasoline boil off first, then kerosene. After removing these two, the distillation may be discontinued and the remaining oil used as fuel oil in industrial and domestic heating. But the demand for gas oil and lubricants has increased tremendously in the last few decades, with increasing industrialization and the use of machinery, that more of these are produced leaving less as fuel oil.

TABLE 7.2 : **Petroleum or crude oil**

Fraction 1	Boiling range 35°C to 225°C	yields gasoline (petrol)
Fraction 2	Boiling range 225°C to 300°C	yields kerosene
Fraction 3	Boiling range 300°C to 400°C	yields gas oil.
Fraction 4	Boiling range 400°C to 450°C	yields lubricating oil

The refining of oil has been further revolutionized by the cracking and hydrogenation process so that it calls for a complete reassessment of the oil resources of the world. There was a time when ten barrels of crude oil were needed to produce one barrel of gasoline. The hydrogenation process has reduced the amount of crude oil required to produce the same amount of gasoline. It has also made possible the conversion of the coal reserves of the world to oil reserves because oil can now be produced from coal. The dividing line between coal and petroleum is breaking down and a rational approach to the use of energy is being made by the industrial countries. Hydrogenation, however, is very costly. Conversion of coal into oil may be technically possible but not economically feasible under normal conditions. What nature has done in the case of oil, has to be accomplished by chemists in the case of conversion of coal into oil. On the other hand, the oil reserves of the world are more limited than coal reserves and the demand for the products of oil is increasing rapidly. It has therefore become necessary to overlook the cost of hydrogenation and use the technology available, particularly in the areas where oil is scarce or absent and capital adequate. In areas where oil is plenty, the increasing demand for the products of oil may justify the use of costly technology. Man may even discover a means by which to reduce the cost of hydrogenation. Efficiency and cost of technology are the major considerations for its use.

The uses of petroleum

The main use of petroleum is as a source of heat, light and energy. It is one of the main sources of heat and energy in industry at present. In a short period of a hundred years or so, petroleum has altered not only the life pattern in the countries that produce it, but also that of a large part of the world. In 1920 oil and natural gas supplied hardly 15 per cent of the total energy requirements of the world. Today it provides more than 50 per cent of the total requirements of energy in industry. It has more or less displaced coal in the field of transportation. Engines using coal are fast disappearing and diesel engines are taking their place. Gas is also being used increasingly in industry, in domestic heating and cooking appliances.

Petroleum is used not only as an energy resource but like coal, it forms the basis of a fast developing chemical industry. Using petroleum distillates as the main ingredient, the petro-chemical industry has emerged to supply all the basic chemicals that were once derived from coal, alcohol and vegetable oils. They form the raw material for plastics, synthetic fibres, like polyester and nylon, and a wide range of synthetic organic chemicals such as dye stuffs, pesticides, synthetic detergents and pharmaceuticals.

Natural gas also forms the basis of chemical industries. It is mainly composed of methane, ethane, propane, butane, and other higher hydrocarbons such as pentane and hexane. Besides hydrocarbons,, natural gas may also contain a certain amount of nitrogen, hydrogen, sulphur compounds, carbon dioxide and helium. Natural gas found in association with oil contains higher quantities of hydrocarbons and is poor in methane. This is considered wet gas, while the non-associated gas contains little of pentanes and higher hydrocarbons and it is called dry gas. Natural gas provides the base for the manufacture of ammonia, methanol and their products and carbon black. The dry gases are suitable for manufacturing ammonia which can feed fertilizer industries.

The gas produced at the refineries (cracked gas) is very rich in olefins and are polymerised to get high octane gasoline. They are also useful in the petrochemical industry. The distillation gases are mostly paraffins and are normally used as fuel. The refinery gases are rich in butane and propane and they are extensively used as domestic and industrial fuel.

One of the most popular amongst the petrochemical raw material is liquid naphtha. Its use in the fertilizer industry, organic chemicals and plastics, was appreciated in India only in the mid-sixties. With the growing demand for nitrogeneous fertilizers in the underdeveloped countries, the market for naphtha is widening. Naphtha on reforming, yields hydrogen which is required for the synthesis of ammonia. To produce one tonne of ammonia one tonne of naphtha is required.

Naphtha cracked produces olefins which are the base for the bulk of petrochemicals such as ethylene, propylene, butadiene, and so on. The cracking of naphtha to produce olefins is a major commercial process. Naphtha crackers are generally so designed as to give variables of olefins according to market requirements.

One of the major uses of naphtha is the production of aromatics. By reforming, Naphtha produces benzine, toluene, xylene, and so on. Aromatics are used for the production of synthetic fibres, high quality gasoline. and so on.

Some economic aspects of petroleum

Petroleum is a liquid or gaseous product while coal is a solid bulky product. This fact affects the mode of transport of the two fuels. Petroleum is usually transported by pipelines or in oil tankers. Pipelines can be laid down successfully only in land of moderate relief. The diameter of the pipes will determine the quantity of oil that flows through it, whatever the capacity of the oilfield may be. Once the pipes are laid, it is difficult to change them. The cost of pipeline transportation is lower than that of freight haulage by rail and thus it is a superior form of transportation for liquids. They are bound by law to charge reasonable rates. Ocean going tankers also carry huge quantities of oil. Almost half of the world's tanker tonnage belong to USA. Both pipelines and tankers are used to carry the refined products but a large part of the products use railroads.

Secondly, petroleum is one of those natural products which yield several other related products, both major and minor. The major products are gasoline, kerosene, gas oil and lubricating oil and others; and the minor products are asphalt, paraffin, coke, vaseline and so on. Unlike related products in economics, like beef and hide from cattle, or wool and mutton from lamb, the products of petroleum are not controlled by nature. Hydrogenation and cracking processes have given complete control over the quantity of the related products that are produced from crude oil. Hence petroleum products are not controlled by the same economic laws that operate in naturally produced related products, so far as prices in the markets for different products are concerned.

On the other hand man has less control over the quantity of crude oil produced than in the case of coal. A considerable amount of petroleum is brought to the surface by natural pressure but no coal will leave the earth's interior without man digging it out. Moreover the quantity of oil that flows into the refinery depends on the diameter of the pipelines once they are laid down. Man has therefore less control over the quantity of crude oil that comes into the market. This lack of control is aggravated by the fact that we have only an inadequate knowledge yet, of the location and extent of the oil reserves of the world. This makes it necessary to continue drilling to prevent any check or stoppage of flow from the wells.

The situation is worsened by certain laws governing oil. In countries where oil resources and other mineral resources are nationalized the danger is not great. But where private companies operate as in USA, these laws have a powerful impact on oil production. The usual law regarding mineral resources is that the subsoil resources belong to the owner of the surface land. This is applicable to minerals which are sold, where their underground occurrence can be fairly accurately traced. But it cannot be appllied to liquid mineral resources where different conditions prevail. Oil is a fugitive resource. If at some point of the oil pool, there is a disturbance and greater draw, the oil can flow from one place to another. To cater to this aspect of oil behaviour, the laws governing oil are something like those operating in water resources but these have also proved to be inadequate. According to the laws operating in oil, unless the underground wealth is actually captured, the onwer of the surface land has no claims to it. He cannot prevent his neighbour from draining his subsoil wealth by pumping more oil from his side. He cannot sue him for damages even if he can prove that the oil originally came from his land. Unless an owner possesses the oil, the oil is not his. This has led to a great deal of wasteful exploitation and speculation in the industry where private companies and individuals operate. There is a haste in "capturing" the oil, regardless of the requirements or prices in the market. The mad race between the drilling companies is threatening to deplete the oil wells too soon, and break down the law of supply and demand.

There is also a powerful element of speculation in the oil industry. Everybody is hopeful of getting rich on oil overnight. This element prevents normal economic laws operating in the industry. Capital normally does not flow into an industry when the market for its commodities is flagging. But the oil producer is driven by the fear that if he does not get the oil today his neighbour might get it tomorrow. Flagging markets do not have any effect on the flow of capital into the oil industry. The producer is willing to risk his last penny in the oil business partly to compete with his neighbour and partly in the hope of getting rich on oil. So far as production of crude oil is concerned, this element of speculation and gamble has broken down the law of demand and supply. The supply is out of control. Prices in the market do not have the slightest effect on the producer of crude oil, unless other factors such as political or strategic considerations intervene.

As long as the refiners were engaged only in the processing and marketing of their products, there was no great danger except to the crude oil producers. But the refining companies have now entered the field of crude oil production. Surplus production of the crude prevents the use of technological improvements which have been introduced in refining, leading to wastage.

Overproduction of crude oil also necessitates its storage. Oil is usually stored in tanks along the pipelines and in the refineries. The most economical place to store the oil is the ground itself. But, as mentioned before the laws prevailing in crude oil production do not permit it to remain in the ground. Storage was also resorted to because there was serious doubt as to the adequacy of the oil and large stocks were accumulated in storage tanks. Oil evaporates on storage and the loss on accumulated storage can be considerable. The storage buildings, tanks and the leases are also quite costly and add to the prices of crude oil. A certain amount of storage is necessary to ensure continuity in supply but overproduction of crude oil leads to unnecessary requirement in storage facilities.

Crude oil is comparatively of less value than the products of refining. Crude oil can easily compete with coal in price. It is the refiner who makes the highly valued products of oil which fetch a far higher price than coal. Coal can produce the valuable products which oil produces but economic conditions permit the processing of only limited quantities of it. The bulk of coal is used in the raw. The demand for the products of coal distillation such as tar, gas, sulphate of ammonia and so on is much less than those of petroleum distillation, namely gasoline, lubricating oils and others. It is only under certain peculiar conditions that coal processing to produce distillates like those of petroleum is economic. The oil industry is, therefore, dominated by the refiner. The crude oil producer is in a weak position in the oil industry. Where both mineral exploitation and refining are in the hands of the Government, the inherent weakness of the crude oil producer may not have an impact on the industry. But in countries like USA, where both mineral exploitation and refining are in private hands and the latter was completely independent of the crude oil producers, at least in the early days of the development of the oil industry, the impact of the refiner on the industry was great. It was more so because the crude oil producers were then small capitalists who were attracted to the industry by the easy accessibility of the oilfields of Kansas, Oklahoma, Pennsylvania and Ohio to the population centres of the east, the availability of water transport and so on. No great capital outlay was required to lay down pipelines through the plains in north-east United States, exploit the oil and find a market in the east, unlike in some other oil producing countries of the world where only big companies with large capital could enter the field of production. In the US two important aspects of the marketing of oil products, namely refining and transport, were gradually controlled by one man, Rockefeller, who, with the huge capital at his disposal and the organization he could command, was able to take advantage of the weakness and the unorganized nature of the crude oil producing sector in the nineteenth century. Rockefeller's Standard Oil Company monopolised the transport, refining and marketing of petroleum till it was dissolved by the Supreme Court in 1911. Later when the Refining Companies began to enter the field of crude oil production, the relationship between producers and refiners became competitive. Each company began to strengthen its own weaker sectors to enable it to compete with the others. The US has a commanding position in the world as an oil producer and consumer and the nature, and pattern of her industry has an impact on the oil producing and refining countries of the world.

The main area of the occurrence of petroleum bearing rocks

in India are in Assam in the north-eastern region, in Gujarat, Rajasthan and off Bombay in the western region, in Jammu-Kashmir, Himachal and the Ganga Trough in the northern region and in the Krishna-Godavari Deltaic Belt, the Kaveri basin and the Kerala coast in the southern region. The main producing areas, however, are north-eastern region and the western region at present. Exploration in the north eastern region started towards the end of the nineteenth century. But the western region now has better prospects and an edge in production over the northern eastern region.

The north-eastern region

The oil fields of Assam lie in the alluvial plains of the Brahmaputra in an area of about 180 miles (228 km) long and 4.5 (72km.) to 65 miles (104 km) wide. The origin of oil here is attributed to the submergence of land and marine invasions in geologic times and the trapping of the muddy deposits subsequently, in suitable structures when earth movements took place. Most of the oil is in the Barail, Surma and Tipam series. The Assam fields are much more difficult to work than those of western India. In 1910 the Geological Survey of India reported that "the country is clothed with jungles and the area has no detailed maps for satisfactory prospecting for oil". Today, however, large areas have been suitably surveyed and mapped and still larger areas are photographed. But the structure continues to present problems in drilling.

There are numerous reverse faults, thrusts and overthrusts and loop faults in the Assam region. These thrusts and faults have a bearing on the distribution and accessibility of oil. Oil wells tend to be scattered. The thrusts cause sudden stratigraphic cuts which make exploration difficult and continuity of supply from working wells doubtful. The anticlines although visible at the top have thrust folds at a depth which make them virtually worthless. Even in the Surma valley where thrust folds are not very common exploring for oil is not easy.

The Assam oil field region is also a deeply dissected region of high relief, heary rainfall, impenetrable jungles and roadless tracts which make transport of oil by pipeline or railroad to the more industrially developed parts of India difficult particularly after the emergence of East Pakistan (now Bangladesh). The best-known fields of the north-easterns region are Digboi and Nahorkatiya.

The crude oil of Digboi is classed as between Paraffin based and Asphaltic based. In carries a very high content of paraffin hydrocarbons but its residium contains asphaltenes associated with waxy hydrocarbons. The Digboi oil contains small proportions of petrol. But the composition of crude oil may vary greatly from field to field in quite small areas. It even changes composition with depth.

Oil in the Nahorkatiya is mainly from the Barail sands. The Tipam sandstones here contain gas but is not known to have produced oil in commercial quantities.

Nahorkatiya crude oil is waxy and difficult to be pumped through pipelines. Its paraffin wax content is smaller than in the crude oil of Digboi and it has a higher proportion of cyclic hydrocarbons.

Western Indian region

In western India oil-bearing rocks occur in the Cambay Basin, Cutch and Rajasthan. Offshore drilling in Bombay High in the Arabian Sea is also being done. The most important field in the western region are the Ankleshwar field and the Bombay High. The geological structures in the western region make oil drilling easier than in the north-eastern region. Pipelines can also be laid with greater ease in the plains of Gujarat.

A pipeline diameter of 16 inches takes the Ankleshwar oil to the Gujarat refinery at Koyali and a special gas pipeline takes the gas to the Utran Power Station to generate thermal power. The Ankleshwar gas also feeds the Gujarat Fertiliser Plant and serves the industries in Baroda through feeder pipelines.

Oil was struck at 2,000 metres in the very first well drilled in the Arabian Sea, 176 km. west of Bombay. It produces about 2 million tonnes of crude a year but its capacity is expected to increase to 10 million tonnes a year. It also produces gas. The latest pipeline constructed is the one to pump Bombay High crude and imported oil from Salaya Port to the Mathura Refinery a distance of 1,222 km. A branch of this pipeline will supply the Bombay High and imported crude to the Gujarat Refinery.

The ONGC has carried out surveys in the Gulf of Cambay, Arabian Sea, Gulf of Kutch, the Coromandal coast, sea off the

Krishna-Godavari delta and off the Sundarbans (West Bengal). They have discovered several structures favourable for oil accumulation. In the Bay of Bengal oil was struck at 2000 meters in the very first well dug, in an area 128 km. east of Paradeep. Oil was also struck off the Kaveri mouth in Madras State.

The organization of petroleum exporting countries

The Organization of Petroleum Exporting countries (OPEC) is a formidable thirteen nation oil cartel which has been trying to control both production and prices of oil. Twice in the past the OPEC has raised the prices of crude oil. But recently the combined efforts of conservation and world-wide recession, have reduced the prices, creating a global glut where once there was scarcity.

By July 1980 the supply excess or glut in world crude which was expected for several months had arrived. The glut occurred because the storage capacity of world crude and products approached capacity levels. The supply excess increased from 3 million barrels per day to about 4 to 5 million barrels per day causing a decline in crude oil prices. But the supply excess did not cause the OPEC crude prices to fall. The function of the OPEC has been successful in the past also in maintaining the floor prices of crude in the face of a supply excess of 6 million barrels per day. The OPEC was not able to maintain their official prices in 1980-81. Saudi Arabia and UAE did not raise their prices to the agreed $32 a barrel but it was expected that they would do so gradually. The OPEC is likely to increase their prices. But the OPEC nations are faced with the painful fact that they cannot control both prices and production at high levels.

The total demand for refined products is also declining, for gasoline by 7 per cent in the second quarter of 1980, 10.7 per cent of distillates and 2.3 per cent for residual fuel oil but the demand for jet fuel and kerosene increased by 0.2 per cent.

In 1982 Saudi Arabia, the group's biggest producer (7.5 million barrels per day) enforced a 9.6 per cent production cut to combat with the slack in the market and to prevent oil prices from falling below the cartel's official price $ 34 per barrel. But once they had agreed to the cuts, Iran, Libya, Venezuela and several others began pumping crude at levels above their ceilings and also cut down the prices to their customers. The prices in the unregulated market dropped to $29 per barrel after touching 42 in 1980. Meanwhile, a world-wide glut in oil has developed (4 million barrels per day in excess of demand in 1982). Saudi Arabia is pressurising the OPEC members not to produce above their ceilings and not to reduce prices. She has also threatened to cut prices to such an extent if the situation in the other OPEC continues, so that all other exporters would be driven out of the market. But Saudi Arabia cannot afford to take drastic measures because a sudden wrenching break in prices would be perilous to all oil exporters and importers alike. Billions of dollars have been lent out since the late 1970s for oil exploration and development in the hope that oil prices will continue to rise. If prices were to collapse the banks will have no other alternative but to write off these loans. A gradual decrease in prices to $ 25 or $ 28 per barrel is considered better for balancing world economy.

India being an importer of oil is caught up in the world oil politics and oil prices as dictated by the major producers and the giant oil cartels. (See Table 7.3)

ELECTRICITY AS ENERGY SOURCE

Electricity is another source of energy used at present. It is derived from falling water (Hydroelectricity), coal, oil, gas and low grade fuels (thermal electricity) and nuclear power. Unlike petroleum and coal, electricity is a manufactured fuel. Yet it is not completely divorced from the physical factor. The supply of water for generating hydroelectricity depends on topographical conditions and climate, mainly altitude and precipitation. Thermal electricity depends on the availability of fuel resources.

Hydroelectricity : estimates and actual supply

The theoretical total water power of the streams of the earth has been computed from figures on mean rainfall and mean elevation of land areas. If all the water could be utilized, there will be at the disposal of mankind, about 360 trillion Hp/hr. yearly which is about eight times more than the present energy requirements.

But only a fraction of this water can be used for generating electricity. Much of the precipitation which falls on land goes into the subsoil. Again the altitudes at all places do not permit an adequate enough fall of rivulets and streams to generate electricity. The gradual descent of rivers is not suitable for

TABLE 7.3 : **World production of crude 1978 in thousand (42 gallon) barrels**

Country	*Quantity*	*Percentage of change over 1977*
1	2	3
North America	*4,100,517*	*+8.5*
Canada*	483,260	+0.3
Mexico*	440,555	+23.0
United States*	3,175,927	+5.5
Cuba*	775	0.0
South America	*1,295,097*	*+0.5*
Argentina	165,195	+5.1
Barbodor	272	+119.4
Bolivia	12,045	—5.0
Brazil	58,527	—0.3
Chile	6,570	—18.2
Columbia	47,815	—5.8
Ecuador	73,730	+10.1
Peru	55,845	+67.8
Trinidad	84,680	+0.9
Venezuela	790,418	+3.2
Western Europe	*643,149*	*+31.4*
Austria	12,486	+0.2
Denmark	3,650	+11.1
France	7,300	—3.4
Germany (west)	37,230	—4.6
Italy+	9,902	+25.5
Netherland+	10,950	+16.2
Norway	129,940	+27.5
Spain	6,570	—4.8
United Kingdom	394,930	+45.4
Yugoslavia	30,191	+3.2
Middle East	*7,884,827*	*—3.7*
Bahrain	19,346	—8.9
Iran	1,900,555	—8.6
Iraq	959,585	+5.5
Israel	365	+42.6
Kuwait	680,725	+4.6
Neutral Zone	170,090	+25.0
Oman	115,300	—6.7
Qatar	176,637	+8.8
Saudi Arabia	1,113,470	—5.4

TABLE 7.3 (*contd.*)

1	2	3
Syria	62,050	—2.5
Turkey	18,225	—6.2
United Arab Emirates	668,680	—8.3
Africa	*2,23,791*	*—1.9*
Algeria*	447,125	+9 1
Angola	47,815	—23.4
Cameroon	3,650	—
Congo	14,956	+24.2
Egypt	169,360	+12.2
Gabon	82,125	+1.2
Libya	727,445	—3.4
Morocco	365	+118.6
Nigeria	697,350	—8.9
Tunisia	36,500	+12.2
Zaire	7,300	—11.6
Asian Area	*1,037,520*	*+2.0*
Australia	158,108	+0.6
Brunei	90,600	+18.2
Burma	8,960	—13.8
India	92,812	+22.5
Indonesia	597,505	—2.9
Japan	3,963	—8.6
Malaysia	75,564	+12.8
New Zealand*	4,423	—18.0
Pakistan	3,650	—1.9
Taiwan	1,825	+14.3
Thailand°	110	+6.8
Eastern Europe and China	*4,963,250*	*+3.6*
Albania°	15,000	0.0
Bulgaria°	730	0.0
Czechoslovakia°	730	0.0
Germany (East)°	2,500	0.0
Hungary	15,695	—6.5
Peoples Republic of China	731,825	+12.0
Poland	3,285	0.0
Romania	100.010	—8.4
U.S.S.R.	4,093,475	+2.6
World Total	22,158,251	+1.2

Estimate; * includes condensate.

Source : Energy Information Administration U.S. Energy Department.

generating electricity. The waters can be harnessed only if they form large rivers, their drop is steep and their flow continuous, unchecked by seasonal changes in climate. Alternatively facilities should be available for storing water in reservoirs and regulating the flow. Development is practical only where water can be impounded with a sizeable head. The lowest practical size of head is about 1 metre. However, high head schemes are more economical than low head schemes, as in the latter, the quantity of water handled is small. The average head of all US hydroelectric plants is 24 metres. The highest head water power plant in the US is the 40,000 kw. power plant in California where the water drops over 3/4 of a kilometre.

It does not seem likely therefore that more than 5 per cent of the estimated power of the streams can be used, that is about 18 trillion Hp/hr per year. The best estimates at present stand at about 8.72 trillion hphr. But estimates are unreliable. The estimates for Africa, much of Asia and South America are mere guesses. Many of their streams have scarcely been evaluated. If the figure be correct it is much less than the present total energy requirements of the world.

Generation of electricity

The first principle underlying hydroelectric generation is that water at any level has a potential energy which can be converted into kinetic energy when it falls. Falling through a height of 150 feet, (45.72 meters) a cubic foot (0.0283 cubic metres) of water can generate 10 K.W. of electric energy.

The second principle used is that when a closed coil moves in a magnetic field a current of electricity is generated. The electrical machine designed to do so is called a generator. The generator consists of a Stator (fixed part of an electric machine) and a Rotor (the rotating part of an electric machine). The stator is the source of the magnetic field and the rotor corresponds to the coils. The rotor, mounted on an axle is connected to and rotated by a hydraulic machine called the turbine. The turbine has an axle with vanes fitted around it. Water falling from a height is led to these vanes, its impact moves the vanes and they rotate. The movement rotates the axle, and the rotor which is connected to the turbine also rotates. The rotor rotates in the magnetic field created by the stator and electric current is produced.

Water has been used as a source of energy since early times. The water wheel is a very old feature of the industrial economy of the present advanced nations of the world. But the use of water power along modern lines and the generation of electricity has been developed only during the past 100 years or so. It has paved the way for an industrial revolution and has given countries without coal, like Switzerland, Italy and Scandinavia, a measure of economic power. It has caused a redistribution of industry and population in the world.

The electrical industry is one of the greatest achievements of Applied Science rivalled only perhaps by the chemical industry. The discovery, like many other achievements of mankind, rests on a series of inventions going back to antiquity. Loadstone and magnetic iron were known to early man. The mariner's compass represents man's knowledge of magnetic properties. In 1600 was published a book *The Magnet* by Gilbert. The subjugation of the electric force was at first slow but later developed rapidly when the hydraulic turbine was invented by Fourneyron in 1827 and the steam turbine by Parsons in 1884. But a series of inventions leading to electrolysis in 1831, the storage battery (1859), the first practical arc light installation (1866), the first practical generator (1870), the first incandescent lamp (1879), the first central power station (1882), the first commercial alternative current generator (1886), first electric street railway (1887) and Mazda lamp (1900), all contributed to the final emergence of electricity in its present form for man's use. In the twentieth century were invented the x-ray tube, Marconi wireless, electric cardiograph, grid low tube, photoelectric cell, television and many others which have widened the use of electricity.

Electricity can now be generated on a large scale and generators of more than 200,000 k.w. are built. Electricity can also be transported over great distances without much difficulty, once the transmission lines are laid down. But the voltage at which electricity is transmitted increases with distance, being roughly about 1000 volts for each additional mile (1.6 km). A high tension line costs five to eight times more than a low tension line. Hence it becomes uneconomic to transport electricity over very great distances. The present economic limit of about 300 miles (480 km.) will require 3,00,000 volts. The grid system, if introduced, would solve the problem of long distance transport of electricity.

Advantages of electricity

Electricity is a clean fuel. Where cleanliness is a factor to be considered it has great advantages over coal and oil. Electricity can also be transported easily and economically than coal or oil. These latter fuels have their own limitations in transport. Water power in its old form could be used only at its source but when converted into electricity it can travel over long distances Science is continuing to increase the transportability of electricity. Electricity also possesses great versatility. It can be converted into mechanical energy, chemical energy, light, heat, or take any form desired for a particular use. It possesses great divisibility. Its energy can vary from a few watts to many thousands of watts. Hence it can be controlled accurately. This control is a great asset to industries where precision in the application of heat is required. In the high grade alloy steels of today electric furnaces are used because of their high degree of heat controls available.

Electricity also permits industries to be diffused and spread over large areas, unlike coal. Coal demands a concentration of the heavy industries in the coal area although changes in location are taking place with scientific advancement. Once the heavy industries are located in a particular place there is a tendency for other industries also to move towards it because of the advantage of the linkage of industries. The finished product or the byproduct of one industry may be the raw material for another industry. A large industrial complex and an industrial region which grows round a coal area, becomes an area of population concentration with a high purchasing power. Consumer industries and light industries which usually seek a market cluster around the industrial complex built round coal. The problems of overpopulation, congestion, problems of housing, concentration of economic and consequently political power in a small area are characteristics of industrial regions based on coal resources, because of its limitations in transport. But electricity can disperse industries and relieve congestion because of the ease with which it can travel over distances.

The disadvantages of electricity

One of the great disadvantages of electricity is that it cannot be stored for future use. It must be used immediately. Coal and oil can be stored although they are subject to deterioration in course of time depending on the quality, type and the facilities for storage.

This lack of storability prevents electricity-using manufacturers from spreading their activities over the year and adjusting production to suit seasonal and market fluctuations. This disadvantage becomes even more serious in the context of erratic nature of the demand for electricity. The generation of electricity has therefore to be adjusted to the maximum demand rather than to the changing market requirements. Since it is more economical to generate electricity on a large scale and construct huge power stations, users must be found to consume the maximum capacity.

If the demand for electricity is low, the per unit cost will be high. The availability of electricity at reasonable rates will depend on creating new industries, new uses, electrification of rural areas and the like. The use of the TV, radio, electric appliances, the services of electricity in the medical field, all have widened the use of electricity, reducing its cost. Multipurpose projects are also designed to reduce the per unit cost of electricity.

The overhead cost of electricity is very high but once installed it will produce electricity regardless of market requirements. So, unless there is a maximum utility of the electricity generated the installation of an electric plant is uneconomic. In some of the undeveloped countries the multipurpose projects are a solution to the problem of low consumption of electricity. The water is used for generating electricity, for irrigation, for fish culture, for recreation (boating and so on) and for navigation so that the total expense incurred in installation and the running cost may be shared by all, reducing the cost of each.

Hydro electricity and thermal electricity : A comparison of costs and efficiency

Like all other capitalistic enterprises the cost of generating electricity falls under two heads, namely the installation cost and the running cost. The installation cost of hydroelectricity as compared with thermal electricity is very high. The installation of a hydroelectric plant requires a great deal of investigation, organisation, surveys of land, involvement in legal transactions for requisition of land and so on. Land and water rights have to be established which sometimes may involve agreements with other countries. Usually water power sites are in remote mountain areas where there are scarcely any facilities. Roads and highways have to be built to improve accessibility. The power and plant structure, reservoirs, transmission lines have to be constructed. Finally the whole period of development of the project stretches over the years which makes it expensive.

In the case of thermal electricity the fuel used can be moved to the load centre whereas hydroelectricity has to be generated at the site of a waterfall. As noted, these sites are generally in remote mountain regions which are thinly populated. Hydro-electricity has therefore to travel long distances to the consumption areas A steam power plant which is located at the centre of use does not need long transmission lines. The installation charges of a steam plant and hydroelectric plant may be in the ratio of 1:2 to 1:5.

The running cost of a hydroelectric plant, on the other hand, is less than that of a steam plant. The running costs consist of administration of the plant, operating cost of transmission and and distribution, taxes, depreciation, production and so on. About one and a half pounds of coal is required for an average modern steam plant to generate one kilowatt of electricity. The cost of coal used will vary with the cost of transport to the site and the type of coal and transport used. But once a hydroelectric plant is put down the fuel costs next to nothing.

Steam plants are also handicapped by higher labour costs, nearly four to five times than that in hydroelectricity. Hydroelec-tric plants once installed require only a skelton staff to look after its satisfactory functioning whereas a steam plant requires much more labour.

Hydroelectric plants score over steam plants in that they are almost 90 per cent perfect whereas steam plants have only about 30 per cent efficiency. There is much room for improvement in the steam plant. It is more likely to deteriorate or become obsolete. The cost of replacement, depreciation charges are higher in the case of fuel power plants.

The seasonal and year-to-year irregularities and unreliabilities of stream flow, however, go against hydroelectricity. This difficulty is overcome by storage reservoirs or by auxiliary stand by plants. Stream flow can be regulated by constructing dams and reservoirs. But very often it becomes necessary to assist a hydroelectric plant by a stand-by steam plant. The steam plants are allowed to operate during low water periods. But a steam plant built only to fill the gap in the operation of a hydroelectric plant, is not economic because it does not operate to full capacity at all times. Further, the transpor t of fuel to the site of a hydroelectric plant necessitates long distance haul so that it becomes costly to set up a stand-by steam plant a t the hydroelectric plant site. Such plants pay only when incorporated into a larger power system.

Hydroelectric plants can be put into operation quickly and cheaply to meet the peak load. Thermoelectric plants are not so flexible. It takes about 4 to 5 hours to put it into operation so that it has to be kept ready almost continuously to function as a stand-by plant. The cost of operating a steam plant at half-load is higher than at full load. Hence thermoelectric plants are not suited to fluctuations in load.

Interconnection

Great improvements have also taken place in the technique of transmission of electricity which have made possible the link-up of small isolated power projects into a power system, covering large regions. A power system may even cross international boundaries. Interconnection permits centralised production by tying up small isolated and scattered plants. The main purpose of interconnection however is the disposal of surplus power. This aspect is particularly important in hydroelectric plants which may have surplus power at certain periods of the day and which may go to waste. Interconnection is for mutual aid.

It is also possible that in spite of the technical efficiency of a hydroelectric plant, accidents might occur and machines might break down. Since the installation cost of modern large units is very high, a unit in reserve is costly. On the other hand, if there is no unit in reserve, the failure of a plant can cause considerable derangement of services. Interconnection is of vital importance in such situations to give continuity in service.

But the economy of interconnection depends upon the nature of power plants and their operation. A steam plant takes some time to put into operation. So they must be kept hot to take the maximum load required of the station. The best boilers are not flexible enough to pick up immediately a great deal of increased load without losing pressure. A steam plant needs a constant load for efficient running. A hydroelectric plant on the other hand can be started and shut off without waste of heat units or energy. It is more suited to fluctuating loads than a steam plant.

The steam plant is very often used for the base load while hydroelectric plants are kept for peak loads. Hydroelectric plants also differ in that some have a constant supply of water throughout the year and no storage and others are equipped with storage facilities. The former can produce a definite amount of power night and day throughout the year. Those plants which are situated on fluctuating streams have to be provided with reservoirs which are expensive to build. These can only partially equalize the seasonal variations of rivers. The market cannot adjust to the varying supply of power. A combination of these plants through interconnection can utilize much of the otherwise wasted power.

TABLE 7.4 : **World electricity production**

United States	2,206,073
USSR	1,200,000
Japan	495,180
Western Germany	353,412
Canada	335,712
United Kingdom	287,652
France	222,552
Italy (1977)	320,299
China (Estimate 1975)	121,000
Poland	115,560
Spain	99,264
E. Germany	95,952
India	100,908
Brazil (1977)	99,864
Sweden	90,180
Australia	85,968
South Africa	84,384
Norway	81,108
Czechoslovakia	69,060
Netherlands	61,704
Romania (1977)	59,856
Mexico (1977)	50,052
Yugoslavia	51,348
Belgium	50,844
Switzerland	42,096
Austria	38,064

Source : (Monthly Bulletin (UN) of Statistics, June, 1979).
(in million kilowatt hours production for 1978)

It makes possible the maximum use of capacity. The load factor is very important in electricity because it determines the cost. Unless the load factor is increased the cost per unit will remain high. The most efficient way of increasing the load is interconnection. It increases the number of users and permits adjustment of capacity to market demands.

Electricity can be brought to the industry whereas industry moves to the source of power when fuels like coal are used. The use of electricity as a source of power has the effect of scattering industries. Any surplus power can be used by small industries, railway and so on. With the increasing use of electricity it is possible that the large and congested cities of the world may disappear (See Table 7.4).

8

THE ECONOMICS OF AGRICULTURE

THERE is a vast difference between a subsistence agricultural economy and an industrial civilization. A large part of the world is still at the level of subsistence agriculture. Industries such as handicrafts, and a certain amount of exchange of goods, facilities for transportation and financial services do exist in such an agricultural civilization but these are only of secondary importance. Agriculture is the dominant function. On per capita basis, subsistence agriculture is inefficient because of inadequate control of energy. But when considered on per acre unit it can be highly efficient. Further, there is a tendency in such an agricultural civilization to an unrestrained growth in population causing an increasing pressure on land, inadequate supply of food, malnutrition and a general lack of progress.

In the developed parts of the world, however, agriculture is carried on within the framework of modern industrial civilization. It has adequate control over energy resources (coal, petroleum and electricity). The per capita efficiency of modern agriculture must be assessed in terms of the services available from the power and machine industries. Agriculture is not a dominant activity in the present industrial world but it is of primary importance because it supports life. Industry can help to increase yields from land. Science can push cultivation to the inhospitable 'frontier lands'. But the products of industry and science cannot sustain life. As more and more attention is bestowed on industrial pursuits dependence on an efficient agriculture becomes greater. Without an adequate agricultural structure there cannot be an industrial civilization. The reverse is also true.

Agriculture in a broad sense includes not merely crop cultivation but also animal husbandry, forestry, plantation, horticulture, fur-oyster-and fish farming, trapping and so on.

Many agricultural products are produced under different environs. From the economic point of view rubber produced in Malaya under highly efficient agricultural and marketing system is different from the rubber gathered from the wild forests of Brazil. Timber comes from the virgin forests of Canada or USSR as well as from man-made forests. There are many products which are now scientifically reared and carefully cultivated which can easily compete with wild varieties. The gap between the developed and the underdeveloped world is, in a sense, wider than before but agriculture in the industrial world has almost kept pace with the machine age. It has become a highly organized industry.

THE ECONOMICS OF AGRICULTURE

Nature of supply and demand

On the whole, agriculture is more dependent on the natural environment than industry. Its relationship with the environment is simple and direct. Soil, terrain, climate, topography, location directly affect cultivation. Thus the agriculturist has less control over the quantity and quality of the products of his farm. He has also little control of the time factor in production. Nature determines the growth period of plant and animal. Science may improve the quality and quantity of the farm output and also cut short the growth period with better seeds and breeding, but the peasant is largely at the mercy of nature even in the highly developed countries. Industry on the other hand has greater control over the quantity and quality of its products as well as the time factor in production. In economic terms, the agriculturist is less able to adjust supply to the demand in the market than the industrialist.

The supply position of the agriculturist is worsened by the unreliability of the weather. Pests, diseases and the like also reduce his output. The lack of quality and quantity control in agriculture necessitates the setting up of an elaborate marketing mechinery which requires capital. Agriculture seldom generates enough capital to set up organizations for marketing, processing, transporting, price controlling and so on. It is for this reason that the agriculturists have a tendency to fall into the hands of middlemen who supply the capital necessary for organized marketing of his products. The impoverishment of the agriculturist, whether in the developed or the undeveloped world, as compared with the industrialist, is inherent in agriculture itself.

Again, agriculture is a seasonal activity. The supply of the products of agriculture is only during particular seasons. There is a glut in the market during the 'in seasons' bringing down the prices, and there is a shortage of supply in 'off seasons'. This necessitates storage for even supply. Since agriculture functions on marginal profits, as mentioned before, the middleman capitalist has to supply the necessary storage facilities. The agriculturist again becomes indebted to the middlemen. One of the most important economic activities thus has certain inherent weaknesses, the impact of which is seen to a lesser or greater degree in the different parts of the world depending on man's capacity to offset them with this technology and organization.

Agriculture in the modern world is highly competitive. Excluding the Polar regions (where also technology has made agriculture possible) 40 per cent of the earth is cultivable and the rest can support animal and plant life. Thus agriculture is a worldwide phenomenon while industry is more localized and confined to certain areas. Although the greater portion of the products of agriculture is consumed locally (unlike the products of industry) some of them do enter world markets on a large scale. The impact of competition in such products is far greater than the small proportion of the total agricultural products that enter the world market. It may lead to worldwide depressions or booms. Agriculture in the modern world has thus to be considered against the background of a competitive economy.

Further, agriculture is not able to use power machinery to its full capacity. Many of them are specialized and made for particular operations. They can be used only during certain seasons, for a week or two. The rest of the year they lie idle. Industry on the other hand can use machinery to their full capacity throughout the year and through an eight hour day period (other things being normal). This inability to use power machinery in agriculture full capacity makes investment on them costly. In the US and Canada there are private owners of such machines who lend their services to the agriculturists of the prairies. In the USSR the state farms rent out these machines at a low rate.

Another feature of agriculture is that the period of prosperity is not the period of maximum output. The price of agricultural products is determined by the volume of production, that is supply determines price. A good harvest usually brings down the prices. In industry, on the other hand, prices determine supply. Thus while the agriculturist has to sell the bulk of his products at low prices, the industrialist can sell his at high prices.

Both agriculture and industry are subject to the law of increasing cost and diminishing returns. But industry can benefit greatly by expansion because the per unit cost decreases by increase in production. The manufacturer can thus put out his product in the market at reduced prices. The demand for the products of industry being generally elastic, he can benefit by an increase in sales at reduced prices. On the other hand, the per unit cost of agricultural products increases by increase in production, as generally poorer quality land has to be brought under cultivation. The demand for agricultural products is generally inelastic and an increase in production does not increase sales.

On the demand side also agriculture has certain peculiar features. Agriculture produces food for man, feed for animals and raw material for industry. The demand for food (not under all conditions and for specialized food) is inelastic. A larger supply of food will not induce man to eat more (unless he is on starvation level). The demand for animal feed is also inelastic. The number of animals cannot be increased (except perhaps in the case of pigs) or decreased with the fluctuating output of the farm. The demand pattern of the industrial crops cannot be generalized. When used for necessities such as cotton for clothing their elasticity is inadequate to meet the erratic nature of the farm output. There are thus very few agricultural products for which the demand is elastic. One of the important reasons which reduces the stability and profitability of agriculture is the inelastic nature of the demand for its products. Most agricultural products also have substitutes. The food requirements of man and animal (carbohydrates, proteins, fats, salts and vitamin) can be had from a variety of food-stuffs. This increases the competition in the products of agriculture and leads to fluctuations in demand.

Inspite of all the weaknesses of agriculture it has to keep pace with the increasing population in the world and to meet its basic necessities, and provide comforts and luxuries. The demand for agricultural products has increased with the industrial revolution. Land has to support more numbers as industry does not produce the food necessary for sustenance.

METHODS OF INCREASING PRODUCTION IN AGRICULTURE

Extensive and intensive agriculture

Both extensive and intensive agriculture are the result of agricultural revolutions to meet the requirements of an increasing population and the demands of a growing market. In the early days when man learned to sow the seed and reap a harvest, virgin empty lands were considerable and cultivation could be extended to these lands. But in modern times vacant land which can be profitably cultivated is limited. Most of the empty lands are very remote, cold, or infertile. From the technical point of view some of these can be cultivated but only at a great cost. Man has, therefore, resorted to extensive and intensive agriculture to increase production.

The aim of extensive agriculture is to produce the maximum amount of a commodity with a minimum input of capital and labour. It is usually practiced where manpower is scarce, and capital is meagre. However, there are areas in the world where huge capital is invested in extensive farming. Largescale use of machinery and farm equipment such as the combine harvester has made extensive agriculture expensive from the point of view of total investment. But the farms are very large and the machines are a labour saving device in labour scarce areas. Hence, the cost per unit of land is relatively small. The best lands for extensive farming are open plains with a gentle topography where machines can be used with ease. The great wheat farms of Canada, the prairies of USA, the wheat lands of Australia and the Pampas of Argentina are flat open lands which can use highly specialized farm equipment at every stage of cultivation. Thus crops can be produced cheaply and with very little manpower. In such areas the cost of production may be even less than in areas of intensive agriculture using human labour. Rice grown in USA costs less per bushel than rice grown in China or Japan, even though the wages in America are five times more than that in Japan and China. This is the economics of large-scale mechanized extensive agriculture. Mechanization may, however, lead of careless cultivation, heavy ploughing and consequent depletion of the soil. The return from the farms may rapidly fall off. Conservation of the soil and checking soil erosion are problems of extensive mechanized farming.

Intensive farming aims at getting the maximum return per unit of land area. It is a method of farming where much human labour is expended and much capital invested to a given unit of land to increase its productivity.

With the development of large-scale industries intensive agriculture has to compete with industry for the use of land. Industry being more capable of generating profits, agriculture is often at a disadvantage. But agriculture cannot stray too far way from the densely populated and industrial areas as the market for agricultural products is in these areas. Further agricultural products being perishable and of low value compared to those of industry, must find a market as nearby as possible. Hence the situation calls for the intensive cultivation of the existing agricultural land. But this requires skill and organization.

An increase in agricultural production can be achieved in various ways, by careful tilling of the soil, by scientific rotation of crops, application of fertilizers, cutting down the fallow period, supplying good irrigation, using quality seeds and stocks through scientific breeding, elimination of pests and diseases, introducing new varieties of crops to suit environmental conditions, mechanization and changes in land tenures. Each one of these is the result of economic, social and cultural changes in society and the pressure on land, with the increasing population. The degree to which these methods of increasing production are used by the agriculturists, is different in the different countries and gives rise to the areal variations in crop cultivation and crop association. The agricultural region evolves out of the needs, skills and attitudes of man and the impact of the physical forces in an area.

Scientific rotation of crops

The purpose of rotating crops scientifically is to restore the nitrogen cycle in the soil. The soil gets exhausted with continuous cropping. The nitrogen cycle is disturbed when nitrogen-extracting crops are cultivated continuously. Some sort of a rotation on a small scale was practiced by farmers all over the world with knowledge gained through experience Land was kept fallow to recoup the fertility of the soil. The three-field and two-field systems in Europe and England were means by which 1/3 or half the land in a farm was left fallow while the rest was cultivated. The rest period gave the soil the opportunity to recoup itself. But the need for land lying fallow for maintaining the fertility of the soil reduced the land under cultivation. It became uneconomic as population increased and the market widened. Land lying fallow also created other problems for the farmer. The soil was exposed to the wind and rain, when the protective vegetation cover was removed, resulting in soil drift and erosion. The infertile, rocky, hard underground layers were thus brought to the surface making tilling and cultivation difficult.

Scientific rotation permits the restoration of the nitrogen cycle without having to resort to leaving land fallow. Nitrogen-fixers are leguminous crops and are generally rotated with an exhaustive crop which removes the nitrogen from the soil. Some of these crops are grasses which can be fed to cattle to increase the output of meat and milk from the farms When pressure on land increased, European farmers grew clover as a nitrogen fixer and also used it as cattle feed. Alfalfa is grown in Argentina to improve the quality of the cattle. Canada grows hay in rotation with wheat for better yields The extensive cultivation of leguminous crops as nitrogen-fixers and simultaneously as cattle feed on a large scale came in the eighteenth and nineteenth centuries, following the industrial revolution in England, and some of the European countries.

Scientific rotation leads to a complete change in farming practices and farming seasons. Yields may increase but the need to grow nitrogen-fixers reduces the area under other crops for human cousumption. However, the discovery of nitrogen-fixers, which are also cattle feed, has improved animal husbandry in countries like Argentina, Canada. Australia and Europe. But where animal husbandry is still not an organized industry as in some of the developing and underdeveloped countries, the cultivation of nitrogen-fixing grasses is not popular or even sound economically. Since population is large and land scarce, priority is given to human feed rather than animal feed in these areas. Growing grass to feed the animals to produce meat for human consumption is costlier than growing food crops for direct human consumption. The demand for animal products would have to justify the cost.

Scientific rotation with a view to increasing production should be undertaken only if there isa market for the increased production and a competent organization to transport the products of the farm to the market without exploiting the rural population. A glut in the market can cause great depressions and rural indebtedness.

Fertilization

Deficiencies in the soil can also be made up by either farm manure or chemical fertilizer. Farm manure is the cheapest and the most balanced manure. It contains all the needs of the plant in the required quantity. But it is a low value, bulky commodity which makes its transport difficult. Chemical manures are costly but easy to transport. They are produced in factories where organization is far more efficient than that at the disposal of the rural community which usually produces farm manure.

In the tropical countries, heavy rain causes great erosion. The fertilizer is washed away along with the topsoil, so that frequent use of fertilizers becomes necessary. The areas needing frequent fertilizing prove to be a heavy burden. Chemical manures which are costly cannot be wasted with erosion in areas where the purchasing capacity of farmers is low. In such areas, farm manure, which is cheap and usually a by-product of the farm itself, is used with more facility.

In certain countries the fertilizers are placed at the actual root of the plant to reduce cost. But this can increase the cost of labour and can be practiced only where labour is cheap. In highly mechanized agriculture, the whole field is fertilized. The cost of production is therefore high.

Chemical fertilizers have to be used after a thorough analysis of the soil and climatic conditions, the degree of percolation and evaporation, the financial capacity of the farmer and the return value of the product of the farm in the market.

Another impact of the use of fertilizers is that it may change the farming system. Chemical fertilizers on a large scale can be used profitably only in large-scale farming. It may therefore lead to a shift from subsistence agriculture to large-scale commercial farming or from a single crop economy to mixed farming. It might also require the import of fertilizers. The extra output from the farm must have a market to compensate for the extra expenditure incurred. The control of the production and distribution of fertilizers in foreign hands as in some developing countries can lead to foregign control of agriculture.

Breeding

Breeding is often resorted to increase yields of plants and animals and to avoid hereditary diseases. But plants and animals become suceptible to diseases in a new environment. Hybrid cotton and wheat introduced in Gujarat were found to be sensitive to disease. In Canada rust affected the cotton plant. The yields in hybrid varieties were also found to be gradually decreasing in a new environment till they were on a par with the local varieties. The new varieties usually adjust themselves to the local environment and attain characteristics of the local breed unless careful breeding is repeated. Breeding, therefore, must be undertaken only after studying the local conditions. Hybrid varieties have to be tested locally. Imported varieties evolved under a different environment may not succeed in a new environment.

Irrigation

Irrigation can increase the productive capacity of the soil and it was practiced by the farmers of ancient Egypt, Mesopotamia, India and China. In India where the rainfall is confined to one season irrigation is necessary for the rabi crop. In all lands where the rainfall is seasonal or deficient, irrigation is the solution for successful cultivation. Its greatest use is in the margins of deserts.

Successful irrigation depends on physical conditions, the slope of the land, the supply of water, fertility of the soils, and facilities for constructing canals. But it has great advantages. The farmer can apply water to the land when he likes and in the amounts needed. Cultivation becomes possible all the year round. Irrigation also helps to reduce certain plant diseases. The output from the farms can be increased in a short time with irrigation.

The initial cost of large irrigation projects in modern times is high. Its maintenance, although not very costly normally, can be difficult and expensive under certain conditions. The indiscriminate use of water could cause water logging. Many of the irrigation projects of the Indus plains have raised the water table in the area to such an extent that lands are becoming clogged, marshy and unfit for cultivation. It can also create problems of leaching. Undesirable mineral salts may also accumulate on the surface of the soil in the dry seasons forming saline crusts eventually. Stagnant water in the irrigation channels and reservoirs may also become a breeding ground for insect pests and cause diseases in plants. If leaching, percolation, erosion of soil and stagnation of water are not checked, the yields of irrigated farms may fall.

Irrigation on a large scale may also require cooperation between different states or countries, heavy capital investment, technical skill, and in certain situations import of technical know-how. The return value of the crop from the farms and the capacity of the farmers to organize themselves to use the facilities effectively for higher production, have to be considered before undertaking costly irrigation programmes.

Dry farming

The purpose of dry farming is to preserve the scarce moisture in the soil to permit the cultivation of crops. It is usually practiced where rainfall is scarce and the summer long. The moisture is preserved in the soil by protecting it with a thin mulch made up of manure and vegetable matter. The mulch reduces or prevents the evaporation of the moisture by the heat of the sun. Dry farming, however, needs very clean cultivation. The growth of weeds during the fallow season has to be checked. On the other hand, the exposure of the soil in the fallow season to wind can cause erosion of the top soil. The soil has to be protected during the fallow period. A scientific rotation can dispense with keeping land fallow and can preserve the soil.

Reclamation of land

Reclaiming marsh land or land from the sea requires high expenditure, but it increases the area which can be brought under cultivation. In the Netherlands a mixture of peat in glacial sand produces a good soil in the reclaimed lands but not all reclaimed lands elsewhere fertile. Lands reclaimed from the sea can be salty and dangerous for crop cultivation. Along the Gujarat coasts the problem of excess salts in some of the soils of the reclaimed lands has resulted in high investment costs and low returns. Reclaiming land involves cost and labour which increases the cost of cultivation. The Pripet marshes, the biggest marshy area in the world, is being drained for cultivation by USSR. The efficiency of the state-owned farms makes it possible to cultivate it successfully. With efficiency in organization and a careful assessment of the possibilities of cultivation in the reclaimed land, the investment can be made worthwhile.

Elimination of pests

Pests and diseases bring down the yield of plants and animals. Every farmer tries to eliminate or check them according to his capacity. Pests are distinct from diseases and there is a wide range of both all over the world. The control of some of these need international cooperation such as in the case of the periodical invasion of locusts from the middle east deserts to the rich river valleys in the nighbouring countries. The control of these pests need long term research and detailed knowledge of plant and animal husbandry, avilability of equipment to eliminate them and capital investment. The high cost will put up the price of the products of the farm.

Mechanization of agriculture

Mechanization increases output per man but it also leads to unemployment. In countries where labour is cheap because of the dense population, mechanization might prove to be a waste of investment costs.

Mechanization can be undertaken only if the farm unit is large. Tradition-bound countries like China and India, where the small land-owning peasants have cultivated only an acre or two of land since ages, cannot easily adjust to large-scale mechanized farming.

Mechanization of agriculture cannot be divorced from the organization and development of various engineering and machine tool industries which serve the needs of agriculture. If the country's industrial development and engineering skills are below par, these tools have to be imported, leading to economic dependence on other countries. It involves high cost and the danger of acquiring machines unsuited to the local environmental coditions. Machinery has to be designed to suit particular conditions of soil, climate, tradition and psychology of the people in the different countries. Industry has to move in step with agriculture and the machinery required for mechanization of agriculture must be evolved with a knowledge of local conditions.

Changing the land tenures and systems of farming

Mere changes in land tenure, unless accompanied by a technical and socio-cultural revolution, cannot contribute much to increasing production. Russian collective farms succeeded because of the mechanization of agriculture and its control by the state. In Argentina land tenures under the Spanish *estencias* had an impact on the cultivation of wheat. In West Africa tribal land-holding hampered the plantation agriculture of the Europeans. In the corn belt of USA the traditional practice of cultivating corn as pig feed in small plots prevented the large-scale cultivation of clover as cattle feed when the demand for beef increased.

Systems of farming differ from country to country. They have an impact on the output of the farm. The characteristic features of an agricultural region evolve gradually through a particular system. In general some half dozen systems can be recognized.

(a) Private individually-owned lands are usually small, worked by the farmer and his family or with a few other hired labourers. Each farmer may cultivate the crops of his choice. The profits from such a farm depend on the efficiency of the farmer and the work he puts in. But since he is producing to keep himself and his family alive or in comfort, he takes a real interest in the farm and tries to get the most out of it. An increase in the output of the farm depends on intensive cultivation and the capital at the disposal of the farmer.

(b) A peasant who rents a plot is less concerned with maintaining and improving the field. He may also be renting scattered plots which cannot be worked with efficiency. Farms cultivated under this system, may also produce a variety of crops as in the privately-owned farms but a rented farm (particularly short term tenancy) lacks the coutinuity of experience required for efficiency.

(c) Share-cropping is a system by which the farmer gives a part (sometimes as much as half) of his products to the landowner who furnishes the seed, stock and farm implements (according to the agreement). Share-cropping was very common in Europe and in the corn belt of USA but it is fast disappearing. In India too share-cropping is found amongst some of the Gujarat peasants. The commitment of the owner of the land is, however, different in the different parts. Share-cropping may or may not encourage an increase in the output of the farm depending on the efficiency and ambition of the actual cultivator. On the one hand are the obligations of the cultivator to the landowner which makes the former apathetic, on the other is his desire to increase his share by increasing the output of the farm.

(d) A fourth farming system is the great estate holding. It was very common in the Mediterranean regions formerly. But these feudal relics (Latifundia) have mostly been broken up and purchased by others. In Latin America the impact of the Portuguese and the Spanish culture evolved the great *estencias* of Argentina, the *haciendas* of Chile and *fazendas* of Brazil. This agrarian system for long withstood the penetration of other systems brought by later European colonisers who wanted the lands opened up for the cultivation of crops (such as alfalfa and wheat, in Argentina). The *zamindari* system of India also was often a deterrent of efficient cultivation. Under such a system lands are often held for prestige rather than for using the full capacity of land.

(e) Co-operative farming has spread to many parts of the world. The producers join together in this system to take advantage of the efficient methods of processing and marketing their products. Cooperation extends also to seed procurement, purchase of farm machinery, fertilizers and other commodities and the equipment necessary for running their farms efficiently. The Californian fruit-growers have made a great success of cooperative farming.

(f) The collective farm is a step further from the cooperative farm. The original small holdings are merged into one single unit (*Kolkhozes*) to enable the efficient use of machinery. The state owns the farm but it is managed by the farmers. In addition there are also state farms (*Sovkhozes*) entirely run by the state. A detailed account is given in the following pages, of the success of such a system in Russia and the methods used to increase the output in a collective farm.

Farming systems in the world are closely linked with land tenures and it is an important factor affecting farm efficiency and the type of agricultural regions evolved. Small farms owned by individual peasants can be worked with care and intensity but they rarely evolve as a commercial agricultural region. The large estates owned by landholders and worked by hired labour are sometimes, but not always, inefficient. Large farms can use machinery and increase yields if they are held by forward looking enterprising farmers. The breakup of the old systems alone, however, does not guarantee higher production. It has to be followed by organizing and educating labour and by making the marketing of farm products easy through a network of transport lines and market organizations.

Yields from by-products

Under organized farming, many by-products can be produced on a commercial scale to increase the profits from the farm and reduce the prices of farm products in the market However, it requires new equipment, more capital investments and technical know-how. Unless there is demand for these by-products the investment would be uneconomic.

None of the above methods of increasing production from the farms can be considered in isolation. Application of science to agriculture, mechanisation, irrigation, control of pests, fertilisation, breeding, changes in tenures, all these require a knowledge of not only the physical conditions of the local area but also its socio-economic patterns The state can step in and control agriculture as in Russia.

The collective farms of Russia

Russia succeeded in collectivising her farms mainly because the great majority of the peasants were serfs under the Tsarist regime. Half the cultivated land was held by a few landlords and the peasants eked out a megre living on the other half. These had no agricultural implements or horses for ploughing. They had to be rented or hired from the landlords. The aristocracy also charged heavily for services rendered, such as fertilizers, water, plant breeding and on so. The landlords were only interested in the export market and the land was worked in a primitive way by human labour. There was not much scientific rotation and the yield was also poor compared to European standards. The revolution came as a relief to the majority of the farmers. The state-owned collective farm brought more prosperity to the peasants than they had ever known under the Czarist regime. But what succeeded in Russia may not succeed in countries where private ownership of small or large plots of land or tribal land laws are deeply rooted.

During the first ten years after the revolution in Russia there were very few changes. The New Economic Policy as an experiment failed to achieve the goals of the revolution. In 1927 an effect was made to organize the farms. Machines could not be used, or rotation on a scientific basis planned, in small farms. It was decided that every one should work collectively. Farm programmes were based on scientific principles. At first co-operative farms were set up to market the produce of the farms. Little by little farmers began to see the advantages of working together. The collective farm emerged with the co-operation of the peasants. Its success of collectivisation was mainly due to the direction given by the state and its organizational efficiency. A number of peasants in a village, for example, came together to collectivise their farms. The boundaries of the individual farms were removed and the new boundaries of the collective farm were determined by the law of the state. The state took over the farm and allowed the use of it to the peasants. The cattle, implements, seed supplies and so on belonged to no individual, but to the farm. No peasant was forced to surrender his land to the collective farm. They were also free to withdraw and their land was returned to them. But the advantages of collectivisation was such, that the poor farmers were only too willing to work for a return which they had not known before. It took several years to be accomplished and the state had to face stiff competition from the *kulaks* or rich farmers. By 1940, 96.9 per cent of the farms were collectivised.

The collective farm is state-owned and state-planned. The individual members of a collective farm have their own house and small plot on which he can work in his spare time. The size of the plot a farmer is allotted varies in the different regions. Where land is valuable (such as irrigated land) it is as little as 5/8 of an acre, while in other regions it may be about 2½ acres. In a dairying region, a farmer is allowed about 2 or three milking cows. In the stock rearing regions, he may possess as many as five cows or other animals. A nomadic collective farmer may be allotted as many as 8 to 10 cows, 10 horses and upto 500 sheep (in places such as Kazakhstan See Fig 8.1).

The workers of a collective farm are paid according to the work done and the quality of the work, and not according to the original land surrendered to the collective farm by each peasant. A work-a-day is the unit in which payment is assessed and the number of hours in a work-a-day differs in the different regions and on the type of work. Most of the work is organized in brigades consisting of 30 to 40 workers and each brigade does the

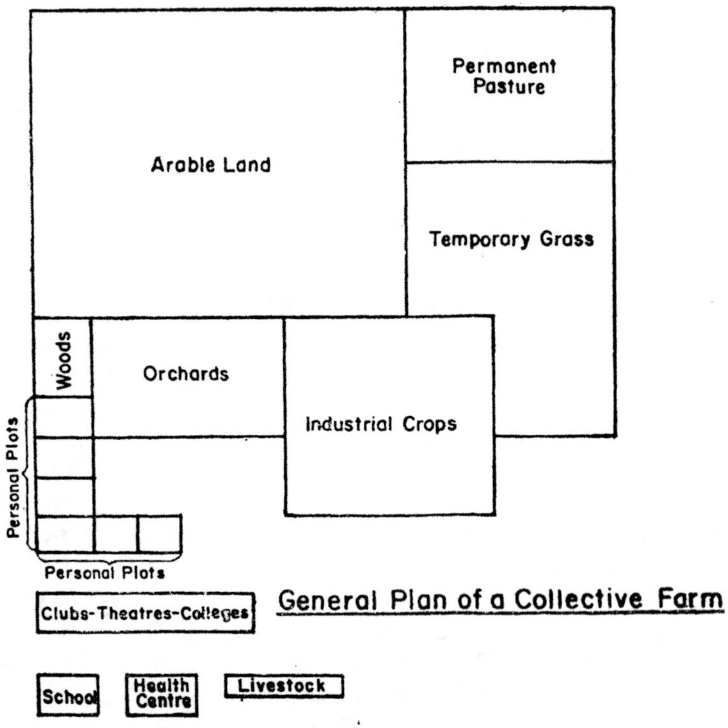

FIG. 8.1

same work in the farm for a whole season. The brigade is also given a definite area of work of a certain number of cattle to look after. The leader of the brigade keeps a record of the individual work done. The brigade is entirely responsible for the equipment given on rent, and the results of the work. Bonuses are given for good work.

The product of the farm is distributed by the state according to its needs and policies. A certain amount is sold to the state at a fixed price. Another portion is given to the machine tractor station for work done in the farm (in the form of rent). A third portion is sold at a slightly higher price, through co-operative markets, to the people in general. A fourth portion is reserved for seeds and emergencies. The remainder is divided amongst the farmers of the collective farm according to the work done.

The portion allotted to the state, the tractor station, the co-operatives, seed supply unit and to the workers, differ in the different years and is decided by the collective farm and the state according to the requirements.

The collective farms are run on democratic lines. The board of management and the auditing committee are both elected bodies. They run the collective farm almost like a factory. The requirements of the farm are placed before the Soviet of the State from where they are sent to the Supreme Soviet. Some decisions are taken at the level of the collective farm, some at state level but issues of national importance, priorities and so on are decided by the Supreme Soviet.

The collective farm is assisted by the state farms. At first, state farms were only large farms for growing grain to demonstrate to the peasant the advantages of large scale mechanised farming. But state farming was extended to stock rearing (cattle, pigs, sheep reindeer and fur breeding animals), cotton growing, orchards (for citrus and other fruits), market gardening, fishing and so on. There are thousands of state farms which do extensive research in evolving farm machines suited to particular soils and climates, in breeding, and in scientific agriculture.

The planned economy of Russia also decided that industry and agriculture must march in step if the revolution was to be made a success. The increased output from the collective farms was possible because of the growth of the engineering, machine tool and tractor industries. Implements and other equipments needed by the farmers were produced by the planned industrial units. Also planned was the development of the fertilizer industry, irrigation, marketing, transport and technical know-how.

The Soviet industry does not supply machines directly to the farms. Agricultural machinery plants are established for supplying the machines required and the machines are rented to the collective farms through particular channels. The agricultural machinery plant at Rostov was producing more farm machines per year just before the Nazi invasion (middle of the third five year plan period) than all the factories together in the Czarist regime. Within ten years of the planned economy, Russia had achieved a production level far superior to that she had known for centuries.

THE USE OF SCIENCE IN AGRICULTURE

The USSR is an outstanding example of the success of the application of science to agriculture.

The main change achieved by the Revolution is a shift from monoculture to a balanced agriculture. This was achieved in the first plan period (1927-32). But even today the tendency is to produce the food necessary for each planned economic region. This is done to save transport costs. The inadequacy of transport particularly in Siberia and the Central Asian Republics, is one of the main problems facing Russia. Each planned region, whether industrial or agricultural, therefore, aims at a certain self-sufficiency in food to avoid long distance haul of bulky products.

The area under crops has been extended. Wheat is now grown further and further north of the traditional wheat growing area of the steppes. It is replacing rye. Clover is rotated with flax in the flax region because the latter is an exhaustive crop. Clover is fed to animals and the flax region is fast becoming an animal-rearing area for meat. The Moscow region is a good market for meat and milk. The upper Volga, Leningrad and Moscow regions are no longer dependent on the steppes for their food. Likewise, western Siberian agriculture is now linked not with Moscow but with the planned industrial regions of Kuznetsk and Karaganda in Siberia and Central Asia.

In the Central Asian Republics cotton is still the main crop but an increasing acreage is used for cattle food. Wheat is also grown in the Caucasian region, southern Ukraine, the Kura Valley and so on.

With the introduction of new seeds Russia has extended her agriculture far beyond the limit of the 60° latitude. Science has helped in evolving frost resistant plants There are collective farms and state farms well within the limits of the Arctic circle. The cold deserts have been conquered by man, atleast in Russia, and potatoes are grown in the Tundra lands. Although the frost-free days are only 90 in these areas there is perpetual light in summer. This partly compensates for the low altitude of the sun. Crops like vegetables can be sown even if the subsoil is frozen.

In the beginning vernalisation was resorted to. The seeds were vernalised before sowing, with a slight increase in temperature and moisture, so that they sprouted earlier. This meant that the seeds which required a minimum of 110 frost-free days could mature in 100 or 90 days. Winter wheat is now grown in areas where only spring wheat was grown earlier. Electric heating of the soil is also practiced in the cold north.

New methods of seeds selection were devised by growing seeds in the nursery. An optimum number of plants are now grown in a given area to give the highest yields.

Irrigation schemes were also undertaken on a very large scale for increasing production. The Ferghana Valley scheme, other schemes in the Central Asian Republics and in Trans-Caucasia and the Great Volga scheme, now irrigate thousands of acres of land. The local collective farms were given the working of digging canals in the Ferghana Valley and a 220 mile (352 km.) canal was completed in 45 days. The valley, which was once partly dry and partly swampy, now cultivates walnuts, pistachio, apples, sugar beet and cotton. In Tadjik thousands of acres are brought under cotton with irrigation. In the Zeravshan valley (near Samarkand in Tadjik) rice is cultivated at 1,220 metres elevation, corn at 1,310 metres, peaches at 1400 metres, grapes at 1,798 metres, millet at 1,950 metres, apricot at 2,103 metres, and barley at 2,438 metres. The altitudinal variation in climate is made use of to cultivate a variety of crops ranging from tropical to temperate. The snow line here is at 3,657 metres, higher than that in the Alps. The foothills of the Pamirs cultivate apricot, almond, walnut, pears, apples, cherries, figs and dates. The slopes are cleared of forest for cultivating vine in certain areas.

In Turkeman also irrigation has done much to extend cultivation. The Amu Darya which flowed westwards across Turkeman into the Caspian sea was diverted to fill seven large depressions in its abandoned channel of the Uzboi and to dig a 480 km. canal with branch canals, to irrigate Turkeman. The waters are also taken to irrigate the oasis of Tashan. Dunes are stabilized for cultivation and the research station at Repetak in the Karakum experiments on growing plants in deserts.

The Great Volga scheme, with dams along Kama and Volga rivers, is developed for irrigation, navigation and electricity. The region between Kuibyshev and Saratov was a dry steppe before, beset with recurring famines. There are two reservoirs, one at Kuibyshev and the other at Saratov, and the scheme irrigates a large area. The Elshan dam on the Samara river and the

Pugachev dam on the Irgis river (tributary of the Volga) have extended the area under irrigation.

The fourth method by which Russia has increased her farm output is by dry farming. In areas where rainfall is scanty, dry farming is practiced.

Draining the peat and bog area is another of Russia's great achievements since the revolution. A great number of watersheds in this area are occupied by glacial lakes. The Pripet Marsh occupying five million acres of land is being drained and brought under cultivation. Flax, hemp and wheat are now grown here. Both Moscow and Leningrad regions have large areas of marsh. The Ob basin is also a marsh land. Along the Azov and the Black sea coast, especially in Georgia, a million acres of land have been drained. Eucalyptus trees are grown in these areas. They absorb a considerable amount of water and are suitable for draining off water from the soil.

Side by side Russia is also experimenting on new plants to suit its climates and soils. Before the revolution few fruit trees were grown except in the favoured areas of the Black Sea coast, Ukraine and Central Asia. Wild varieties of fruit trees growing in Siberia and Canada were crossed with cultivated varieties and the new varieties were created. Fruit growing was pushed further north and now reaches Leningrad and beyond 60° north latitude Vines are grown as far north as Kiev, Kuibyshev and south Urals. Several fruits were evolved by crossing known varieties like plum and apricot. There are many thousands of acres devoted to orchards.

Before the revolution Russia was growing very few plants of economic importance. Wheat, barley, oats, rye and potatoes amongst the food crops and flax and cotton amongst the fibre crops, were the major crops. Industrial planning in the first Plan period opened up the market for raw materials and industrial crops. Rubber, vegetable oils, dyes, cork, vegetable fibres and so on were required. The policy of the USSR is to grow them herself.

Soviet Union has no climate for growing rubber. Plants were tested which yielded rubber-like substances. Three such plants were found in the Tienshan mountains and these were suited not only for the semi-arid deserts but could also be grown in areas as far north as 60° latitude. They were cultivated in several acres of land by 1937, in Kazakhstan in Central Asia, western Siberia, Trans Caucasia and White Russia (Bylo-Russia).

Another plant introduced was the Soyabean in Ukraine and north Caucasus. This is grown for flour and oil.

Drought resisting plants like the millet are grown in the dry areas of Kazakhstan and south Ukraine.

Several new vegetable fibres found in most of the subtropical areas are now cultivated round the Black Sea region, Lower Volga, the Chu basin, Central Asian river basins, Crimea, south Ukraine and the Caucasus. Potatoes are crossed with tomatoes and the plant yields both potatoes and tomatoes. But this may still be in an experimental stage.

Animal husbandry also was improved on scientific lines. Tremendous strides were made in improving the type of stocks which has increased the yield in wool, milk and meat. The native stocks are crossed with imported strains to improve the variety.

Feeding the animals is also undertaken on an organized and scientific basis. Natural pastures were the chief source of fodder in the past. But arable farming and pasture are carried on side by side in White Russia, Ukraine and in the Moscow region. The food of animals in Russia vary from potatoes to sugar beet, pulp and maize. Animal husbandry is fitted into the varying crop rotations of the different agricultural regions. There was always a scarcity of food for animals in winter but this was overcome by producing hay and by storing fodder crops in Silos attached to the collective farms.

The fur bearing animals are now scientifically treated. Certain animals are protected during certain seasons and no senseless plundering of these animals is permitted. Practically every agricultural region has a sanctuary. It is meant for research to acclimatise the animals, for cross breeding and for other experiments.

In USSR is seen the success of applying science to agriculture and of a planned economy. The directing authority is the state but at the lower levels, in the collective farms, the set-up is democratic. Production and distribution are controlled by the state and there is no room for haphazard planning or inefficiency in organization. The discipline, the state has been able to instil into the workers, is because the experiment has largely succeeded in bringing prosperity to the millions of peasants who were struggling to eke out a poor living under the autocratic rule of the Czars and his nobles.

The USSR is an outstanding example of how agricultural production can be increased through technology and careful planning and organization. However, it is not necessary to have a totalitarian form of government to harness science and technology to agriculture. Knowledge is at the disposal of any government or individual determined to bring about the necessary changes. In the US production is at a very high level although land and industry are privately owned. But evils of capitalism are bound to affect the smooth running of a government on democratic basis. On the other hand a government invested with the fullest authority may become corrupt as in some of the Afro-Asian countries.

TYPES OF FARMING IN THE WORLD

Different types of agriculture is practised in the different parts of the world. The organization, the size of farms, the way they are worked, the types of crops grown, the degree of mechanization all vary from place to place and from time to time as technology advances. They have a close bearing on the efficiency of agriculture and the cost of the farm output. Today commercial agriculture has more or less displaced subsistence agriculture in most parts of the world. The economic geographer who seeks the causes of the variations in agricultural patterns must concern himself with the efficiency and cost of the different types of agriculture, their characteristic features and the stage of technical advancement in the different areas. Robinson enumerates ten types of agriculture (including stock-rearing)

Subsistence agriculture

In the tropical regions the general type of agriculture is subsistence agriculture. The peasant is mainly concerned with growing food crops for himself and his family. There is generally no attempt made at producing a surplus for the market. Subsistence agriculture in the tropical regions includes both shifting cultivation as well as sedentary agriculture. In the former the trees are felled, cut and burnt, and the ashes provide the fertilizer. The land is ploughed by simple tools like the hoe and the digging stick. In the hot wet tropical forests, however, the soil gets depleted once the vegetation is removed. The humus which is largely derived from rotten vegetation and animal refuse ceases to form, once the forests are cut down. Rain water flows unchecked by vegetation causing erosion and loss of the valuable top soil exposing stony soils. The heavy rain also causes the removal of the minerals in the soil. The heat of the sun encourages capillary action bringing an undesirable quantity of salts to the top soil. Laterisation also takes place where the base rocks are siliceous. Tropical soils, therefore, become infertile once the forest is removed and the soils exposed to the rain and wind. Then the peasant has to shift to a new place, make a new clearing and start cultivating again. The abandoned land takes more than twenty years to grow forest trees again. Sometimes they revert permanently to bush and scrub. Shifting agriculture is inefficient and in a sense costly because of the wastage, low returns and the lack of permanency.

In some parts of the tropics where land is scarce sedentary agriculture is carried on. In this type, cash crops are also grown along with food crops but normally food crops predominate. Shifting and sedentary agriculture of the subsistence type are, found in Africa, Asia and South America. In the tribal areas of the north-eastern states of India, and in the hilly regions of central India and Gujarat shifting agriculture is still practiced and sedentary subsistence agriculture is found in many states.

Plantation agriculture

This is also a feature of the tropical lands. But it was introduced with foreign capital, foreign organization and foreign technical know-how. When European countries colonised the undeveloped regions they introduced plantation agriculture on a large scale, making use of cheap labour in the undeveloped countries. Plantation agriculture occurs in selected areas where conditions like climate and soil are suited for a particular crop. It is a system favourable to crops which do not give immediate returns. A tropical farmer cannot afford to wait for years for a return from the land. He does not have the capital nor the technical know-how for large-scale plantation agriculture. Plantation agriculture must have a good organization for marketing, for processing the commodity and for maintaining price levels in the markets. It is a characteristic feature of colonial economy where the mother country extended her agriculture to the colonies for commercial purposes

Plantation agriculture (coffee, tea, rubber, cacao) in the tropics is much more efficient and organized than native farming. Some of the native farmers gradually took to plantation agriculture on a small scale eventually but they have not been able to compete with the large-scale holdings of the foreign companies, their organization and their techniques. Plantation agriculture is generally characterized by large holdings. The average holding in the rubber plantations of Malaya varies from very small (under 25 acres) to very large (over 100 acres). It requires heavy investment in the form of processing units, light railways and shipment facilities for the disposal of the product to the port of export and to distant countries. Labour is usually native and thus cheap. During the colonial days labour was often forced and paid very poorly. The weakness of plantation agriculture from the economic point of view, is the concentration on one single crop and the overdependence on outside markets. Plantations usually being developed for large-scale commercial purposes, the price of the commodity is dependent on the total world production and the total demand. The producing countries sometimes enter into agreement to maintain the prices.

Intensive agriculture in the monsoon lands of Asia

This is also a kind of subsistence agriculture but the peasants are much more advanced than the shifting and sedentary agriculturists of the tropics. Rice is the main crop and is cultivated with care and the land is intensively used. The chief features of this type of farming are small holdings, hand tillage by spade and hoe or ploughing with the help of bullocks or buffaloes. The yields are often high. In the dry season when rice cannot be cultivated, the land is put under millet, beans and vegetables. These are raised to increase the total output of land as well as to keep the land clear of weeds. By a skilful rotation of crops, usually gained through experience, the farmers maintain the fertility of the land. Irrigation has been practiced in these areas from time immemorial as rice needs plenty of water. The dry season crops can also be made to yield more with irrigation. To increase production from a given unit of land, intercropping, double cropping and terracing are characteristics of this type of farming. Fertilizers are usually the locally available farm compost and human excreta Land is a scarce commodity in the monsoon lands because the population is very high. Every method known to the native peasant is used to increase the production of crops for human consumption. There is very little land to spare for raising animal feed. Hence stock-rearing is not very common in these regions. Except for poultry and some scavenging animals like pigs, which can feed on refuse, there is no scope for animal husbandry.

Mediterranean agriculture

The Mediterranean climate is hot and dry in summer, cool and moist in winter. When the plants need moist water (summer) there is a dry spell. For this reason cereals are grown during the winter rains. Soils are also thin and stony as most of the lands surrounding the Mediterranean are mountainous. But there are valuable deltaic lands and river valleys which are intensively cultivated and are very fertile. The subsistence crop in these regions is mainly cereal while commercial farming is mainly in fruits (citrus fruits, vines, peaches, figs and market garden fruits).

The major problem in the Mediterranean regions is the shortage of water. Irrigation is necessary here and has been practiced since long.

Animal husbandry in the Mediterranean is confined to sheep and goats because of the shortage of pasture for successful cattle-rearing. Mountain pastures are poor but adequate enough for sheep and goats. Transhumance is a characteristic feature of Mediterranean animal husbandry. Transhumance is the vertical movement of flocks up and down mountains according to season in search of fresh pasture. In a sense it is a kind of nomadism.

Cultivation in the cases of deserts is similar to Mediterranean agriculture. The Mediterranean lands are actually on the edge of the deserts. But while the Mediterranean regions have a comparatively adequate system of transport to reach their commodities to the world markets, the oases in the deserts are still isolated. Further, the Mediterranean culture has long since been commercial in nature and some of the earliest centres of civilization are in these lands The oasis culture is still nomadic.

Large scale mechanized grain farming

The type of farming is different from the intensive grain (rice) cultivation of the monsoon lands. In the lands where labour is scarce, extensive grain farming is the general practice. In the interior plains of USA, Canada, Argentina, Australia and so on, open land is available for profitable cultivation but labour is scarce. Large-scale commercial farming of grain in these regions is made possible with mechanized agriculture. The steel plough, the combine harvester, the barbed wire and underground water opened up the prairies for extensive grain cultivation. The tough prairie soils could not be ploughed with the wooden plough. The crop once cultivated was liable to be damaged by wild animals unless the farms were fenced. Fencing large farms of thousands of acres could be done only by the use of barbed wire. The prairies also lacked water. Being in the interior they have generally unreliable rainfall (particularly on the margins). Water had to be pumped from underground reservoirs to irrigate the crop. The growing season being short, quick-growing varieties of crops had to be discovered by the application of science to agriculture. Soil erosion by wind in the dry season (winters are cold in the prairies and summers short with light rain) had to be checked by technology. It was a combination of science, human persistence and the needs of the market that opened up the prairies of USA and Canada, the Pampas of Argentina and the Murray-Darling basin of Australia for wheat cultivation. Some parts of the prairies also cultivate corn as animal feed.

Monoculture is the rule in these regions and the main crop is wheat. It is cultivated for the world markets. The agriculture is highly mechanized and human labour is scarce. The per hectare yield is low compared to the intensive grain cultivation of the monsoon lands. The man-land ratio is very low. The real difference between the two regions of grain cultivation is that the intensive cultivation area has a high output per hectare and the extensive cultivation area has a high output per capita.

One of the main weaknesses of the extensive grain cropping is its dependence on one crop. If it fails there can be a national and even world-wide depression. The second weakness is that the product of the farm is dependent on world prices of the commodity. The competition between producers is international and not within the purview of the country's government. The producing countries have to enter into international agreements to control production and prices.

Mixed farming

This type of agriculture devotes itself to the cultivation of a variety of crops usually for commercial purposes. Animal husbandry is also practiced. The mixed type of farming enjoys more security than monoculture. The farmer has a varied source of income.

He is self sufficient in food (grain, root crops, fruit, hay, milk, eggs).

The size of the farms is small and usually worked by the family. The farmer has to evolve a well developed system of rotation to enable him to cultivate several crops in one farm. A high degree of capital investment, (in the form of tractors, machines and other farm equipment) and the use of fertilizers, (mainly green manure but also chemical fertilizers) are other features of mixed farming.

Mixed farming is the result of a combination of several geographical phenomena, physical, social, economic and historical. A special climate and soil are required to raise both crops and animals. Secondly, the farmers produce mainly for the market and their commodities being largely perishable, they have to be near the market. They must also have cheap and speedy transport facilities. Thus mixed farming has economic limitations Thirdly, it has cultural limitations. Its demands skill, foresight and adaptability on the part of the farmer to enable him to succeed in cultivating several crops for the market. Mixed farming is largely confined to Western and Central Europe and the north-eastern parts of USA.

Dairy farming

Dairy farming on a large and organized scale has emerged with the demand for milk in the large cities. Dairy farming regions are usually those which are too cold and wet for cereal cultivation but are quite suited for growing grass and for the production of hay such as north-eastern Europe, south-eastern Canada, north-eastern USA and so on. Highly specialized centres of dairy farming are Denmark, Holland, Switzerland, New Zealand, England and Eire.

Natural pasture is normally one of the factors that determine the development of dairy farming. In general, however, all dairying countries grow leguminous forage, root crops and grain. In Denmark where there is a shortage of land, great reliance is placed on feed stuffs such as grain and root crops. Livestock have to be shed fed. In India the main problem of dairy farming is lack of pasture, natural or cultivated.

Commercial dairy farming is dependent on an urban market where population has a high standard of living and high purchasing capacity. Butter, cheese, cream and fresh milk are the products of dairy farming. Of these milk must be produced near to the consuming centres. It cannot travel more than 300 km without spoiling. Butter and cheese can be carried over long distances. Refrigeration has furthered the distance to which dairy products can travel. Dairy regions have a tendency to specialize, for example, New Zealand and Denmark specialize in butter while Netherlands and Switzerland specialize in cheese. The economy of dairy farming is dependent on the competitive prices offered by the countries specializing in the products and the quality of the goods.

A characteristic feature of dairy farming is that it is associated with pig-rearing for skimmed milk is a good pig feed.

Horticulture

This is a highly specialized intensive commercial farming usually carried out on a small scale. The term horticulture originally referred to the cultivation of a garden. In the modern and broad sense it includes market-gardening, hot house and glass house cultivation, flower cultivation, plant nurseries and commercial fruit cultivation. In a general sense it means the cultivation of vegetable, salad, fruit and flowers on small plots. It requires more care and intensiveness than field cultivation.

Like dairy farming the development of horticulture is dependent on an urban market where the high standard of living makes the market effective and reliable. Thus the regions of horticulture are around urban areas. The urban areas of western Europe, north America and other areas of white settlement are the main areas of organized horticulture. But it is also practiced remote from urban areas provided with good, speedy and cheap transport. At present specially equipped trains, refrigeration facilities and air transport have encouraged horticulture in areas away from the towns. Fresh cut flowers are now transported at very high cost from the Riviera to Paris. Rhubarb goes from West Riding to London and from Florida to north-eastern USA in refrigerated trains.

In France, flowers are cultivated for the scent industry and they are comparatively on a large scale. But the plots are small as great care has to be taken in raising the flowers.

The land is intensively cultivated in the areas of horticulture and it is heavily fertilized. High skill is required to make horticulture a success. Special packing techniques (in boxes and containers) are necessary to transport the products to the market. The cost of production is, therefore, very high. But the commodity fetches a high price in the market.

Nomadic herding

The herding of livestock by nomadic people is a very old trade, but it is slowly disappearing. Robinson is of the opinion that livestock ranching found in USA is the present form of nomadic herding.

Nomadic herding is confined to areas which are too cold or too dry for raising crops. It is depended on two factors, the availability of pasture and water. Nomadic herding is subject to disasters because of its dependence on natural environment. The pastures may fail, water holes in the desert may dry up, locust plagues may invade the region and eat up everything green, the moss and lichen may burn up in the heat leaving no pastures for the animals. Animals may also be subject to disease. The herding is done by people who are technically backward and the industry is very disorganized and on a primitive level.

The livestock reared vary from cattle, sheep and camel to reindeer depending on the region. Along with them are also raised work animals like horses and asses.

The nomadic way of life is still followed in Sudan, East Africa, in the arid zone, Mongolia, Lapp and Eskimo regions, the Central Asiatic Republics of the USSR and so on. In the Central Asiatic Republics, however, the planned economy of the state has wrought great changes. The nomads are settled in great big collective farms and induced to give up their nomadic ways for better returns from their livestock.

Nomadic livestock-rearing yields very few products for commercial exchange. It is largely a self-sufficient existence. The farmer himself shears the sheep, makes the carpet or rugs and sells them, or he cures the leather for himself or for a small neighbourhood market. Life is migratory since the farmer has to go in search of pasture and water which may be miles away.

Livestock ranching

Livestock ranching, unlike nomadic herding, is developed on a commercial basis. It produces a variety of commodities. Cattle are reared mainly for beaf, and sheep mainly for wool. It also produces meat, hide and hair. Livestock ranching is geared to the market. They are a characteristic feature of the world's natural grasslands, particularly the drier and less peopled areas where cereal cultivation has not encroached upon natural grass. Ranching has displaced the more nomadic type of herding in the technically developed countries. The difference between the two is not only in their organization and the technical skill used, but in the purpose for which the animals are reared, in the intensity of production and the care taken in breeding high quality animals. The emphasis of the modern rancher is on quality because he has to compete in a world market. The nomad herder's emphasis is on number because his prestige in society depends on the number of animals he owns. He has no thought for the prices he can fetch in the market because production is low and the market limited.

One feature of herding, whether nomadic or commercial, is that the ratio of animals to area is very low. The density of animals per hectare of land is particularly low in Australia and South America. In general the carrying capacity of land in such areas is low due to scanty pasture and poor quality grass.

Agriculture in any area, on the whole, is influenced not only by climate and topography but by the methods of cultivation, the organization of farms, types of farming, technical skills, social customs, market, government policies and international controls. The relative importance of each of these factors vary from place to place and from time to time. An agricultural region is the result of the combined impact of all these influencing factors but it changes its function, form and structure when the factors that produce it, change. A few examples of how an agricultural region evolves during course of time and how various factors influence its growth as a distinct region helps in understanding economic patterns in the world.

9

ORGANIZATION AND STRUCTURE OF MODERN INDUSTRY

NATIONAL income depends on high efficiency in the economic sphere. Industrial efficiency is the means by which the greatest results are obtained with minimum cost. It increases production but the first impact of industrial efficiency is unemployment. A hundred thousand men will be required to produce the same quantity of iron by the old indigenous method which a modern blast furnace can produce with thirty men.

But the purpose of industrial efficiency is not unemployment. As long as unemployment, following industrial efficiency, is not eliminated, the gains of industrial efficiency are worthless. But improvements take time. The savings may be inadequate to provide the capital necessary for new ventures or the entrepreneur may take his time to expand. The absorption of displaced labour into new industries depends on the growth rate of the industries. In state-owned enterprises the growth rate can be adjusted to meet the unemployment situation. But individual firms have to consider not only the gains of growth but also the cost of growth. It is a competitive world in a capitalist society and competition might tend to establish firms other than of optimum size, regardless of unemployment.

Modern industry being on a very large scale is located in factories functioning under factory laws. To understand the present organization of large-scale factory industries one has to have a fair idea of the antecedents of modern capitalism. There is no reason to believe that mankind became suddenly cleverer and more inventive during the industrial revolution in the different countries in the world. Modern capitalism grew from the family and household system under certain special incentives. A clear-cut division of the stages of development is not seen in the actual course of history but Robertson distinguishes four stages for purposes of discussion.

The family and household system

This is a system in which the family produces all its wants. It raises its own food, makes its own clothes, untensils, and so on. There is a vague division of labour between man, woman and child. The various activities are completely integrated. Productive capacity is limited to the requirements of the family. Industries are scattered. A hangover of this system is seen to this day in the underdeveloped and the developing world. But the impact of this system on modern industries in the developed world (particularly in such countries as Japan) is quite evident.

The handicraft stage

The household system evolved into the handicraft system. A man specialized in a craft such as wool, metal or stone work. He no longer supplied his own needs but exchanged his products for those of others. This system recognized the principle of the division of labour and differentiation in labour. The village blacksmith, coppersmith and goldsmith are survivals of this system. Production was still limited to the small size of the market. In the different stages of the handicrafts, industries showed a tendency towards localization at particular places. But they were still scattered over urban and rural areas.

In the handicraft stage Robertson recognizes four sub-stages:

(a) The simple craftsmen like the mason and carpenter, whose market was confined to the village or the immediate neighbourhood.

(b) With the improvement of communications and water transport the market widened and production increased. The craftsmen began to concentrate in towns where the purchasing capacity was high or the nobility patronized the crafts. A broad distinction between the manufacturer and the agriculturist came into existence particularly in the west. The industries become more localized. Production was on larger scale than before. But where communications remained inadequate the progress from one stage to the other was slow.

(c) In the third stage the craftsmen became more specialized. They were no longer metal workers and stone workers but makers of special commodities from metal and stone. In the textile industry the dyers, printers, weavers and spinners became distinct. They were specialized in a particular stage of the industry which prepared the final product. Separation of such functions was not universal but developed under particular environmental conditions and incentives. Specialization led to some increase in production and exchange but the market was still restricted due to poor transport. As specialization became more effective the localization of industries in favoured spots became increasingly necessary. Villages and towns came to be known for special products.

(d) In the fourth sub-stage of the handicraft system there was a return of the industry from the urban areas to the rural areas. But this was again not a universal feature. With the migration of the crafts to the rural areas they became diffused and more decentralized. The craftsmen in the rural environment turned farmer in his spare time. There was thus a re-integration of craft with agriculture. In some of the Afro-Asian countries this integration of craft with agriculture continues to the present day.

The merchanting system

Robertson calls the third major stage in the development of manufacture, the merchanting system. At this stage the individual craftsman came to be controlled by the merchant class. As the craftsmen ceased to be concentrated in particular places, the industries once again became scattered. The merchant community took up the responsibility of delivering the goods to the consumer. It is not known when the merchant gained control of the distribution of goods and the supply of raw materials. Some sort of a control of the kind existed in the handicraft system also but it became more pronounced when manufacture became decentralized. The consumer had no access to the manufacturer and the producer had to get all his raw materials. The merchant became the middleman for both. It was in the merchant stage of the crafts that the division between the producer and those who controlled production and distribution, became important. The craftsmen now worked to order. It was the merchant who decided what quantity he should produce, what designs and patterns he should follow and where he should sell his goods. The craftsman (producer) lost his direct contact with the consumer. He was, for all practical purposes, a wage earner of the merchant who controlled production and distribution. This type of organization continued well into the nineteenth century. The merchants of the various East India Companies thrived on this system. From the control of production by the merchant to the control of industry by the capitalist was a short step and it came with the factory system

The factory system

The industrial revolution was the result of a long and complicated series of inventions. The revolution is still spreading to the different parts of the world. The stage at which industrial development has reached differs from country to country and an assessment of it is necessary to understand the structure, location and distribution of industry which is the concern of the economic geographer. From the technical point of view the leading feature of the factory system is that the simple hand-driven tool of the craftsmen was substituted by complicated and expensive machines driven by steam or other mechanical power. This change in manufacture required the concentration of labour in a centralized establishment which was called the factory. During the days of the East India Company the trade depots of the foreign companies were also known as factories. From the factory of the trading merchant were practically born the factories of the capitalist.

The machines driven by steam were expensive and required maintenance. Huge capital had to be expended to set up a factory with the necessary equipment. The ordinary craftsman—producer who had no capital was forced to be a wage earner in the factory. Thus the factory system also induced the control of production by the capitalist and the concentration of industry in particular places.

The machine age also brought with it other characteristic features of modern industry, the regimentation and discipline of a large body of workers and standardization of products. The organization of such a large body of people under routine disciplined conditions required good management. Managerial skill was required to run factories efficiently, raise capital, control production, maintain prices, and so on. The directors of the industry, and the quality of organization became crucial factors in industrial development.

Modern industry is on a very large scale where investment costs are high. Machines left idle can bring about great losses to the management. A continuity of production has to be ensured if the factory is to be a success. This means that there must be a continuous supply of large amounts of raw material and a stable market for the products. Factory industry therefore cannot be isolated from other facilities such as an efficient transport system, organized market centres, development of primary activities, availability of capital, supply of power, development of technical skills, a responsible attitude towards disciplined work, government policies and international controls.

Modern industry is not easy to define with accuracy. It consists of many firms, each often producing several commodities inside a single plant. Iron and steel industry is not one single industry but several industries producing several commodities. Each one tries to make goods slightly different from the other and create a special market for his goods. By creating a separate market he can command higher prices than the market price for his goods. Most industrialists seek exclusive markets so that the factory system has also ushered in a particular pattern of marketing, other things remaining the same. However, the price fixing policy of one producer depends on that of the other producers of the commodity. The complicated production and marketing requrire keen business acumen to run the industry.

But changes in the techniques according to Robertson did not always go with good and competent organization of industry. There were factories, he says, even before the machines and there are also machines which can be worked by isolated producers. It is not easy to say where the factory begins and ends. He adds it is not the machinery, the use of mechanical power or the factory building that really distinguishes a factory, but the sharp cleavage between the one who commands, that is the capitalist, and the one who obeys, namely the worker. In modern industry it is the capitalist who is the organizer, the manager, the planner and the controller. It is the complete cleavage between the capitalist and the worker that brought in the evils of capitalism forcing the world to turn to socialism, communism and state control of industries. Industry today functions under both the capitalist system and under state control. The structure of industry differs under the two systems and the economic geographer must be acquainted with these, to understand the characteristic features and the location of industries in the different countries.

The factory system came into force not by accident but

because certain factors favoured it. The industrial revolution which was ushered into England in the eighteenth century gave rise to the factory system. But the revolution came to England because of the long period of prosperity it enjoyed following overseas colonization by merchant companies. The rich merchants accumulated capital and became merchant capitalists. The acquisition of territory in the east opened out a wide market for its machine-made goods. There was enough wealth and inducement to experiment with new techniques and new organizations. A revolution in road and canal followed and then came the railroad and the steamships Efficiency in land and water transport widened the markets still further while the establishment of the Empire and colonies gave England a monopoly control of world trade. Finally, the increase in population in England itself was a challenge to increase production and invest capital in enterprises in the Empire and colonies as well as in other parts of the world. The factory system therefore is not the by-product of the steam engine but the natural outcome of a combination of phenomena which operated at a given time in a given place. But it had a deep impact on the location and structure of industry. The technical skills which the revolution brought are still unevenly distributed over the surface of the earth which in turn explains the character and location of manufacturing in the different parts of the world. The economic geographer has to consider all these factors when analysing the location of a particular industry in any region.

LOCALIZATION OF INDUSTRY

With the emergence of the factory system, there rose the need to localize industry at particular places. It was uneconomic to scatter expansive power using machinery at all places. Modern industry needs access to large quantities of raw material, access to power resources and access to markets. These factors more or less control the location of industries except under conditions of state ownership of economic enterprises, when political and other factors may assume greater force. But even state planned industries have to be located in places where there are some facilities for procuring power and raw material and a market for the commodities produced. Besides factors like the long traditions of a people, the social and cultural factors, government policies also affect the structure and location of industries.

Access to raw material

Access to raw material or nearness to raw material is an asset particularly when they are bulky and of low value, to stand the cost of long distance transport. But with the development of quick and cheap transport, proximity to the source of raw material is becoming less important to the location of industries. In certain countries concessions are available to transport certain commodities like coal as a measure for developing industries. Where transport is controlled by the state, costs can be reduced to the minimum for the welfare of the state. In a competitive world transport costs of the raw material is a crucial factor in the location of industries. But even here more and more raw material is being transported over long distance to take advantage of the market. Iron and steel industries which were once considered to be economic only when located near the raw material are now seeking the market area or even an intermediate location between the market and raw material. The deciding factor in such locations is the transport cost of the raw material against the transport cost of the finished product to the market. It was felt that if the finished product can be transported the raw material can also be transported It is this consideration that led to the location of the cotton textile industry in Lancashire. The cotton was imported from America (in the early days and later from India and Egypt) and spun in Lancashire for the Indian market. It was an unstable location and was made possible only because Britain controlled the economic policies of India. Accessibility to raw material is an asset for the development of an industry in a particular environment but not all industries, not even heavy industries at present, need be tied to raw material.

Access to power

This is one of the most important causes for the localization of industry since the industrial revolution. Coal is still the chief source of power for heavy industries because it is the cheapest. But its bulk and low value does not bear the cost of transport. So it lacks mobility. Hence it became the practice to locate industries in the coal area and transport other raw materials to the coal area. The great manufacturing industries of the nineteenth century in Britain, Germany and USA were all in the coal area. Even the industrial regions of USSR are planned with coal as the nucleus. This aspect of the industry needs no elaboration. But new sources of energy have been discovered by man since the advent of coal. Petroleum and electricity have reduced the dominance of coal for the localization of industries. Petroleum can be transported easily by pipelines and tankers and it has more mobility than coal. In fact industries are seldom located in the petroleum area because of the danger of fires and the need to maintain the petroleum wells free of any obstructions like buildings and factories. Electricity has actually decentralized industries because of its great mobility. The attraction of electrical power for the location of industries is at present not as great as when coal was the sole fuel. Though with new techniques and skills in the conservation of power and new methods of transport, coal has become less essential.

Access to market

A steady market is necessary for large scale production. Expansion is dependent mainly on demand. Concentration of industries in the market area usually occurs when the transport of the finished product is costlier than the assembly of the raw material. Light industries using electricity as power, consumer industries, service industries and so on are better located in the market area.

LOCALIZATION OF INDUSTRIES DUE TO FACTORS SUCH AS HISTORY

Some factors influence localization of industry because they attract other service facilities. Once an industry is established in a particular place because of certain facilities accorded to it in a previous period, it would prefer to continue in the same place because the cost of shifting is very high. Its location over years in a particular place also generates other advantages such as availability of skilled labour, interlinkage of industries, availability of capital, market and such necessary infrastructure. But inadequacy of transport; machinery, labour arising from redundancy and of obsoleteness are undermining these locations making them unstable. There are many examples of such locations all over the industrial world (see Chapter 2).

Integration of industries

There are successive stages of production in modern industry. Sometimes, these are performed in independent plants. But more often it is under single control. When the different stages of production are under a single managerial control the industry is said to be integrated. This tendency for integration varies with the different industries. The iron and steel industry shows a tendency towards integration, from the stage of the extraction of coal and iron to the final stage. This is because the product of one stage is somewhat dependent on the other for the raw material. Secondly, energy can be conserved by concentrating the different stages under one roof. Thirdly, the many by-products of coal can be utilized profitably by integration. Coal and coal tar produce goods which can be used for medicines, dyestuffs, textiles, explosives and so on. Fourthly, iron and steel industry has the flexibility to switch over from one product to another. During World War II Germany's steel industry could switch over to explosives and armaments at short notice. When the successive stages of an industry are under one control it leads to vertical integration, while the production of commodities apparently dissimilar (like the products of coal tar) are under one control it leads to lateral integration. Iron and steel industry shows a tendency to both. Steel magnates even enter the building industry to induce export and import or the hotel industry to maintain contacts.

In the cotton industry on the other hand the tendency towards integration is less. Spinning and weaving can be carried on separately although it is not a universal characteristic. This is because of the uniformity and standardization of the cotton yarn available in the market. The weaver can get his exact requirements in the open market. There is no need for spinning and weaving to be under one control. But spinners will locate themselves near the weaver because of the ready market. The woollen industry on the other hand prefers spinning and weaving to be integrated because standardization of the yarn is not as perfect as in cotton. As techniques improve the woollen industry will show tendencies to vertical integration. A second reason for lack of integration in the textile industry as a whole, is because not all the products of the different stages are interdependent. While the weaver is dependent on the spinner, the spinner does not need cloth for his industry.

The distinctions in the structure of the industries explain their location and the reason for the iron and steel industry becoming the nucleus of an industrial complex at the heart of which is coal and iron, while cotton industries are widespread.

In the case of industries using animal products, where the raw material is widely diffused the motive for integration is the desire of the manfacturer to be independent of the raw material producer. It was the desire of the meat packers of Chicago to control the raw material that led them to invest in the ranches of Argentina and New Zealand.

Large-scale industries today have the trend of integrating subsidiary processes into the main industry. This is advantageous, because it reduces cost of production in the long run and increases its capacity to compete in the market. If the main industry is highly localized, other firms specializing in subsidiary products and processes will soon get established in the neighbourhood thus inducing the growth of an industrial region.

Combinations

Another feature of modern industry is the combination. Firms combine to take advantage of the economies of large-scale production. Small units are uneconomic in the context of the large-scale production of modern times. Combinations increase the tendency to concentrate power in the hands of a few. A combine can influence prices and production which a small producer seldom can

THE JOINT STOCK COMPANY

In modern times industrial enterprises are so large that they require a great deal of capital. Individual owners and partners of the old order can hardly acquire the capital necessary for the giant companies of modern times. The joint stock company enables the industrialists to gain command over financial resources far beyond their capacity to supply. A licence is obtained by a few people, from the government, to start a company which entitles them to invite the public to provide the capital necessary for the enterprise. Those who invest in the company or buy shares become shareholders. They are part-owners of the company and the properties acquired by the company. But the individual shareholder's liability is very little. He may lose the money he has invested in the company but not the whole of his fortune. He can also sell his shares to any one at any time. Although he has voting rights he can seldom influence the company's policies because few individual shareholders have controlling shares.

The company can also command the savings of the public through bonds and debentures. These holders of debentures and bonds are not part-owners of the company as the shareholders. They are entitled to the punctual payment of interest and repayment of their capital at a definite date. Being only a 'creditor' of the company who has lent capital for a short period he has no share in the management or the policy of the company.

The economic features of the joint stock company

In a joint stock company is seen the complete separation between those who operate the industry and those who provide the capital. The board of directors direct the policy of the company but they seldom expend much time or attention to the working of the company. The managing director (president or chairman) devotes most, or the whole, of his time to the company. He is a salaried officer working under the board of directors (who are also entitled to a remuneration). Under the managing director are many salaried officers. The board of directors control the policies of the company. The concentration of power in the hands of the board is helped by the tendency of the individual shareholders and bond-debenture holders to invest in many companies to avoid risks. This cuts down his influence to direct the affairs of any company. Secondly, a certain amount of secrecy is maintained and the individual shareholders are seldom acquainted with the operation of the company. Thirdly, the directors being responsible for policies, they must also have a say in how the profits are to be distributed.

The merits of the joint stock company

The company more or less acts as a bank by inviting the small savings of the public. These savings which otherwise would not have found their way into large-scale industries are concentrated in the hands of the entrepreneurs who can utilize them and take advantage of the economics of large-scale production.

There is a continuity in a joint stock company which the private individually-owned companies do not possess. In the latter legal complications arise with the death or the retirement of the owners or partners.

A joint stock company can also utilize the talents of the individuals by taking them up as salaried officers. With the financial resources at its disposal it can pool the human resources of a country and concentrate them for the development of an industry.

The defects of the joint stock company

When the company becomes old and established it tends to become rigid and less adaptable than the private company. It has all the defects of a large-scale organization. The success of the system depends on business integrity. Where this integrity does not exist it can be a complete failure.

The fact that the company's directors are trustees for others is a disadvantage. A trustee may be too timid to embark on ambitious policies and take the risk of implementing new ideas and new techniques. The capital invested is usually far beyond the capacity of the directors to make good. On the other hand there is also the danger of the company becoming too ambitious embarking on a policy of disastrous expansion.

It is the control of finance in the hands of a few that characterizes the joint stock company. The directors themselves are substantial shareholders. They have also control of the shares of the public. As it advances in age the company becomes autocratic The dictum 'where risk lies, control also lies' begins to operate. It is then that the evils of capitalism express themselves. In the joint stock company and the multinational combines are seen the social evils of capitalism at its worst. The gap between the rich and the poor, the developed and the underdeveloped world, the 'haves' and the 'have-nots' becomes wider. Industries tend to concentrate in certain regions of the world and agriculture in others. It is the control of industries and other economic enterprises in the hands of a few that ushered in the socialist and communist revolution and the state control of production and distribution (discussed in Chapter 12).

Investments of the capitalist countries in the developing and underdeveloped countries for the production of food for their growing industrial population and for raw material for their industries become a necessity and it was often achieved through economic exploitation and military might.

Stock exchanges

These have also come to stay with the emergence of the joint stock company. The saver of small capital can now acquire the rights of ownership in an expensive and big industry because of the emergence of organized markets where the securities can be bought and sold.

Such concentration of finances by a few capitalists, and the organization of industry under the modern capitalist system are of importance to the economic geographer, to understand the structure, pattern and location of industrial activity.

10

SOCIAL AND CULTURAL FACTORS

IN THE introduction to the *Social History of England* Trevelyan says 'Without Social History, Economic History is barren and Political History, unintelligible'. A geographer could adapt this statement to 'without Social (and Cultural) Geography, Economic Geography is barren' (and political geography unintelligible). The attitude of a people to economic progress depends very much on their traditions. their social and cultural setting, their level of education, their beliefs and their religion and a host of other factors which condition a community's approach to life in general. These differ from people to people and from country to country. Social and culture geography have drawn the attention of geographers only in the past few decades but their impact on regional variations in economic development has been so deep in certain countries that economic geographers have also had to take cognizance of these factors to understand the nature of economic development in the different parts of the world.

SOCIAL FACTORS

Social conditions impinge on economics directly in two ways (i) the impact on labour and attitude to work, (ii) the attitude towards land.

The attitude to work and impact on labour

The attitude to work differs from people to people and from community to community. In the western world material development is the one single goal that drives people to work. Materialism is a great asset to economic growth. As an example of the impact of this materialism or progress, can be cited the growth of Dallas in Texas. Dallis is situated in a monotonous, barren plain and has no particular physical facilities superior to that of any other town in north central Texas. But the Dallas people took up the challenge of the inhospitable land and worked to make it as accessible as possible. In the early days of its existence there were other route centres in the area which could have easily competed with Dallas. The ferry service on the river, provided by its founder, was not at a particularly advantageous place. During the period of the stage coaches, the Dallas people set up a staging post in their town to improve its accessibility. Then came the railways. The railway company, having run out of a capital, was forced to terminate the line at Dallas. For a few invaluable years of its life Dallas enjoyed the status of a railway terminus. It was the outermost limit of the railway line which connected the vital markets of the east with Texas. The drive, skill and the energy of its people took full advantage of the situation and made it into a thriving commercial and business centre. Today its merchants are determined that their city should dominate wholesale trade. They have constructed waterways and roads to improve its nodality.

Its businessmen are equally aggressive and are fully conscious that any cessation in the expansion of Dallas would be catastrophic. Although the oilfields of Texas are at some distance, Dallas is the oil capital of the country. It is the Dallasites who provide the essential services to the oil industry.

Side-by-side with its new traders and industrialists are those who live in feudal glory, having made their fortune in oil. Steeped in Spanish culture they enjoy life to the hilt and take pride in their eccentric tastes.

There are also the Negroes in Dallas whose attitude to work is that of the economically deprived. Thus three distinct approaches to life and work, of three separate groups of people, have made Dallas what it is today.

The same drive of industrialists and traders of Dallas is seen amongst the fruit growers' cooperatives of California, in the oil and automobile industry, in the transport industry and in the trade of USA. The American approach to work is one of survival at any cost, to 'keep moving to avoid decay'. Cut-throat competition is the driving force behind successful business.

In England too, idleness was considered evil in Victorian times. With the prosperity ushered in by the Empire and the Colonies, the idea that leisure is an absolute necessity for efficiency in work gradually replaced Victorian ideals. Today an England faced with economic recession, mounting unemployment and competition from other countries, is reverting to the traditions of the East India Company's aggressive economic policies. But her techniques of achieving the goal is different from that of America. An English man believes fully in his capacity to achieve his goal and in his country's future. He has the persistence, the power of persuasion, the skill to negotiate and make his opponent believe in what he himself believes in. Material progress in England has always depended on the philosophy 'never say die'.

The efficiency of Japanese labour has helped the country to become one of the leading industrial nations today. The Japanese are considered to be the world's most dedicated workers. Their discipline has been achieved through cooperation, the traditional attitude of the people towards their elders, their neighbours and to society as a whole, largely a remnant of the old order. The stress is on group action, cooperation and consensus of opinion and not on the individual. While most of the workers of the world are conscious of their rights the Japanese worker is conscious of his obligations. He believes that he is his own quality inspector, responsible for maintaining the quality of the products of his company, and building up cultures to induce dedication and self-respect.

Independent India also began its life with such slogans as 'idleness is evil' but these have not been able to rout the age-old unmaterialistic outlook on life and the belief in *karma* and *dharma*. From the vedic period great insistence was paid to 'moral purity and self restraint', and in the unquestioned acceptance of life's vicissitudes. Such beliefs and acceptance, have drained the average man of any initiative and independent thinking, the ambition to create a goal and fight for it, and of the desire for material progress. The thoroughly ritualized life has resulted in a contempt for things worldly. The restraints and disciplines preached by the Vedas have paradoxically created a lethargy, indifference and irresponsibility to work.

Apart from the spiritual approach to life, the division of society into caste groups in India has deeply affected the attitude towards work. Each caste was allocated certain functions and their trade from father to son. The centuries-old traditions produced a society with rigid caste-function segregation which had a deep impact on the economy of the country. While the system preserved certain crafts, despite the foreign onslaughts on them, it is creating problems for modern industrial organizations. The trade each caste learned was limited. It did not produce the educational base necessary for large-scale production and factory industries. Independent India's efforts to abolish caste have only partially succeeded. Economic progress without corresponding social and educational advance can create dangerous tensions in such a society.

Besides India has also a vast tribal population. They are skilled in many trades but have so far produced only for the household or for a limited local market. The integration of a tribal economy with a national economy is a complex process which can be achieved only through education and social advance. There are no major industries in these tribal areas. One of the main difficulties in their industrialization is the apathy of the people to take to factory industry. Much of the borderlands of India are occupied by tribal people who have no awareness of a national economy.

In the Middle East also clan loyalties are very strong. The Bedouins are traditionally wandering nomads used to a tent life. The discipline and organization demanded by an industrial economy sit lightly on the nomad. A similar social structure is found in the Central Asiatic Republics of the USSR and amongst the Eskimos in the northern parts of the Russian Federal Republic. Special autonomy is given to such tribal groups while inculcating into them the need for economic regionalism in the planned development of the USSR.

The attitude to industry in primarily agricultural or backward countries creates problems. It does not benefit the entire nation equally. The skilled and educated people reap the benefit of industry. The people in the rural areas do not share the industrial gains. Many of them remain poor, thus widening the cleavage between the rich and the poor and the urban and rural. To balance industrial technology with agricultural and tribal technology, the gap between the urban and rural must be closed. The urban outlook on economy should be to cater to the rural needs. But the traditions of economy in most of the former colonial countries, which in general have remained backward and agricultural, have not contributed to the development of an integrated urban-rural economy. Farmers changed their ways and were encouraged to cultivate commercial crops to cater to the industries of the developed countries. Raw materials were exported while manufactured goods were imported. This heritage is now standing in the way of an integrated urban-rural development in these countries.

Further, there is the attitude of the agricultural and industrial community towards population and family planning. In an agricultural community a child is an asset. He can learn his trade early in life and help his seniors. This is true of any trade which is on a cottage or household level producing for a small community. Thus in the underdeveloped countries there is the problem of overpopulation and pressure on land because the skills developed are too meagre to take the best out of the land while the desire to increase the labour force to increase production is keen. The people of the industrialized nations on the other hand have a background which prevents the increase in numbers. Urban facilities are few for very large families. With mechanization the opportunity for work is conditioned by skills acquired through specialized education. The capital required for such training also restricts the size of the family. Thus while the developed countries are facing the danger of a decreasing rate in population growth, the undeveloped countries have not only to tackle the problem of overpopulation but also of lack of skilled workers for industry with the right attitude towards work.

Further, there is the problem of imported labour in some countries. The difference in the wages of imported and local labour originally stemmed out of racial prejudices. The Indians in Malaya and Ceylon, the Chinese in Singapore, the Negroes in America, or the skilled and highly paid technical labour from the developed countries, all today are sources of tension amongst the local population leading to economic regression and political unrest (see Chapter 4).

In south Africa colour bar is a potent factor in the evolution, structure and pattern of economy. The struggle of the minority white population to control the economy at any cost, has generated the problem of aparthied. There is a wide gap between management and labour usually prevalent in exploitation economies. The leaders of industry have seldom any sympathy for the aspirations of the labour force which lives in squalor and poverty, in areas allotted to them. They hardly benefit by the industrial and the mining prosperity of the country. Today the blacks are being divided to perpetuate the minority white rule.

In east Africa, there is a threefold division of society. the white, the Asiatics and the Africans, each with its own economic goals. The whites and the Asiatics have generally been the directors, managers, technicians and entrepreneurs and they have together exploited local labour. Many of them have migrated to other countries after independence was conferred on the east African countries. But the African attitude towards work, his apathy and his lack of education and drive, have put the economy out of gear. The solution to the problem must come from education and a belief in the necessity for a national economic development for the stability of the country.

The problem of racial discrimination and the consequent impact on labour exists also in the developed countries. The American Negro can claim equality with the white American only in the Constitution. Many 'technical hurdles' stand in the way of his achieving that equality. Hence squalor and overcrowded neighbourhoods are seen coexisting with affluence and wealth.

In England too race prejudices are deeply rooted in society. In fact the Englishman's antagonism to the so-called inferior races is supposedly greater than that of the average American. But so far these races did not come in contact with the English in their own homeland to any great extent. Their dealings with the underdeveloped people were in the Empire and Colonies where administrative control permitted them to pass whatever laws they wanted to impose subjugation Today the discrimination against races in England has become a crucial political and economic problem But many of the social welfare institutions and economic units are sustained by Asian labour. While the English entrepreneurs and government are willing to attract Asian labour because it is efficient and cheap, they are not willing to accord to them equal status or equal wages with English labour. Asian labour resents the colonial approach of the English to Asiatic labour.

The individual attitude towards work and labour in general make up the society's viewpoint on economic problems arising out of labour. It has an impact on trade unions and the understanding between labour and management. The ultimate aim of all trade unions is the fixation of minimum wages and the attainment of better facilities. America sees advantages in trade unions while England with its colonial background looks upon trade unions as parallel to a communist upsurge. In some tribal areas of west Africa, the West Indies, the Middle East and so on, membership of trade unions is looked upon as equivalent to disloyalty to the tribal chief and defiance of tribal laws.

Attitude towards land

The attitude of people to land also differs from country to country and it has an impact on the economy. The Chinese traditionally have a veneration for ancestral land which communism and collectivization of farms have sought to remove. Industrialization on a large scale has succeeded to some extent in removing age-old beliefs but China is struggling between two worlds, the world of state controlled economy and the four thousand year old attachment to ancestral land.

The attitude of the tribal people in the different parts of the world towards land differs according to the tribal laws. Some are very attached to the clan land while others are loyal to the tribal chief and the clan laws. The tribal land, which was originally won laboriously from forest and wild beasts, was jealously guarded by the clan from outside thrusts. Thus a strong exclusiveness grew, based on kinship. The tribal concept of land rights is one of the commonest causes of major disturbances in the north-eastern states of India. In Manipur, for example, the two major groups are the Nagas and the Kukis. The Nagas are the most advanced of the tribes in the north-eastern region. For their participation in World War II, Britain had planned to give the Nagas an independent Nagaland. In 1945 Sir Pawsay had formed the Naga Hill District Tribal Council for uniting the Nagas of Assam, Manipur, Burma, the then NEFA and Chittagong. Just a year before India got independence the Council became a political organization demanding independence for the Nagas. Britain's aim was to make Nagaland into a separate Crown Colony and Phizo became the leader of the Naga independence movement. He had the full support of the British. Welfare work was easy amongst the Nagas and a large number of them were converted to Christianity through the efforts of the British and other missionaries. After the war, many of the demobilized Naga soldiers were settled in the hills region of

Manipur as permanent horticulturists and they grew oranges and other fruits. The hills region, however, is dependent on the valley of Manipur for food. Transport between the two is inadequate. The Nagas are very attached to the land and their settlement as permanent horticulturists has created problems for the Kukis. A Naga does not tolerate any encroachment on his land. Whether modernized or not he carries with him traditional tribal customs. The Nagas also consider forests their private preserve and resent any interference. After independence the Nagas have continued to be the most advanced of the tribals but their concept of land ownership is that of the tribal Naga. The creation of Nagaland, to the north, the compactness of the Nagas as an ethnic group, their comparatively advanced technology and their expansion into the hills region of Manipur as permanent horticulturists, are some of the main causes for the economic, political and social unrest in the north eastern region, hampering the development of the states and union territories.

The Kukis are comparatively backward. They are widely spread out in the hills between Burma, Manipur, Kachar and Arakan. There are many clans amongst them and the Kukis prefer to be identified by their clans rather than as an ethnic or racial group. The British, before they left India, had not made any effort to organize them into a political group as they did with the Nagas. There is no great cultural or social affinity between the Kukis of the different areas. But every Kuki looks upon jhooming as his right. They consider their rights in the forests as a way of life and will not tolerate any encroachment on these land rights. They are not attached to the land as such. When a Kuki leaves his village he has to surrender everything he possesses to the chief. He has no individual property. The settlement of the Kukis as permanent cultivators has not been as easy as amongst the Nagas. The acute shortage of land for *jhooming* following the settlement of the Nagas in the Manipur Hills Region, is making the Kuki resentful. The force of the traditional indifference to boundary lines in the forests, the attitude of the tribal people towards forest and grazing land, the lack of an awareness of a national economy and the tribal concept of land rights, are obstructions to the economic development of these areas. The Kukis find the Nagas too strong politically to stand up for their jhooming rights in the forests.

In Africa there are the tribal laws of the Negroes and the

White Man's law. The tribal laws stood in the way of the plantation economy of the whites. The existing social system and tribal land laws had to give way to permit the introduction of plantations. The shift from tribal land-holding to ownership of land under colonial laws caused the disruption of the old social order and the removal of tribal land boundaries. The indifference of the European planters to tribal laws was the cause of much of the disturbances in western Nigeria during the colonial days.

In Argentina, the attitude of the Spanish nobility to land-holding discouraged wheat cultivation by tenants. To the Spanish, the possession of great estates was a matter of prestige. They parcelled the land to tenants only to keep it free of weeds. The tenants, who did not have a permanent right over the land, were discouraged from developing it for more profitable commercial crops. Yet it was under these precarious land rights that the wheat cultivation in the Pampas took root.

Laws under which land is held in the different parts have thus a great impact on agriculture and industry. The economic geographer must be acquainted with the different rights under which land is held, in the region he is investigating for a full comprehension of the development of its economy. The *zamindari* and *ryotwari* systems in India, the *estencias* of Argentina, the *haciendas* of Chile, the *fazendas* of Brazil, cooperative farming in Denmark, New Zealand and so on, share-cropping once popular in western Europe and parts of USA and the collective farms of USSR are all relevant to an understanding of economic geography.

CULTURAL FACTORS

Cultural factors also affect the economy of a country or region. Literacy is one of the main cultural factors which has an impact on economy. Literacy is the foundation on which agricultural and industrial skills are developed. The availability of skilled labour is one of the reasons for the location of industry in a particular place. At present there are technical and engineering colleges as well as agricultural colleges in most parts of the world to impart the necessary education for the economic development of a country. But the people can avail of such facilities only if the standards of literacy are high. It is through the proper education of the people that the national and regional economies are developed. It is also possible to spread knowledge through the radio, a purposeful propaganda machinery and so on. But such mechanisms lead to exploitation if the people are illiterate and ignorant.

Language is another cultural factor which affects economy. It is the means of communication. In some countries where several languages are spoken, the national outlook on economy suffers. In India language is the basis on which the state boundaries are delimited. The constitution permits a certain amount of economic autonomy to the states so that very often national programmes for economic development have to be sacrificed for state programmes and ambitions. Irrigation and electricity schemes, the development of the textile industry, iron and steel industry, the transport industry, mining, petroleum and other industries are faced with the problem of the regional interests of the states and the national interests of the central government. Some of these are centrally controlled to ensure development without conflicts but the state governments are increasingly becoming conscious of their 'rights' to regional resources.

Very often language barriers prevent the assimilation of knowledge. In Tibet, China and Arab countries where technical skills are still rudimentary, the lack of knowledge of a technically developed language is a drawback. The vernacular of some of the countries has great limitations as science itself has not developed in these countries. A language becomes rich in technical and scientific terms only if science and technology are developed amongst the people who speak that language. Such backward countries have to imbibe the knowledge necessary for economic development through a borrowed language at least temporarily. In India too the educational institutions are faced with the dilemma of developing a national language against the background of developing regional cultures and the need for a foreign language for technical advancement. Technical skills in the world have advanced very rapidly in the last few decades so that a country which cannot keep pace with knowledge is in danger of being exploited economically. Commercial contacts, marketing and banking on a world-wide scale become difficult with language barriers. A modern industrial and commercial country has also to understand the tastes and fashions in other countries, the likes and dislikes of the people, their way of life if they want to expand their market and language may become a barrier to such commercial expansion.

RELIGION

Religion has a powerful influence on man's activities in certain countries. In the medieval period the domination of the church curbed the development of science. In Germany Bismarck's attitude towards Catholicism and later Hitler's antagonism towards Zionism directed the course of German economy. The conflict of Moscow with the Roman Church drove Russia out of the European continent. The Muslims whatever country they belong to are bound by religion and it has an impact on the economy of the Muslim countries. There is no colour or functional segregation amongst the Muslims. As a contrast to this is the elaborate caste system of the Hindus which subdivides labour into functional groups. Certain functions are handed down from father to son and they are confined to certain castes. The economy in India is still caste-ridden despite all efforts to abolish caste under the new constitution.

An example of the direct influence of religion in agriculture and livestock industry, is the religious prescription about eating fish. It may militate against fish culture. Buddhism advocates vegetarianism which explains partly the poor development of animal husbandry in China, Korea and Japan. Hinduism venerates the cow. Amongst the Muslims, Jews and the Hindus pork is a forbidden food. The Muslims consider the pig, an unclean animal. Thus in many parts of the world pig-rearing is prohibited on religious grounds.

The impact of religion is seen very much in the layout of towns and villages in some countries. Social, cultural and religious factors affect the morphology of settlements. The ideal town in China was laid out in accordance with ritual prescriptions. Certain features are comm on to all long-standing towns of China. The Chinese religion places China in the centre of the universe while the rest of the world is considered its younger bretheren, to be guided and educated. In the centre of the town was, therefore, the palace It was enclosed by walls and formed a town within the town. The arrangement and form of the palace was repeated in miniature in the houses of the nobles, each surrounded by a wall. Double walls surrounded the towns, the outer enclosing the whole area and the inner the actual town area. The encompassment by the wall expressed the Chinese concept of the universe and the highly integrated town reflected the Chinese gift of organization and systematic arrangement. These old towns have given way to new industrial and commercial towns but old concepts are still reflected in their layout.

In India too cultural and religious factors had an impact on the layout of towns and villages which neither the Muslim nor the British conquests have completely obliterated. The elaborate caste system of Dravido-Aryan India allotted an economic function and an area to each caste. A caste function zoning is seen even today in most Indian towns.

In Russia the cultural and social factors of a bygone age are evident in the settlement patterns. Russia is spiritually and materially Asian. The Russians have their foundation in social collectivity and their actions are not unlike those of the Asians. Mysticism is a marked feature in Russia. This fact explains the trend of settlement right up to the revolution. The citadel formed the centre of the town. Within it were the administrative buildings, the main churches, the prison, the arsenal and the homes of the officials and soldiers. It was a town within a town as in China and India. The ordinary people remained outside the town which was called the free district.

The most characteristic and the best known type of town in Russia is the old Kremlin town. The centre is the Kremlin. The ground plan is concentric with a network of arterial roads converging on the centre. Between them is a mass of secondary roads. Moscow is the Kremlin town par excellence. In the centre of old Moscow was the castle and market. The craftsmen lived outside.

The rapid industrial and agricultural development under the planned economy of Russia has somewhat changed the functions of towns particularly in Siberia, and thus its morphology. But the impact of old beliefs and traditions remain.

Social and cultural factors influence the economic patterns and structure in every country whether developed or undeveloped. But the criteria by which to detect and measure the impact have to be chosen by the economic geographer to understand fully the development in the area investigated, whether it be the impact on the general economic patterns or on the more specific settlement patterns. He has to be aware that such factors do influence the structure and pattern of economy so that while investigating the causes of regional variations in the area of his choice, he is competent to choose the right criteria to explain the differences.

11

CAPITAL AND ITS ROLE IN ECONOMIC GEOGRAPHY

CAPITAL is a prerequisite for economic development. The only real capital is manpower and the capacity to work. Capital in its true sense is the productive capacity of a country. Money is the medium of exchange and a measure of value and wealth. The capacity to produce goods depends on the availability (both external and internal) of raw material as well as the technical skill, organization and discipline of the labour force. The simplest type of economic development requires trained workers, transport, machinery, rolling stock and a host of other things, all of which require investment of capital.

In any capital investment, the time gap between investment and the return expected has to be considered. This period may be short or long depending on the type of economic enterprise. In the developing countries where capital is scarce, entrepreneurs cannot afford to wait for returns. This time element in capital investment and production has a restricting effect on the free flow of capital.

The requirements of capital also vary at the different stages of development of an enterprise. Any delay in investment at the proper time may cause damage to the whole project. In backward countries capital is inadequate to meet the cost of a developing economy and they have to resort to borrowing.

The capacity of a country to borrow, however, depends on its political and economic stability and strength. A country that is independent can chalk out its own fiscal policies. But a colony or dependency is subject to the economic policies of the metropolitan country. However, an independent country need not necessarily be strong economically.

The political status and stability of a country also influence the flow of private capital into its economic enterprises. When India became independent its alleged commitment to socialism prevented private entrepreneurs, both indigenous and foreign, from taking the risk of investing in its enterprises. The indigenous sources of private capital were however negligible at the time of independence. The revenues at the disposal of the government accruing from taxation were also not adequate for the country's ambitious economic programmes. Borrowing at government level was possible only from countries where governments controlled economy as in the USSR. The government, therefore, stepped into the field of production. Side-by-side the Indian government also encouraged private enterprise. Rapid economic development required the tapping of capital from all sources. It resulted in a mixed economy where both government and the private entrepreneurs were partners in economic activities. But as private capital accumulated, with increasing per capita income and the economic stability of the country, pressures mounted, not only from indigenous private entrepreneurs but also from entrepreneurs of the capitalist countries, for a larger share in the enterprises of the country. It resulted in an unhealthy competition between private and public enterprises and in an alliance of internal and foreign capitalists. Today USA, UK and the western European countries are quite anxious to invest in India. But the private capitalists in these countries are willing to invest only in private enterprises. There is pressure on India to give up its nonalignment and its socialistic goals to avail itself of aid from the capitalistic west.

In Argentina, where no government was in power for long, there was difficulty in attracting private capital to economic activities. This was true to some extent in France also until a few decades ago.

A stable banking system can attract private capital. An increase in the bank rates can induce the small earner to invest his surplus earnings in the banks. A bank enables the utilization of the capital resources of the small man in productive activities which otherwise would be frittered away. The banks with the accumulated deposits at their disposal can initiate economic development programmes. In countries where the banks are privately owned, these deposits are generally used to boost up the private industries owned by the bankers. But where the banks are nationalized the government has access to these deposits. However, nationalization of banks by itself does ensure economic development, unless the government also initiates policies for the utilization of the capital for furthering the industrial and agricultural interests of the country. A banking system, privately or otherwise managed, enables a country to put to good use the savings of the nation. However, the government and the private banker must both be aware of their obligations to society when they utilize the resources at the disposal of the banks.

In most countries the industrial houses themselves encourage deposits from the public. They give high interests, often higher than those of the banks, on deposits to attract capital to their own enterprises. The public can also buy shares and debentures from a company and indirectly help in the economic programmes without taking the risks usually attached to the promotion of economic enterprises.

The capital for economic development must come either from home resources or through aids from foreign countries.

HOME CAPITAL RESOURCES

Home capital resources are the savings of the people, and the state's revenues from taxation. The state itself can get involved in certain industries or transport with the capital at its disposal. In a country where the banks are nationalized the state has also access to the private earning of the people. The amount of savings that a people can accumulate depends on the per capita income and the standard of living. Agricultural countries can rarely generate adequate capital to promote industries unless its agriculture is on an extensive commercial scale. It is industry that can generate capital surpluses which, if ploughed back into new enterprises, can stabilize the economy of a country. The taxation policies of a country give the clue to the amount of capital at the disposal of the government after expenditures are met. A government which uses its revenues wisely for the welfare and development of the country can alone achieve stability and command the respect of the people.

DEPENDENCE ON OUTSIDE SOURCES OF CAPITAL

Whether a country decides to generate internal capital resources for economic development or borrow from outside countries depends on its political and economic policies. The USSR after the socialist revolution decided to accumulate capital from its own sources when it launched its nationwide economic development. But the Afro-Asian countries, after their independence, have chosen to take aids from foreign sources, partly because of their inability to generate capital for ambitious economic programmes and partly because of a lack of knowledge of the implications of foreign aid on the economic and political future of their country.

Prior to World War I loans were raised in London. The situations changed after World War II. The USA was the only country, immediately after the war, which could give aids and loans. Even the war-damaged western European countries looked to USA for aids to reconstruct their industries. But today the west European countries have recovered from the war damages and are not only in a position to give aid but are also anxious to get involved in the economic programmes of the developing world in order to gain control of their economy. The oil-rich countries also have surplus capital which they are willing to invest in the developing world. The fiscal policies of some of the backward oil producing countries are directed by the capitalist countries.

Loans can be had for a short term or for a long term. Short term loans are unsatisfactory because of the gap between investment and profitable production in economic enterprises. Most developing countries therefore, seek long term loans for developing programmes such as irrigation, electricity, transport and steel. The loans are given on interest. The USSR generally charges very low interests while the interests charged by the capitalist countries are, on an average, high. Both the capital and the interest are repayable within a stipulated period under terms of agreement.

Economic stability cannot, however, be achieved through a perpetual dependence on loans and aids from outside. If the receiving countries utilize the aids efficiently and wisely they can generate enough profits to enable them to repay the loans within a reasonable period. Such aids are to be looked upon as a temporary feature to tide over a difficult period in the economy of a country. All countries at some time or other must be able to generate its own capital. If its economic policy fails, repayment of loans becomes a problem. The country's economic dependence undermines also its political independence. The aiding countries or organizations often advance loans with a view to gaining a stranglehold on the economy of the receiving country. A country which is subject to the dictation of the aiding countries or organizations, like the IMF in its economic policy, find it difficult to achieve any stability. As for example, India took a loan of Rs. 5,000 crores from the International Monetary Fund in 1981. Experts were of the opinion that the loan was no solution to the country's difficulties and that instead of helping the country it was actually making the situation worse because of the terms and conditions attached to it.

One of the conditions attached to the IMF loan of 1981 was the liberalization of both industrial and import controls. The Indian government accordingly introduced the open general licence for imports. This was accompanied by an increasing dependence on multinational corporations and big industrial houses to accelerate industrial growth. The government made efforts to control imports in view of the adverse developments. But opposition mounted from the multinational corporation and some of the big industrial houses in India. There was also danger that if India reversed its policies of liberalization, the IMF may cut off the balance of the loan or impose new conditions.

Further, it was felt that the loan may not be used for the development of industries nor for narrowing the gap in trade deficit but frittered away in unnecessary imports, leading to economic recession, devaluation of the rupee and so on. India's efforts to increase exports to the aiding countries met with little success. The IMF also restricted India's freedom to borrow from other sources which was detrimental to her economic independence.

Aids are also given in kind such as food grains (wheat loan of USA to India) equipment, technical know-how, services and so on. But these have also to be paid back according to the terms of the agreement.

Some countries are willing to give aids and loans on attractive conditions. The USSR for example advanced loans to India on the basis that India agree to her purchasing Indian goods in the

Indian market to the equivalent of the loan. India was not required to pay back the loan in Russian or Indian currency, but in kind. It was a great relief to India as home capital resource was scarce. There were several commodities which India could offer Russia to clear her debt. But the situation is not the same in the case of the USA, she has a surplus of both agricultural and industrial products and can produce more if necessary. There is very little that she needs to import from India. Paying back in kind to USA is also made difficult because of her political ambitions in the developing world. She is interested in India as a market for her industrial and agricultural surpluses and as a producer of goods. However, 'to tide over India's dollar crisis', USA agreed to accept rupee payment. It was considered to be a great advantage to India at the time. But Indian currency, accumulated in the USA began to be used to further her political and economic interests in India. The US presssurised India to agree to her investing the rupees in Indian industries, transport, mining, fertilizers, pharmaceuticals and so on. The situation was eased only when the dollar ceased to reign supreme and India began to seek aids from countries which could be paid in kind or from the soft and medium currency areas (see Chapter 13). Countries which seek aids have to steer clear of the stringent conditions attached to these aids and loans as they would gradually undermine the economic and political stability of the country.

Before 1914 Britain also welcomed payment in kind. She was a top-heavy industrial country and her large industrial population had to be sustained by imports of food and raw material from the dependent countries or from countries where she had investments in economic enterprises (as in Argentinan railways and wheat farms). She could dump her manufactured goods in these countries and draw upon their food resources to support her industrial population. In spite of all the disadvantages of such an economy, England could be paid back in kind. Trade was mutual although prices and trade terms fixed by the mother country were often unfair to the dependent countries. The US on the other hand, is the biggest creditor and the biggest exporter, a situation which cannot last. A multilateral trade, as existed when Britain was the leading trading nation in the world, cannot be emulated by USA. A country which exports must also import. The US is an exporter of both agricultural and industrial products. She cannot continue exproting without opening up her market to other countries. Already there are signs of an economic recession and forceful cut-down of production to maintain prices. With the recovery of western Europe from war damages, the formation of the European Union and the Common Market, the rise of USSR as an economic power, the competition from industrial Japan and the accumulation of petro-dollars in the hands of the oil-rich countries, the US is no longer in a position to dictate the terms of international trade and international capital investment. The ability to exchange goods is a necessity to maintain world trade but the developing countries have not been able to catch up with world production and world trade so that loans borrowed have accumulated making these countries economically and politically vulnerable. Stabilization of their economy can be had only through increased productivity and extended trade.

12

THE ROLE OF GOVERNMENT IN ECONOMIC DEVELOPMENT

THE impact of government policies, acts and regulations, tariffs on export and import, taxes and duties and so on affected the location and structure of economic units only indirectly till the socialistic revolution of the USSR ushered in the planned economy and state control of production and distribution. The success of the state enterprises of Russia induced other states to follow in her footsteps. Governments woke up to the responsibility of planning economic enterprises and directing their courses. Planned economy is now an accepted fact. Planning of economic enterprises, whether by the state or by the individual capitalist, has, however, to consider certain fundamental principles of location. But in state-planned economies the role of the government is crucial. The industrial and agricultural development and location of economic activity under the various governments being somewhat different, the economic geographer must be acquainted with the types of political organizations which direct or control the economic policies of a country.

A brief survey of political concepts

Five main philosophies of social organizations can be recognized in the development of political thought in the west, anarchism, liberalism, socialism, communism and fascism.

Anarchism does not accept any organized political authority. It is an extreme form of individualism and believes that man is born free and has the right to remain free. The anarchists advocate a state of lawlessness where there is no security to property. But they also believe that human beings have a natural inclination to cooperate for mutual benefit. Thus collective and cooperate work is inherent in anarchism. While some of the eighteenth and nineteenth century anarchists pleaded for a peaceful transition to cooperation and collectivism, others supported violent revolutions. The Russian revolutionary, Bakunin (1814-1876) proposed a decentralized socialism. According to him revolution was the work of the masses and not that of the political leaders. His slogan was 'anarchism, collectivism and atheism'. The Marxists, on the other hand, proposed an authoritarian socialism. The struggle of the Bakunists with the Marxists ended in the eclipse of the former in 1872. Tolstoy was a religious anarchist. The state according to him was against the tenets of Christianity and as such people should not pay taxes nor enter military service nor recognize the authority of the court. He believed that love should bring about the welfare state. In India the principles of non-cooperation and non-violence of Gandhi can be traced back to the concept of the freedom of the individual of the anarchist and the philosophy of Tolstoy. But non-cooperation breeds hatred and hatred breeds violence. Thus the two are incompatible.

Liberalism is a product of western Europe. It was a reaction to autocratically governed states. The feudal lords controlled the common man in Europe and the peasants of Russia lived in a state of serfdom. There was lack of individual freedom and a great disparity between the rulers and the ruled, the nobility and the common man. Liberalism rests on the philosophy of Locke. Man, he said, is born free and lived in a state of nature with rights of liberty and property. But when might became right, man resorted to the social contract by which he placed himself under an authority for protection of his fundamental rights. The weakness of liberalism lay in the claim to natural rights. But the social contract established the responsibility of the government to the common man.

Liberalism found expression in two fields, political and economic. In the political field it laid the foundation of modern democracy. In the popular sense it advocated change. To understand the influence of liberalism on economy, a brief survey of the changing economy of England during this period is necessary.

With the discovery of America and the sea routes to the East, world trade shifted from land to sea. But trade was still largely in luxury goods in the Tudor Period. By the seventeenth century oceanic trade across the Atlantic had switched over to bulky goods. The West Indies began to specialize in the cultivation of sugar to the exclusion of food and depend on England for all necessities.

The trade with the English American colonies also grew rapidly. Till well into the nineteenth century America remained an agricultural country and drew their manufactured goods from England. Her chief raw material was cotton. A sea trade in bulky goods from the American colonies and the West Indies and a return traffic in manufactured goods (particularly cloth) from England developed. In the Stuart period the change was only rudimentary. But the population of England increased from 5½ million in 1700 to 9 million in 1775 and that of America and the West Indies from 350,000 to 3 million. The importance of the colonial market grew, thus the independence of the American colonies did not circumscribe.

Britain was also opening up the eastern markets. The East India Company was expanding its trade and acquiring territories in India and the Far East. The tropical commerce far exceeded the American trade by the close of the century. Trade grew in bulk and value with increased demand and new tastes. The demand on British industry was enormous and it could be satisfied only by new methods of production. The English merchants had amassed enough capital in trade. Expanding commerce and the Indian conquests had produced it. For the first time the 'millionaire' appeared as a phenomenon in England. These capitalists could invest in industry which was calling for more production. Banking services enabled the common man's small savings to be concentrated in the hands of capitalist entrepreneur. Joint stock companies became very much more common in the eighteenth century than in the previous century. Roads and canals were improved by private companies which made a profit in tolls. Such changes were taking place in some other European countries also but they fell far behind England by the eighteenth century. None of them could retain their eastern colonies as England did.

These developments had their impact on political and economic thought. English thinkers realized that the country was going through a great revolution. From the earliest times English Governments had levied duties on commerce with two motives—to increase the revenue and to favour some merchants against others, by means of discriminating rates. The Tudors did not protect home production by making exports free of the duties. But the English merchants enjoyed favour against the foreign merchants. Duties were levied on both exports and imports. The heavy wars of William III (1689-1702) necessitated raising of duties. The Whig merchants were satisfied as long as foreign merchants paid more than they did. But the Tory landholders, objected to the high price of imported goods and opposed protectionism. They advocated free trade. By 1783 British tariffs were hindering trade far more than they protected it. So high were the duties on foreign goods that smuggling became a common activity. The smugglers were called 'free traders'.

Political philosophers were not found wanting to break through the economic controls. In France the physiocrats came to the conclusion that protection was an unsound policy. They held that the regulation of trade by the state was bad and they coined the watchword laissez faire ('leave things alone'). They advocated management of business by private men without interference from the state. In France it received little support. But in England it was taken up by Adam Smith (1723-1790). He attacked protection and state regulation of trade. His *Wealth of Nations* published in 1776 was a vindication of free trade. Adam Smith converted the younger Pitt who took up office in 1783, determined to improve British trade and finances. He reduced duties and step by step initiated free trade. But his success was only a promise.

Then came the industrial revolution. The character of British manufacturing was greatly altered. The population of England and Wales also doubled in eighty years and stood at $13\frac{3}{4}$ million in 1831, upsetting the man-land ratio. Further, the depletion of the forests caused scarcity of fuel for the iron industry. Coal was already being used as fuel for the industry but surface mining proved inadequate. There were no safety appliances or organizations to guarantee the safety of the miners in deep mining. The mining industry was, however, extremely profitable and it spread rapidly. Iron deposits, never touched before, came to be mined under perilous conditions. The steam engine was improved by James Watt and factory industries financed by the capitalists made their appearance. Profits accumulated in trade, flowed into industries and a class of rich capitalist industrialists grew while the workers lived in the evergrowing slums of the big cities.

Society split into two.

As the population depending on tertiary activities increased, more food had to be raised. Improvement in livestock and plant called for scientific breeding and the segregation of herds, for which there was no provision in traditional agriculture. Landlords began to introduce agricultural innovations of root crops from Holland. The new system of farming necessitated the cultivation of open pastures and the enclosure of fields. The enclosure movement, started a full century ago, became intensive after 1783 and the Enclosure Acts were passed. They ignored the rights of the cultivator who had no written proofs of their claims in the manorial estates. Big properties came to be held by fewer and fewer people and a class of landless peasants grew.

Reaction had set in even before the end of the eighteenth century. Thomas Paine published the *Rights of Man* in 1791. The common man, for the first time began to be conscious of politics. They became suspicious of the rich, and doubted their sincerity in representing their cause in Parliament. Jeremy Bentham (1748-1832) taught men not to take political and economic institutions for granted. He became the brain of radicalism. The ideas of the French Revolution also filtered into England (liberty, equality and fraternity). The fight of the common man against the unfair distribution of wealth continued as the industrial and agricultural revolutions accumulated wealth in the hands of the privileged few. In countries where capitalism was deeply rooted a form of regulated capitalism was introduced. In others socialism was the answer to the unbridled development of capitalism.

Socialism evolves from Marx. But since then socialism has taken various forms such as Guild Socialism, Syndicalism and State Socialism. Guild Socialism advocated the revival of medieval guilds along modern lines to restore the rights of the common man. Industries according to them, were to be nationalized. Trade unions were to take over their respective industries and were to be organized as the guilds of the medieval period. Guild Socialism is a Britain variant of syndicalism.

Syndicalism advocates the ownership and control of all industries by the workers. They prefer direct action and accept strikes and 'work to rule, methods rather than parliamentary methods to establish the rights of workers. Syndicalism thrived in Britain and many of the European countries but the movement dwindled after World War I when its protagonists turned to communism. The fascist concept of the corporate state is influenced by syndicalism. Socialism, in some form or other, is a relevant factor even in the twentieth century capitalist Britain and in many other developed countries.

In state socialism, the state controls economic activity. Socialism advocates collective control of basic industries and collective control of income divisions. Socialism does not advocate collective consumption.

Communism is much more extreme than socialism. It believes that the wealth of the state is vested in the commodity. Modern communism is based on the political philosophy of Marx as modified by Lenin (1870-1924). New forms of capitalism had come into force after Marx. The producers of the earlier stages of capitalism had given way to huge combines and trusts. Lenin was convinced that the government was collaborating with the capitalists to achieve its ends. The capitalists were getting the support of the skilled workers because of the high wages paid to them. The working force was thus divided in their interests. The poor unskilled labourers remained poor whose cause was betrayed by the government, the capitalists and the skilled workers. Both Marx and Lenin believed that the government (state) was an instrument of the ruling class and that the proletariat should take over the state machinery. Communists however advocate that this should be achieved in stages, from socialism to communism. Under socialism the principle 'from each according to his ability to each according to his work' is effected. But there are still class distinctions between the intelligentsia and the common worker. Communism is guided by this principle 'from each according to his ability to each according to his needs'. Communism aims at a classless, stateless society.

Society according to the communists passes through four stages of development before it reaches the final goal. In the first stage the bourgeois capitalist class is overthrown. In the second, the class conscious people capture power. The intelligentsia steps in and directs the course of events. In the third, the state controls both production and distribution. In the final stage emerges the classless, stateless society. The USSR claims to have reached the second or third stage of development and the revolution is still continuing. Within the USSR there is complete control of production, distribution and consumption by the state. The 1934 constitution says that 'he who does not work shall not eat' which is in opposition to the principle 'each according to his needs'. Under state-planned economy, Russia which was primarily an agricultural country before the revolution (1917), became one of the foremost industrial powers. Her economy has been developed by a series of five year plans.

Fascism came as a force against Communism. It is an extreme form of nationalism. Like communism it demands the supreme power of the state. The movement claimed to be neither capitalistic nor socialistic and advocated the founding of a corporate state. After Mussolini assumed power in Italy in 1922, the Fascist party became the only authorized political organization in Italy. Italian fascism generated a number of other similar movements in other countries. The national socialism of Germany and the slogan 'Germany for the Germans' led to the eviction of Jews and ended in World War II. In England too, a fascist movement called the British Union was active between 1931 and 1939.

In advocating the supreme power of the state, fascism allows private economic enterprise only when it is beneficial to the state. Such a system can be sustained only by military power.

The running of a political unit and the efficient functioning of its economy has problems whether it is a capitalist or socialist state. Modern economic and political units are very large. Athens, for example, was one political and economic unit in one particular environment. But USA today is not one economic unit. Its population is heterogeneous and complex administrative and economic systems are required to run the state. Centralization has its limits. Hence most large states are federated states. The USA is a federated state. The USSR is also a federated state of some sort. In a federated state power is divided between the centre and the state (provincial) governments. This division of authority can be one of the main stumbling blocks to political and economic development. The central government usually handles defence, foreign affairs and other matters of national interest. The individual states retain some control over their internal affairs.

The supreme court interprets the constitution. The rights of the centre and state are usually clearly defined to avoid dispute over decisions taken by the federal government and amendments can be made with the consent of a fixed number of states in the federation. On the whole, however, the state and centre are usually extremely jealous of their powers. The problem is how much power should the states have and how much the centre. In many of the newly developed federal states, national and state economic programmes get delayed with such disputes. In India the states are given great autonomy in economic planning and since they are also linguistic states, the separatist tendencies of the cultural unit stand in way of national economic planning. The tension between the centre and the state becomes more strained when one party is in power at the centre and another in the state. Even though the central government is expected to balance the states' interests within the national economic plans whatever party is in power in the states there is a tendency to pressurize the states, mainly by withholding finance and delaying development plans.

The economic policies of each country depend very much on its government policies and the economic commitments of the party in power. Most parties, if they are politically mature, have clear cut economic policies. The economic geographer has to be acquainted with the policies and commitments of the different governments and parties, to understand the pattern, the structure and the location of economic activity. He would also understand the economy of his own country better if he is aware of the changing policies of other countries. No country can remain isolated economically in modern times. The policies of one country influence the economy of the other countries. The tariffs and duties, subsidies, bounties, trade contracts and agreements, trade policies and so on are the responsibility of each government and have a bearing on the production, trade and economic activities of other countries.

Tariffs and duties

The government imposes tariffs and duties on goods as they pass the international border. They are more commonly imposed on imports. But tariffs on exports may be justified on the ground that they increase the revenues of the government and advance the interests of the producers of goods.

The aim of import tariffs is to raise the price of imported goods so that the home industries are protected. In infant industries import tariffs are advantageous because they help to avoid competition. One argument in favour of such protection is that the products of the home industries may have to seek a home market, thus strengthening it. But industries built behind tariff walls are loathe to give up protection. Restrictions on imports by high tariffs cut off imports, resulting in a favourable balance of trade (that is, an excess of exports over imports) which is considered advantageous. But a cut in imports results in a cut in exports as well, thus reducing the country's total volume of trade. No country can have a favourable balance of trade covering all payments. An import tariff also undercuts the principle of geographic specialization.

Some countries follow an open door policy. There is no discrimination between one country and another in the export and import of goods. In 1890 Brussels adopted such a policy to increase its revenue. In 1919 Versailles Treaty declared that there should be no discrimination in trade. But many countries adopt discriminatory policies in trade.

The Gatt (General Agreements on Tariff and Trade) in the post-war world, for example, is an affort to regulate trade amongst the different nations. It was enunciated 35 years ago (1947) and has been subject to several revisions. Some 87 member countries met in Geneva recently and in Tokyo nine years ago for negotiations. Such trade agreements and concessions divert the trade of particular commodities to particular countries with which the agreements are made.

Economic self-sufficiency

Some countries advocate economic self-sufficiency atleast in particular. fields Complete self-sufficiency is not possible for any country and it is not even advisable. Certain industries like the defence industries may seek self-sufficiency for strategic reasons. Self-sufficiency in food is a protection against war. World War I strengthened the idea of economic self-sufficiency. Germany protected her agriculture in 1914. But self-sufficiency clearly runs counter to international trade.

Dumping

In the pre-war world dumping the surplus goods of the mother country in the Empire and colonies was a means of expanding and protecting the home industries. But this is largely out of date in the post-war world. Most countries are free to draw up trade agreements on the basis of "most favoured countries" or otherwise.

Subsidies and Bounties

These protect home industries. The effect of subsidy is to lower prices which enables the industry to compete with imports. Subsidies are sometimes disguised.

Currency depreciation and appreciation

These also complicate international trade patterns. If a government decides to depreciate or appreciate the value of its currency in terms of the currency of another country with which it has trade connections, it will have a deep impact on the latter's economy in terms of export and import of goods (see Chapter 13). Since the planned economy has become such a force in the world, an analysis of state planning of economic activity in the USSR would help to understand the role of the government under a totalitarian state.

PLANNED ECONOMY

Since the emergence of USSR as a major economic and political power, her economic organization under planned phased-out programmes, has been taken up by other countries with variations regarding the degree of control by the state, consequent upon local traditions and political and economic goals. India has a mixed economy. It encourages economic enterprises both in the public and private sector.

Some major projects in India particularly irrigation, petroleum and heavy steel are planned and directed by the centre. There are also projects planned and controlled by the state governments. Side by side also flourishes industries in private sector. The socialistic goal of the constitution was aimed at a fair distribution of wealth among the people and prevention of the accumulation of wealth in the hands of a few. But as time passed, her economic policies resulted in an unhealthy struggle between the public and private sector.

The major problems of USSR, so far as rapid economic development under a planned system is concerned, are its vastness and inadequacy of transport, the emptiness of Asiatic Russia and the cold north, the multi-ethnic nature of its population, the vulnerability of its frontier republics and areas and the need to maintain its image as a superpower to offset the influence of the capitalistic states in the underdeveloped and developing world. State plans therefore have to consider not only the availability of raw material and power resources but also the inadequacy of transport, the social and cultural background of the people, where planned modern economy is introduced, and the political factor.

The purpose of USSR's planned economy is to make the maximum use of the country's resources with the minimum cost, and to catch up with the advances made in industry by the western countries. The economic transformation was to be accomplished in stages and the five year plans were to chalk out the stages, sectors and regions of development. These were incorporated into the regional (area) planning, sectoral (industrial and agricultural) planning and macro-regional planning. In the context of an inadequate transport system and the vastness of the country, each planned economic region had to be somewhat self-sufficient in food and raw material. Secondly, the emphasis of the planned economy was on industrial development to catch up with the developed world. But agriculture and animal husbandry were to go hand-in-hand with industry while industries were also planned to cater to the needs of agriculture.

The general principle on which planning is based is 'maximum productivity at minimum cost'. But the plans also considered the availability of transport, market, raw material, labour and factors such as the possibility of expansion, integration and the existing pattern of economy. Industries were then grouped into five categories.

Industries dependent on availability of raw material

Group one has those industries in which the weight of the finished product is only a fraction of the raw material. Quantitative methods were used to assess the amount of raw material required per unit of the finished product and to locate the industry rationally. In such industries the transport of raw material is wasteful and the industry is best located in the raw material area. Metal intensive industries, thermal power stations and such are influenced by accessibility to raw material.

Group one also includes industries such as processing perishable material. (canning, wine making, fish processing) wood work enterprise, saw mills, pulp and paper making mills. All these are material intensive industries and best located in the raw material area except when they are in remote places and transport of the finished product to the market is costly.

Market oriented industries

Group two includes those industries which are best situated at the point of consumption. It includes enterprises which produce goods of great weight such as building material, (bricks, re-inforced concrete) and furniture, baking, confectionery, distilling, brewery and so on. The finished products are costly to be transported over great distances They are best located in the market area.

The transport of oil has been revolutionised with the development of pipelines and oil refineries are also located in the area of highest consumption. Tin smelters and rare earth metals are located in the consumption areas because the deposits are usually small (in Russia) and it is uneconomic to build factories in the raw material area.

Labour oriented industries

Group three includes labour intensive industries. The availability of labour is a crucial fact or in Russia. It is an important factor in the location of any industry but it is a deciding factor in some industries. The group is heterogeneous. It includes the manufacture of precision instruments, polymers, electronics and so on which require highly skilled labour. It also includes the textile industry, knitting, clothing, footwear. Some of these latter industries are located in the predominantly steel manufacturing areas like the Donbas and Kuzbas to enable the employment of women who are generally not employed in steel works. These industries can make use of female labour which otherwise would remain unutilized, and solve also the problem of utilizing the by-products of coal mines and coke plants (coal tar product)s.

In the small and medium-sized towns, labour is put to the maximum use by setting up industies which require limited and not very highly sophisticated labour. There are usually industries which can be integrated with the bigger industrial complexes. The small and medium sized towns near an industrial complex can make use of its labour in such industries.

Power oriented industries

Group four consists of those industries which are oriented towards fuel or electricity. Thermal power stations and certain branches of the chemical industry such as the synthetic fibre industry are attracted to fuel. The aluminium industry is strongly affected by the energy factor. This also applies to magnesium, zinc and so on. Areas with cheap power supplies are best suited for electrolytic production of ferro-metals and non-ferrous metals. The grid system is, however, widening the range of areas suitable for energy intensive industries.

Industries whose location is influenced by two or more factors.

The location of iron and steel industry is influenced by more than one factor, the availability of raw material (mainly iron) and the availability of fuel (coal). The most favourable sites for such industries are those where both are available. The nearness of the iron of Krivoyrog to the Donetz Basin coal, together with the fact that they are situated in European Russia, encouraged the growth of an early iron and steel industry in Ukraine. But some of Russia's best coals are in Siberia and her largest and best iron resources are at the southern end of the Urals (Magnitogorsk). The coal of Kuztnetsk (Siberia) is separated from the Magnitogorsk iron by thousands of miles. When the revolutionists took over planning there was only the Siberian railway connecting the two and the terrain between was little developed. Hence the planned economic region of the Kuznetsk-Ural Combine was developed to utilize the raw material and fuel at minimum cost. The empty area between the two was rapidly developed and several towns now dot the area. Branch lines of the Siberian railway now link the smaller areas of development within the Ural-Kuznetsk region. The macro-region centred on these sources of iron and coal is one of the rapidly developing planned regions of the USSR. Since basic industries are given emphasis particularly in the earlier five year plan periods, the economic regions of Russia are in general planned round coal and iron.

The location of large chemical complexes are also influenced by more than one factor. They consume vast amounts of raw material, electricity and water. Synthetic fibre needs a considerable amount of electricity and raw material. Some chemicals like ammonia, polythelene, acetylane require more than 1000 cubic metres of water per tonne of the product. The use of gas as fuel in the chemical industries and the fact that petroleum, like coal; is the source material for many of these industries is extending the range of possible sites for such industrial complexes.

Group five also includes industries in which the weight of the finished product roughly equals that of the raw material such as flour milling, cotton spinning, sugar refining and whole sale dairy industry. When locating such industries the transport cost of assembling the raw material at the point of production as well as the cost of delivering the goods to the market, is considered. Such industries are located either in the market area or in the raw material area or even at a midway point depending on the transport costs.

The industries which produce a large number of commodities such as the iron and steel industry, are grouped into homogeneous groups to enable their rational location. The engineering industry, for example, is subdivided into six groups on the basis of the consumption of metal and the requirement of labour and their location planned accordingly.

Planning in the agricultural sector

Agricultural planning is secondary to industrial planning in the USSR but the rational development of agriculture in the geographic and economic regions is given emphasis in planning to increase farm output.

Planners recognise the fact that in agriculture, the factors of influence are different from those of industry. Climatic factors and soil conditions strongly influence crop cultivation. Certain temperature, water and soil conditions are required for certain crops. But the range of the zones where many of crops (such as industrial crops like cotton, flax and so on) can be grown has been extended in the USSR with irrigation and the progress of science. But science has only been able to lessen the effect of the physical environment, not completely eliminate them. This is true of animal breeding also.

As in industry the main purpose of agricultural planning is to guarantee maximum returns with minimum cost by a rational use of land. To achieve this goal planners have introduced scientific rotation of crops, combination of crops, irrigation and so on. Russia has also to consider the cost of transport of the products of the farm to the market while planning crop cultivation and animal husbandry. The products of both are bulky and in the context of its vastness and the emptiness of a large part of Asiatic Russia, there is a tendency for agriculture to be developed near the planned industrial regions and urban areas. This ensures a certain amount of self-sufficiency in food for the industrial population. But where stock-rearing is the main activity as in the central Asiatic Republics and the northern cold regions, industry takes second place and caters to the needs of the stock-rearers. This is true of the predominantly agricultural areas like the cotton and the fruit regions of the central Asian Republics. The purpose of such planning is to increase efficiency and reduce costs. The Russian planned regions are highly integrated complexes.

13

MECHANISM OF EXCHANGE AND INTERNATIONAL CONTROLS

THE factors of production namely land, labour, capital, resources and technical skills are unevenly distributed over the surface of the earth which in turn have a bearing on the location of economic activity. It is obviously cheaper to produce goods in an area where the factors of production are comparatively abundant. It is the capacity of one area to produce surplus goods or cheaper goods that induces exchange of goods between countries leading to international trade. In very few countries is the economy absolutely free of international controls.

THE ADVANTAGES OF INTERNATIONAL TRADE

Under free competition goods are produced where the cost of production plus the transport cost to the market are the lowest. But the world is cut up into different political units with different governments, economic policies and currencies, that production is not always located where it is cheapest to produce them. A country may benefit by exchanging its goods with those of another country even if the factors of production are favourable for producing them herself.

Supposing there are two countries, *A* and *B* and the factors of production cannot move from one to the other, only goods can move. Country *A* has suitable factors for growing coffee but not flax. Country *B* on the other hand can produce flax but not coffee. A trade between the two would benefit both because they can get a product which would otherwise be unobtainable in the country.

Supposing both countries can produce both coffee and flax but country *A* can produce coffee more cheaply than *B* and country *B* can produce flax more cheaply than *A* because the factors of production are favourable to the growth of these crops respectively. With the application of *X* factors of production in *A*, it can produce 100 units of coffee but only 50 units of flax. Country *B*, on the other hand, can produce with *X* factors, 100 units of flax but only 50 units of coffee.

Suppose *A* specializes in the production of coffee and *B* in the production of flax, 2*X* factors of production in *A* will produce 200 units of coffee in *A* and the same 2*X* factors of production will produce 200 units of flax in *B*. Specializing in the products which are cheaper to cultivate, the total output of the two countries with 2*X* factors of production each is 200 units of coffee and 200 units of flax, instead of 150 units of flax. Clearly, there is a gain of 50 units of coffee and 50 units of flax.

Supposing the exchange rate is 1 unit of coffee against 1 unit of flax. Country *A* can exchange 80 units of coffee for 80 units of flax and thereby have 120 units of coffee + 80 units of flax. Country *B* can also have 120 units of flax + 80 units of coffee by exchanging her flax for coffee from *A*.

But supposing country *A* can produce both coffee and flax more cheaply than *B*, *A* can produce either 200 units of coffee or 200 units of flax or it can produce 100 units of coffee and 100 units of flax. An extra unit of coffee costs one unit of flax in the country. But *A*, desirous of being self-supporting produces 150 units of coffee and 50 units of flax.

Country *B* being less favourably endowed by natural and human factors can produce both flax and coffee only at a higher cost than country *A* but she can produce flax at a comparatively greater advantage than coffee, conditions being more suitable for the growing of that crop. The same quantity of factors of production can produce 80 units of coffee or 160 units of flax or 40 units of coffee and 80 units of flax in country *B*. An extra unit of coffee in country *B* costs 2 units of flax. *B* in order to be self-supporting produces 40 units of coffee and 80 units of flax.

Suppose *A* specializes in coffee and *B* in flax. Given the same factors of production *A* produces 200 units of coffee and B produces 160 units of flax

Country *A* can give 45 units of coffee in exchange for 60

units of flax from *B*. *A* can now get 155 units of coffee and 60 units of flax. *B* can have 45 units of coffee and 100 units of flax. Both countries have gained by specialization and exchange.

All the above examples fall under one general principle, the principle of comparative costs. *A* country will gain by specializing in the production of those commodities in which its comparative cost advantage is greater or in which its comparative cost disadvantage is less and exporting those commodities in exchange for commodities in which its comparative cost advantage is less or its comparative cost disadvantage is greater.

In fact the absolute cost of producing a commodity in a country which exports it, is always lower than in a country which imports it. Why then do we bother about the principle of comparative costs ? Why do we not simply say that goods will be produced where the money costs of production are the lowest ?

The reason is that money costs of production are made up of prices paid to the various factors of production. These prices are different from what they would be if there were no international trade. The existing factor prices and, therefore. the existing money costs in a country are particularly the result of international trade. The principle of comparative costs gives a fundamental explanation of why trade takes place. The 'costs' to which this principle refers to are not 'money costs'. The term 'costs' seems to relate to the quantity of factors required to produce a unit of coffee or flax But in fact we have been using the term in the sense of 'opportunity costs.'.

Any community must decide what goods to produce with the available factors of production. If it decides to produce more of some goods it must divert more factors of production towards those industries and must produce less than before, of other kinds of goods. In order to produce more coffee, *A* had to produce less flax. *B* in order to produce more flax had to produce less coffee. The opportunity cost ratios in the two countries *A* and *B* for the production of the two commodities are clearly different. It is this fact, and this fact alone, that makes it profitable for them to specialize and trade with one another.

But these opportunity cost ratios in a country do not remain constant. Some soils in country *A* may be very good for coffee cultivation but as demand increases and coffee cultivation is extended, country *A* will have to cultivate coffee in less suitable soils. Hence after a point of expansion of coffee growing it may involve more costs. If all other things remain the same its production in country *A* will be expanded only to that point at which further factors of production can obtain more flax by producing it directly than by producing coffee and exchanging it for flax.

A second reason why countries produce for themselves goods which they can import at lesser cost is because, in the above examples, the relative cost of transport is not considered. The cost of production includes transport cost to the market. The cost of transport is not directly related to distances on the ground but to economic distances. These costs can be very complicated as they are influenced by many factors. It may even be advantageous for one part of the country to import a particular commodity while another part exports it. Thus Hamburg imports coal while Ruhr exports it. The cost of transporting coal by sea from Britain to Hamburg is considerably less than from Ruhr to Hamburg by land.

A country may also be induced to produce certain commodities which it can import if what is produced at home is different from what it imports. France imports wine but it also produces a great deal of wine different from what it imports. She is both an exporter of wine and importer of wine.

A country may decide that it is 'desirable' to produce certain goods at home and aim at a degree of self-sufficiency in some products. They may subsidise home production of certain commodities depending on the country's economic policies.

Further, country *A* may be obliged to produce some of the commodities herself because its requirements of a particular commodity may be greater than it can import from B. Country *B* for example may specialize completely in flax but still not be able to meet the requirements of country *A*. *A* will then have to supplement its imports by producing flax herself or look for other sources.

Terms of trade

A country which engages in international trade produces goods and services some of which are consumed at home, the rest being exported.

But the extent to which the country gains by international trade may vary with the terms of trade, that is the rate which her exports exchange against imports.

Taking the third example again, for country *A* the opportunity cost of producing one unit of flax is one unit of coffee. She will therefore be prepared to exchange some coffee for some flax at any rate which gives more than one unit of flax for every unit of coffee exported. For country *B* the opportunity cost of producing one unit of coffee is two units of flax. This means that the terms of trade between the countries will be somewhere between the opportunity cost ratio in each. One unit of coffee will exchange for more than one unit, but less than two units of flax. Exactly where the ratio will lie between these two limits will depend upon the relative demand for coffee as against flax in both countries.

As time goes on a change in the terms of trade may take place. Suppose the price level of imports in 1982 in *A* was only 55 per cent as high as in 1974 and the price level of her exports was also lower than in 1974 but only 33 per cent lower, then a given quantity of A's exports in 1982 would have exchanged for 22 per cent more than in 1974.

If a change in terms of trade is due to a change in demand, the country whose exports are demanded more strongly, will gain. For example, Australia exports mainly wool and wheat. If the demand for wool and wheat increases and the prices of goods which Australia imports rises less, or does not rise at all, then clearly Australia can obtain more imports than before in exchange for a given quantity of wool and wheat. The great fall in the price level of British imports in the depression years of 1929 and early 1930s was due to the heavy fall in the prices of food stuffs and raw material which she imported mainly from her empire and colonies. While it enabled the great bulk of the population of Britain to maintain a higher standard of living during the depression than they had ever enjoyed before, these years were conversely very hard for the overseas colonies and empire which specialized in raw material and foodstuffs. England as the mother country at that time was able to cut down the prices of the goods she imported.

But less clear cut are the consequences of a change in cost position associated with a change in terms of trade. Thus if the coal deposits in country *A* became more difficult to mine because the more accessible coal has already been removed, the people of *A* may get a higher price for her coal on the world market than before, conversely the increase in motor production may result in a lesser price for the export of cars.

Finally, the significance of a change in the terms of trade will clearly be greater for a country which exports a relatively larger proportion of her output than which exports a small proportion of her output. Empirically a small country is likely to export a larger proportion of her output than a large country because she is less likely to possess a wide range of climates, soils, minerals and other factors.

CURRENCY BLOCS AND INTERNATIONAL TRADE

World trade is also hedged in by currency blocs. A free flow of goods can take place only with a common currency. Multilateral trade requires a convertible currency. The currency aspect of foreign trade must be grasped to throw light on the problems that beset the free flow of goods from the country of origin to the country where there is a market.

If a country imports more than it exports it has to pay for the excess of imports. If it were not for the matter of payment, the flow of goods into a country and an adverse balance of trade, would have been a good thing because the country gets richer in commodities which is real wealth But payments have to be made for all imports. Every country tries to pay for its imports by its exports, so that the problem of payment does not arise.

In the past the difficulty of payment was not very great. For example if country *A* had a favourable balance of trade with country *B* (that is an excess of exports over imports) and an unfavourable balance with country *C*, it could adjust the surplus with *B* against the deficit with country *C*. All that mattered was the net overall balance. But the world today is cut up into currency blocs, the most prominent of which are the dollar bloc and the sterling bloc. How did these blocs come into existence ?

Till 1931 the International Gold Standard was in operation. The currency value of every country that mattered in international trade was fixed in terms of gold. A country could pay in any currency. If it had a surplus in sterling and a deficit in dollars, it could set off the gold value of one against the other and arrive at a net balance.

But one of the essential requirements for the success of such a system is that no gold moved steadily from one country to another only goods moved. Unless a country is a very large producer of gold, a steady export of gold for any length of time would not sustain the system.

People who supported the system, however, believed that if a country exported much more than it imported and if payment is made in gold, a large amount of gold would flow into that country on account of its excess of exports over imports. The value of gold in the country would then go down because there is a surplus of it. As the value of the currency is equalled with gold, the prices of goods will rise in terms of its currency. Its exports would then automatically slow down as there would be less demand in the world markets for its high priced goods. On the other hand its high prices would make it very attractive for selling goods. Its imports would therefore increase. The adverse balance of trade with less exports and more imports would force the gold out of the country in payment for the excess of imports. The situation, it was argued, would correct itself.

But the prediction of the theorists proved wrong. The USA was the main supplier of goods to Europe and England at this time. She had an excess of exports over imports. Gold flowed into the country in payment for its exports. But USA adopted certain monetary policies. She did not permit the prices of goods to rise. Secondly, she imposed heavy tariffs on her imports which prevented any substaintial increase in her imports. Neither of the two situations predicted by the protagonists of the Gold Standard theory came true. The controlled prices in USA and the high tariffs prevented any large imports, and her exports continued at a high level. USA continued to have a favourable balance of trade. Great Britain, the leading commercial nation at the time was therefore forced to go off the Gold Standard in 1931. Many other countries who were actively enagaged in trade, but whose currency reserves and exchange reserves were backed up by sterling and not gold, had to follow Great Britain. All the British Empire and Commonwealth countries (except Canada) automatically joined Britain. Some other countries outside of the Empire and Commonwealth such as Portugal, Iran, Latvia, the Scandinavian countries and so on chose to join the sterling bloc. Others like Japan and Argentina maintained a fixed value for their currencies in terms of sterling. In the beginning any country was free to equate its currency in terms of sterling and also change its value according to the country's monetary policies. Hence when Denmark and New Zealand chose to change the value of their currencies against the sterling no one in the sterling group interfered. It could be done without reference to Britain and the sterling group. The fact was that a large number of countries was not only willing but found it convenient to trade in terms of sterling. The sterling, instead of gold, became the medium for settling balances in international trade. The reason for the acceptance of the sterling was because the sterling group of countries between them controlled a substantial portion of the world's trade. Great Britain, with her Empire, the Commonwealth and her colonies, and her vast mercantile marine, banking services more or less had a monopoly of world trade as a consequence of which she had a sound economic system and a stable currency. The pound sterling had a definite value in terms of goods and Britain saw to it that this value was maintained without much variation, not only in the sterling countries but also in the other countries engaged in trade. No other currency in the world had the stability of the pound sterling.

During World War II the neutral countries withdrew from the sterling group. A common currency meant free movement of goods between countries. England also found it necessary to restrict the movement of funds, capital and goods to enemy countries. Thus a system, which evolved for convenience in trade, became defined in war time to permit restrictions. The sterling bloc, as it was called later, came into existence and it still exists. India is a member of the sterling bloc.

Members of the sterling bloc are to settle their balance of payments arising between them on account of trade or services, in terms of sterling. Since all the member countries have a substantial reserve of sterling, any adverse balance between them is settled by drawing upon these reserves. Trade between the member countries of the sterling bloc does not, therefore, create a crisis.

But this does not mean that a member country can continue to have an adverse balance of trade for any length of time with another member. Each country has to take into account the reserves of sterling it possesses and the general condition of its economy before drawing on its reserves too rapidly.

These reserves were accumulated in Britain when the member countries were exporting much more to Britain than they were importing. By 1913 it was obvious that Britain had an adverse balance of trade and that she was making up the gap with her 'invisible exports' such as investments abroad, the earnings from her mercantile marine and banking services. India had a favourable balance of trade with England during the imperial days, that is, she was exporting much more to England than she was importing from it. Much of her earnings on account of her exports, however, went to pay interest on British investments in India, (like tea estates, British Indian industries, railways and so on) and to meet the expenses of the British military and administrative officers, British embassies, British education and so on. On the eve of independence Britain also scored off a large amount of India's sterling balances, on the excuse that her war debts had mounted. Yet India still had a sizeable balance in sterling when she became independent in 1947. If England is to liquidate this debt to India she has to export goods to India. On the other hand India can also draw upon these reserves and finance an adverse balance of trade with the members of the sterling bloc and outside countries. It would, however, not be in her interest to draw upon these reserves too rapidly. India chose to remain in the sterling bloc after independence partly because her economy was not stable and partly because her currency had no great value in the international markets. A trade with the backing of the sterling was advantageous. Trade between the member countries of the sterling bloc is thus comparatively easier than with members outside the bloc because of the availability of a common currency to settle accounts.

But there are countries outside the sterling bloc which today control a substantial part of the world's trade. Britain has lost her premier position in world trade after the war. USA is able to supply a large quantity of the goods required in the world market. Japan has become a major competitor in international trade. USSR, for political or other reasons, has entered the markets of the world. United Europe (the European Common Market) is also a strong competitor. As their economies stabilised themselves and their trade increased, their currencies are also gaining in strength. The sterling bloc today does not command world trade.

What happens when a member of the sterling bloc trades with a country outside the bloc ? The country which exports goods to a member of the sterling bloc will expect to be paid in her own currency while the sterling bloc countries will want to be paid in sterling which they can easily convert into their own currency. On the other hand, every time the sterling bloc countries export goods to a country outside the bloc, they earn some currency of that country. They can use the foreign currency thus earned for their imports from that country. Thus if the sterling bloc, as a whole, exports goods to an outsider more than it imports, the problem of paying does not arise. Any surplus of currency of that country thus earned can be used to import goods from that country. In other words so long as the sterling bloc as a whole does not spend more of the currency of a country it has earned through its exports, there is no problem in paying. Imports must therefore be balanced with exports to avoid the crisis of payment.

In general all the earnings of the foreign currency of a member country (mostly on account of its exports) of the sterling bloc are accumulated in a Central Reserve, from which each member can draw the foreign currency required for importing goods from an outside country. Therefore the capacity of the sterling bloc to import goods from a country outside the bloc will depend on the total reserve of a particular currency available to the bloc. This in turn will depend on the capacity of the bloc as a whole to export goods to the outsider and earn that currency.

For example the sterling bloc may not find it difficult to import goods from France because the bloc as a whole may be exporting more goods to that country than it is importing. The sterling bloc therefore may have a good reserve of francs on account of its favourable balance of trade with France. Any member of the bloc who wants his sterling reserves converted into francs and import goods from France will not find it very difficult, although restrictions may be placed for reasons other than the ability to pay. But this situation will continue only as long as the bloc as a whole exports more to France than it imports from it. As long as the block has a surplus of francs at its disposal than there is demand for it from the members, the French currency will be a soft currency for the sterling bloc. The softness and hardness of a currency is in terms of the sterling bloc and its capacity to export more to an outside country than it imports from it.

On the other hand, the sterling bloc on the whole imports far more from dollar group of countries than it exports to it. After World War II USA became the main supplier of food, equipment and technical know how, services and so on to the world at large. Britain's commitment to USA during the war and after, was so great that France, which had stepped upon a period of economic development along with the Union of the European Six, (France, Luxembourg, Belgium, Netherlands, Italy and West Germany) was doubtful about including Great Britain in the European Union and the European Common Market. Although the economy of Europe has improved considerably since the war and England has gained entry into the European Common Market in 1971, the dollar continues to be a scarce currency in the sterling bloc. The dollar group of countries now control a major share of the world's trade. Many of the old British Colonies, the Empire countries and the Commonwealth have established direct trade contacts with the dollar group. After independence, some of the former colonies and the Indian Empire countries, have ushered in the Five Year Plans for their economic development, as a consequence of which their imports of capital goods have increased. The industries of Europe and Great Britain having been destroyed during the war, USA was the only country (along with a few other dollar countries) which was in a position to supply the necessary goods for economic development. The capacity of the sterling bloc to earn dollars by exporting goods to USA was very limited. The excess of imports from the dollar group to the sterling bloc, over its exports was so great that the dollar became the scarcest currency for the bloc. Hence it was termed a hard currency in terms of the sterling bloc. Any conversion of the sterling reserves of a member country into dollars had to be watched carefully. But the hardness of the dollar eased slightly with the devaluation of the dollar, Britain's economic recovery from war damages and her success in the European Common Market. Britain has also succeeded in establishing closer trade contacts with the Commonwealth countries like Australia, New Zealand and Canada than during the period immediately after the war.

But Britain's successes in trade and in the European Common Market have not eased the situation for India. India along with the other countries of the sterling bloc, faces the dollar problem. India's position in the sterling bloc with regard to the dollar was further weakened because it was subjected to a variation. After independence and with a food shortage following partition and the separation of Burma, India was forced to import large quantities of wheat from USA. Her ambitious Five Year Plans also necessitated the import of equipment, loans, technical know-how and services from USA. Her dollar deficit became critical. Britain refused to shoulder the responsibility of converting her sterling reserves into dollars except in limited quantities fixed by an agreement each year, which on an average was about 10 to 15 million dollars. This amount was wholly inadequate to meet India's dollar deficit. As a consideration for this rigidity in the conversion of sterling into dollars with regard to India, Britain permitted her to keep her 'dollar earnings' to herself, that is she was not required to surrender whatever dollars she earned on account of her exports to the dollar group of countries, to the Central Reserve. Her exports to USA being negligible, in spite of frantic efforts to increase them, her capacity to earn dollars was very little. The limitation placed by England on the conversion of India's sterling balances into dollars made the dollar the hardest currency for India. Financial collaborations, loans, aids, services, technical know-how and so on added to the dollar deficit. The position improved slightly when India decided to get more of the goods she needed for economic development, from countries such as Eastern Europe and USSR to which she could export some of her own goods. when western Europe recovered from war damages, India was also able to get some of the machinery and equipment she required from countries like France, UK, Germany, the Scandinavian countries and Italy. But the dollar continues to be a hard currency for India

However, India along with the other member countries of the sterling bloc, also faces the hard currency problem with countries other than USA, that is the hardness or softness of a currency depends on whether the bloc as a whole has an adverse or favourable balance of trade with that country and not on the pattern of trade of the individual members. For example, India may have a favourable balance of trade with Belgium, and may be one of the major contributors of the Belgian currency to the Central Reserve. But if the sterling bloc as a whole has an adverse balance of trade with Belgium and the Belgian currency is a scarce commodity in the reserve, then India must also treat the Belgian currency as a hard currency in common with the bloc. Her imports from Belgium will have to be limited even though as an individual country she may be have a favourable balance with

Belgium. This does not mean that India is a loser by remaining in the sterling bloc. Any surplus amount of the Belgian currency the sterling bloc earns on account of an excess of exports over imports to that country will be treated as a net earning of hard currency and India can convert her sterling reserve into Belgian currency.

Similarly if India has an unfavourable balance of trade with another country outside the bloc, except USA but the bloc as a whole has a favourable balance of trade with that country and it has a surplus of its currency, then India can use her sterling balances to settle her adverse balance with that country and she will be able to treat the country as a soft currency area.

Apart from the two groups of countries of soft and hard currencies, there are countries whose currency is termed Medium Currency. These are countries whose currencies would have been hard for the sterling bloc (that is the sterling bloc exports less to them than it imports) but for certain agreements drawn up to meet some of the difficulties of trading with a hard currency area. These are usually in the form of 'payments agreement'. The two countries who wish to trade may agree to trade in terms of sterling to begin with, and come to an understanding that only outstanding debts on account of an excess of imports will be paid periodically in other country's currency. A payments agreement is usually on the understanding that each of the two countries will 'hold' a certain amount of the other country's currency so that when one country is faced with an unfavourable balance of trade and the payment for the excess of imports does not exceed the sum agreed upon, the other country does not ask for immediate settlement, on the understanding that the excess of imports will be paid for by an excess of exports in the future. It is therefore necessary that a payments agreement must have some commodity which the other country requires and which the latter can import in the future. It is also necessary that an agreement of this kind is followed by suitable measures to control export and import so that the unfavourable balance does not continue indefinitely to make the payments agreement ineffective.

If certain hard currency countries can be converted into medium currency countries by payments agreements and trade agreements why do we not adopt the same procedure with regard to all hard currency areas ? The answer is that the deficit the sterling bloc may have with these countries is so large to permit such treatment. Again the country may not have any commodity which it can export to the other country at a later date (after development). Unless the sterling bloc is able to curtail its imports from these countries of hard currencies it will continue to be a hard currency area.

In terms of goods and commodities the explanation for currency difficulties lies in the fact that certain countries in the world are low productivity areas. Immediately following the war, even the productivity of Europe was at a low level. But the European countries have more or less recovered from war damages and their dependence on USA and the dollar group is much less than before. But while conditions in England and western Europe have improved considerably since the 1960s the low productivity of the developing world continues. Certain of India's productive forces have even suffered a regression since 1962.

With the world divided into currency blocs India's balances of trade has to be reviewed in the sectors separately.

Before World War II India's imports from USA was less than 6 to 10 per cent of her total imports. USA took something like 8 to 15 per cent of India's exports. India had a favourable balance of trade with the USA throughout, which made her one of the major dollar earners for the sterling group. But after the war the situation changed. Imports from the USA increased in value and volume while exports did not increase. India began with an unfavourable balance of trade with USA at the dawn of independence. In 1949 India's imports from her were to the value of Rs. 104.23 crores and her exports were only to the value of Rs. 70.64 crores. To this deficit was added loans and aids, payments on account of items other than trade such as interest, payment for technical know-how and deficit from other hard currency areas. By 1948 India's dollar deficit mounted to 45 million dollars and in 1949, 93 million dollars. Of this, 75 million dollars were on account of import of food. It was quite clear that if India could step up her food production there would be a substantial decrease in her dollar deficit. The import of food was also not creating the capital equipment necessary for developing her economy. The First Plan concentrated on increasing food output but the break through, which was envisaged in the Fourth Plan period, was only partial although import of wheat under PL 480 scheme was stopped in 1970. The problem became even more critical when in 1948, barely a year after independence, Britain refused to shoulder the responsibility of India's dollar deficit, cutting down the conversion facilities of her sterling balances into dollars to a small sum of 10 million in 1948 and 15 million in 1949. The amount, on an average, does not exceed much more than this figure each year. India was forced to borrow from the International Monetary Fund. The scale of borrowing reached the maximum possible permissible under the regulations of the fund, and by 1977 she was required to pay back the loans.

By 1961 India's food supplies had increased but recession set in, in industry after the Chinese the aggression of 1962. In the Second and Third Plan periods, efforts were made to increase India's trade with the soft currency countries. This was made increasingly possible with the economic recovery of the Western European countries and with her close contacts with the Communist countries.

It was found that the prices of goods were much higher in the hard currency area and competition to sell to those countries was very keen. But the fact that India had some critical products like manganese, mica, iron and so on placed her in a better bargaining position.

An increase in the export to the hard currency area was also mooted in India. The commodities required by the hard currency area were jute (manufactured and raw) tea, lac, mica, manganese, fruits and vegetable, hides and skins (raw and tanned), raw cotton and waste, spices, vegetables and so on. A shift to the production of commodities such as that required by the dollar group saw the increase in the production of jute in Bengal, expansion of hybrid cotton in Gujarat, Maharashtra, Punjab and other States, the establishment of leather institutes in the public sector for the production of high quality leather, the organization of the Tea Board for reorganizing the tea estates and the export of tea. But many of these projects were bogged down either because of pressures from the foreign countries or because of the apathy of the government and people to tackle the economic problems of the country from its grass roots. There was no substantial increase in India's exports to the dollar group. Jute cultivation in Bengal petered out with political unrest and lack of direction. Its export was subject to licencing and although licences could be had for the asking, farmers did not show great enthusiasm to shift over to jute,

Cotton export had to meet with severe competition from other countries. Hybrid cotton was costly to cultivate and subject to diseases. Farmers were faced with lack of marketing facilities. The production of high quality leather could not be solved by the mere establishment of leather institutes without tackling the problem of producing hybrid animals which yielded hides and organizing animal farming for large scale commercial production. The Tea Board was crippled because British Tea Estates were not nationalized after independence. British policies and pressures continued to operate bogging the efforts of the Tea Board to rennovate the tea estates and control production by Indian participation in the ownership of the estates and export of tea. Indian economy threatened to be geared to a foreign market with sole purpose of earning dollars. But the dollar group was not willing to buy Indian goods except on their own terms. India reached the maximum of her exports to the dollar area at the expense of a stable economy at home. The wisdom of such a policy began to be questioned when conditions from the dollar group tightened with grave impacts on the political and economic independence of India. The competition for selling in the dollar group was so great that prices offered were low. The productivity there was also very high that demand was less keen. A forceful diversion of India's trade to the dollar group with government aids, subsidies, trade agreements and so on proved unsound. In the Second and Third Plan periods efforts were made to increase India's trade with the soft and medium currency areas. The Second Plan also laid down the foundation of a heavy steel complex in the public sector with help from the USSR, Germany and UK, and of engineering industries, with a view to increasing the indigenous capacity in capital goods and machine tools. Major develoments were also sought in the fields of fertilizers, basic chemicals, essential drugs and petroleum refining without any reduction in the outlay in agriculture. Self-sufficiency through industrialization and agricultural development became the policy of India from the second Plan period. But as the Third Plan progressed pressures mounted. The rivalry between the public and private sector gathered strength with full support from the western capitalist countries. The private sector in India argued that the flow of private capital from abroad could be increased if it was allowed to be invested in the private sector and that the requirement of 51 per cent controlling shares by Indian capital was preventing the countries from giving aids to, and collaborating with, Indian industrialists. In USA, the major dollar country, where private ownership dominated the economy, Government to Government collaboration was not considered feasible. The Chinese Aggression of 1962 became the excuse for deviating from the accepted policy of self-sufficiency and socialism of India and for getting rid of the powerful socialist lobby in the government. But the government that succeeded a couple of years later in 1965 was amenable to following in the path of self-sufficiency and non-alignment. However, it could not effectively stem the economic decay that had set in. The ratio of foreign capital to Indian capital in Indian projects was gradually increased and the Third Plan Period saw a slow shift from the public to private Sector in industries and from self-sufficiency to dependence on foreign aids, particularly that of USA and the western capitalist countries With the Chinese aggression a Plan Holiday was also advised extending the Third Plan Period upto 1969. In 1965 came the Pakistani War, 1967-68 the Israeli war on Egypt and in 1971-72 the Pakistani war on Bangla Desh and India. As nonalignment in the political sphere ceased to be of any consequence at the United Nations, with the regression in Egypt, India, Afghanistan, the Arab World, the African countries and South East Asia, economic pressures increased. The Plan Holiday in India lead to severe industrial regression particularly in the core industries. It took 10 years for the iron and steel industry to reach the level of the 1966 production.

The Fourth Plan was started in 1969. India's plans to increase exports failed. The capital producing industries which were set up in the Second and Third Plan periods were faced with bad management and neglect. Most of them were working below capacity so that India still faced a shortage of capital goods which she had to import. It led to an enormous waste of the capital investment of the Second and Third Plan periods.

The situation at the end of the Fourth and Fifth Plan periods was no better. An effort was made about 1970 to improve the working of the public sector and give a purposeful direction to the economy of the country. It succeeded to some extent but the Pakistani war of 1971-72 put back the clock of progress. But measures taken by the government paid off showing an increase of 12 per cent in the output of steel in 1974-75 over the previous year. The government was determined to fall back on self-sufficiency and trade with countries which would permit her to balance her imports with exports. The trend was again stemmed with the change in government. Sudden changes in policies made entrepreneurs timid. The Fourth and Fifth plan did not bring much relief. The income per capital increased but the rupee value had gone down to 27 np. per rupee. The Indian currency had no value in international trade and the markets for Indian goods did not substantially increase in the dollar group areas. On the contrary there is a danger that even the industries which were developed after independence like the steel industry, engineering, chemicals and drugs, dairy and petroleum may be captured by the western capitalist countries. The move of the European Common Market to sell the enormous surplus of milk products in Europe by diverting them to India, is likely to ruin the indigenous dairy industry of India. India will be committed to importing dairy products from the European Common Market and her sterling reserves will once again have to be expended on consumer products which can easily be produced in this country. The import of consumer goods will be at the expense of capital goods which are urgently required for her economic development. In 1975-76 India still had an adverse balance of trade, her exports being to the value of Rs. 39,430 million and her imports being to the value of Rs. 51,578 million a gap of Rs. 12,148 million. The gap is said to be narrowing and it is hoped will ease her foreign exchange crisis. India had a dollar debt (on account of aids) of Rs. 10,563.8 million in the same year. India continues to have an dverse balance f trade

BIBLIOGRAPHY

Anderson, MS, *Geography of Living Things*, English Universities Press, 1951.

Ashley, William, *Economic Organisation of England*, Longmans Green, 1949.

Ashton. T S, *Industrial Revolution*, Home University Library, Oxford University Press, 1948.

Berri, L ya edited, *Planning Socialist Economy*, Vols. I and II Progress Publishers 1977.

Bonavia, M R, *The Economics of Transport*, Cambridge University Press, 1948.

Brown Coggin, J and Dey, A K, *The Mineral and Nuclear Fuels of the Indian Sub-Continent and Burma*, Oxford University Press, 1978.

Cairncross, Alec, *Introduction to Economics*, (Butterworth & co.), 1951.

Clapham, J H, *Economic Development of France and Germany*, Cambridge University, 1951.

Cohen, R, *The Economics of Agriculture*, Cambridge University Press, 1949.

Crankshaw, Edward, *Russia and the Russians*, Macmillan, 1947.

Cressey, George B, *The Basis of Soviet Strength*, Harrap, 1945.

Darby, H C, *Historical Geography of England*, Cambridge University Press, 1948.

Debenham, F, *The Use of Geography*, English Universities Press, 1949.

Deshmukh, C D, *Economic Development of India*, 1946-56, Asia Publishing House, 1957.

East, W G, *Geography Behind History*, Thomas Nelson, 1948.

Fay, C R, *Great Britain from Adam Smith to the Present Day*, McGraw Hill, 1941.

Fearsides, W G, Bulman OMB, and Meakin, Walter, *The New Industrial Revolution*, Victor Gollancz, 1928.

Gadgil, D R *Industrial Revolution in India* 1860-1939, Oxford University Press, 1971.

Harrod, R F, *International Economics*, Cambridge University Press, 1949.

Hartshorne, Richard, *Nature of Geography*, (A.A.A.G. Vol. XXXIX, No. 3 and 4), 1939.

Hartshorne, Richard, *Perspective on the Nature of Geography*, Rand McNally A.A.A.G., 1959.

Henderson, Hubert, *Supply and Demand*, Cambridge University Press, 1948.

Jain, P C, *Industrial Problems of India*, (Kitabistan), 1942.

James, Preston, *Latin America*, (Cassel & Co.), 195.

Kendrew, W G, *Climates of Continents*, Oxford University Press, 1937.

Kendrew, WG, *Climatology*, Oxford University Press, 1949.

Kostyukhin, Dmitry, *The World Market Today*, Progress Publishers, 1977.

Krishnan, M S, *Geology of India*, Higginbothams, 1956.

Krishnaswami, S. *India's Mineral Resources*, Oxford I.B.H. Publishing, 1979.

Lavrishchev A, *Economic Geography of the USSR*, Progress Publishers, 1969.

Mitchell, J B, *Historical Geography*, English Universities Press, 1954.

Mohr, E C J, and Van Baren, F A, *Tropical Soils*, Interscience Publishers, 1954.

Ogilvie, A G edited, *Great Britain, Essay in Regional Geography*, Cambridge University Press, 1958.

Patterson, J H, *North America*, Oxford University Press, 1962.

Peel, R F, *Physical Geography*, English Universities Press, 1952.

Pirenne, H, *Economic and Social History of Medieval Europe*, Routledge and Kegan Paul, 1949.

Podkolzin, A, *Short Economic History of USSR*, Progress Publishers, 1968.

Plumb, J H, *England in the Eighteenth Century*, Pelican 1951.

Rao, B S, *Surveys of Indian Industries*. Vol. I, Oxford University Press, 1957.

Ramchandran, P.R., *Decay of Indian Industries*, Taraporevala, 1935.

Robertson, DH, *The Control of Industry*, Cambridge University

Press, 1948.

Robinson, E A G, *The Structure of Competitive Industry*, Cambridge University Press, 1949.

Robinson, H, *Geography for Business Studies*, Macdonald and Evans, 3rd Edition, 1979.

Robinson, H, *Economic Geography*, Macdonald and Evans 1979.

Robinson, E A G, *Monopoly*, (Cambridge University Press), 1949.

Semple, Ellen C, *Influences of Geographic Environment*, Constable 1947.

Smith, Russel J, *Commercial Geography*, Henry Holt, 1925.

Smith, Russel J. and Phillips, Ugden H, *North America*, Bell and Sons, 1942.

Smith, Wilfred, *Economic Geography of Great Britain*, Methuen, 1949.

Spate, O H K, *India and Pakistan*, Methuen, 1957.

Thatcher, W S, *Economic Geography*, English Universities Press, 1949.

Thompson, Warren S, *Population Problems*, McGraw Hill 194 .

Thomson, David, *England in the Nineteenth Century*, Pelican 1951.

Wadia, D N, *Geology of India*, Macmillan 1961.

Whitbeek, R H, Williams, F E, and Christians, WF, *Economic Geography of South America*, McGraw Hill, 1947.

Zimmerman, EW, *World Resources and Industries*, Harper and Brothers, 1933.

INDEX